How to Complain

www.southbankpublishing.com

other books by this author

Chris Waddle (the authorised biography)
Danger Zone
Gazza, My Life in Pictures
Ha'way The Lad: The Authorised Biography of Paul Gascoigne
How to Succeed as a Sports Agent
Marked Man
McGovern's Horses (as Tim Elsen)
Race Against Time
Rags to Riches
Red Card
The White Corridors
White Lines

How to Complain

Mel Stein

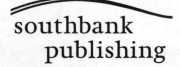

southbank
publishing

First published in May 2005 by Southbank Publishing
P.O.Box 394, Harpenden, Herts, AL5 1XJ

www.southbankpublishing.com

Complaining is a lonely and subjective business and the views contained herein represent my personal feelings. Many of the companies to whom I have complained have reacted positively and even where they have not, nothing in this book should be interpreted as meaning that they are nothing less than *excellent* companies who as far as I am concerned have merely had a bad day at the office. Whatever the outcome of my complaint I would like to thank each and everyone of them for making this book possible and I hope they will take everything I have said in good part and allow me to use their services again.

A CIP catalogue record for this book is available from the British Library.

ISBN 1 904915 02 7

2 4 6 8 10 9 7 5 3 1

Typeset by Avocet Typeset, Chilton, Aylesbury, Bucks
Printed and bound in Great Britain by Cox & Wyman Ltd, Reading, Berks

For Lucinda, my trusty P A and Marilyn my loyal wife, both of whom were entitled to complain about me much more than they did.

CONTENTS

CONTENTS

INTRODUCTION

It was William Gladstone who said, "Never complain and never explain."

How wrong could he be? My motto (and hopefully yours too by the end of this book) is always complain and always explain, because a complaint without any explanation is worthless. Ranting and raving is bad, controlled complaining is good. Don't go away feeling angry or disappointed. Let the people who caused the anger or disappointment not only know about it, but know why you feel the way you do. You never know, they may even agree with you.

The Book of Common Prayer says, "For a while I held my tongue: my bones consumed away through my daily complaining."

And that's so right. The feeling you've been cheated, that something you've looked forward to has failed to live up to expectations … if you fail to do anything about the feeling then the worm of disappointment will eat away inside you, making you feel even worse about events. But at least the worm should exist. He exists in me, and he certainly has a healthy appetite, and what I want to do is to make you realise that it doesn't have to be like that. If you simply walk away, turn the other cheek and do nothing, then the mysterious THEY have got away with it. Maybe the perpetrators know, maybe they are simply incompetent innocents, but either way they'll do it again to someone else unless you stop them. So you have a duty, not only to yourself, but also to society to do something about it.

As my late lamented maternal grandmother used to say, in her broken English, "If you don't ask, you don't get." (At least I think that's what she was saying … the English was very broken.)

Anyway, if you don't ask and don't complain, then you certainly won't get. That's what this book is intended to be about, although I reserve the right to drift off at a tangent and that's a disclaimer which means you can't complain about it. I want to teach you how to recognise that there is something worth complaining about, to explain to you how to complain about it and then to demonstrate exactly what you can achieve by complaining, both by way of self-satisfaction and material gains.

It was Spike Milligan who once rang the BBC and said:

"I've got a complaint."

"What's that?" he was asked.

"Malaria," he replied.

So, ignoring the pun, complaint does have more than one meaning. A moan, an illness, a lawsuit, but perhaps they are all the same meaning if you think about it. Complaining can become an obsession and can turn into litigation. You begin to look for things that might go wrong and are almost disappointed if they don't. My P.A. used to judge the depth of my enjoyment of a holiday by the length of the complaint letter I wrote on my return. But now, even I realise that you have to strike a balance, to ensure that the one overwhelming aim you have to seek to achieve is justice ... and there speaks the lawyer in me.

But this is not a legal textbook, it's more of an autobiography (with the juicy bits omitted). Of course you can go to a solicitor if you think you've been seriously wronged, but mostly the matter that has given rise to the complaint simply won't justify the cost. So if the depth of your pocket runs to the price of this book, but not your lawyer's hourly rates, then hopefully this will be your DIY guide to complaining. Always remember – you need to complain *to* someone and not *about* someone.

Well, before you sit down to contact me or the publishers, complaining about the length of this introduction, let's get down to the nitty-gritty. Are you sitting comfortably? You're not? Well, where did you purchase your chair? Who manufactures it? Let's set about telling you how to complain about it ...

1

OH, I DO LIKE TO BE BESIDE THE SEASIDE

For many people, the annual holiday justifies the other fifty weeks of work – although, as we become more and more of a leisure-oriented society, the old fortnight a year holiday is often transmuted into the new six weeks a year holiday. Cheap flights, time-shares, last minute offers and the general desire to see beyond one's nose (and Blackpool) have made the world a smaller place.

In any event, whether it is a weekend break in the Cotswolds or a round the world cruise, there are always certain expectations. Expectations may well be fuelled by the price or the relative price. Without being condescending, (and I am not, I am really not!) the couple who scrimp and save for their week or so in Spain may have far higher expectations than the millionaire who jets off to New York for the weekend. As you will see as this book progresses, technology is not my strong point, which has always given my complaints about anything that involves a switch or a button a deeper significance.

What I am getting to is that it is not just about value for money, it is also about the experience fulfilling your expectations – or, in many cases, your dreams. If it doesn't in any shape, form or size, then you all know what you have to do, don't you? I am waiting … I can't hear you … No, he is not behind me … Yes, that's right – you complain. You complain at the time, you complain on the phone and – most importantly of all – you complain in writing.

Now, as I said, I wouldn't call myself a technophobe, more of a Luddite really. In my mind, nothing beats pen and paper. I even wrote this book out in longhand originally, using a nice pen and a fresh pad. Mind you, my pen leaked which did mean my taking some time out to shoot off a letter to the manufacturer. See what I mean? It's all about expectations.

But returning to my point, once something is down in black and white and winging its way (at times with proof of postage) to the recipient, then the long, winding trail to Complaintsville is on the map.

Now, let's look at a few examples and the practicalities. This is your main holiday of the year. You have booked a villa in Spain from a brochure. You are taking your kids and you have a few particular requirements. It has to be near the beach. The sea has to be clean and you have to be able to swim in the sea without any danger. In addition, you need your own pool and you need shops nearby so that you can buy your food, as you are not renting a car. You want some maid service so that you don't have to be forever clearing up as you do at home. You have spent a bit more than usual on the villa so you need to cut back on the travelling arrangements and you book a budget airline flight. It's a real bargain at £60 per person but you know there are conditions attached. It's a set time flight on a set day and you can't change it. If you make a booking like that, always be careful to read the small print of the booking conditions. In order to complain you must always have right substantially on your side and if the small print says it's a three-hour check-in and you turn up half-an-hour before departure to be told that your seat has gone, then cutting down all the rainforests in the world to write your letters of complaint will do you no good at all.

On this occasion, you are told that check-in is two hours before the flight. You pack the night before and, after the customary row with your wife about who is taking up most of the suitcase and why she has the need to take ten pairs of shoes to a country that manufactures the best bargain shoes in the world, you actually set off in good time and arrive at the airport at 8.00 in the morning for an 11 o'clock flight. That's good. You snatched a coffee before you left but you could kill a breakfast right now. Then you see the queue to your check-in desks and you lose both appetite and confidence. It goes on forever. Who are these people? Are they veterans of Wimbledon or Cliff Richard concerts? Did they never leave after the last holiday but merely began to queue up for the next year with their blankets and thermos flasks? I have never yet met a person who was first in line for a check-in. I think they are airline plants, just as I never have spoken to anybody whose baggage has come off the carousel first. I truly believe that the first few bags are decoys to encourage you that the real stuff is not too far behind. Fat chance! Meanwhile, back in the queue, you despatch your other half for the last minute purchases you planned to make – suntan lotion, books, games for the kids, foreign currency.

Reluctantly, she takes the offspring with her and you are left with a huge pile of baggage behind a large man in a loud Hawaiian shirt and shorts that he must have bought at a camping exhibition. But he seems to have no luggage, just a bag on his back. He strikes up a conversation. There's no escape. "Emigrating, are you?" he says, with a nod at the baggage. "Fortnight. Wife and kids," you reply, leaving the number of children unspecified so that he may be lulled into thinking that you also run an orphanage, the majority of whose inmates are accompanying you on this trip.

He shakes his head, and fat ripples across him like lard in a frying pan. "Phew!" He must be a builder. It's that "Phew" you get when you call in a new builder to rectify your last bloke's effort. "They're tough on baggage allowance, this airline." You smile brightly. You've read the small print. You put the bags on the scales the night before and you know you are going to be fine; or at least you think you do.

By the time your wife returns with two crying children, one reeling from a politically incorrect slap across the face and the other because "She" wouldn't spend £300 on a new portable video game machine, you have moved forward about five metres. You now have two and a half hours to the flight and half-an-hour to the appointed check-in time. Twenty-five minutes more pass and you still need binoculars to see the counter. You have to do something – but what? You have a vision of reaching the desk and being told that your seats have been re-allocated.

This is where it all begins for you, *if* you want to accept the challenge of a meaningful complaint. You leave your wife with the kids and *Hawaiian Shirt* (who is telling her that he is on a flight that leaves at six in the evening) and go to the head of the queue. By the time you get there, you are hot, sweaty and out of breath and have burned off the same number of calories you usually kill on the treadmill in the gym. You seize your moment and lean on the counter to tell the girl at check-in that you are here for the eleven o'clock flight to Malaga and that you were told that you had to check in by nine. It is now five to nine and you are here, but you are a long way away in the queue. She tells you that everybody is checking in for that flight and not to worry. You do worry because you know *Hawaiian Shirt* isn't checking in for that flight. You tell her that. "He is in the wrong queue then," she says, which lifts your spirits a little. "Don't worry," she says, "as long as you have a ticket, you'll be fine."

Now, make a mental note of that conversation and her name (let's call her Margo) and also jot down the time that you spoke to her. It may be useful evidence. So ... back to the queue. The quandary you now have is whether or not you tell *Hawaiian Shirt* he is wasting his time, or enjoy it when he gets to the counter and gets sent away to another, longer queue which gives him little or no chance of being in the air by the evening. However, an hour later, when you finally get to the counter, they ticket him quite happily and he vanishes into the crowd, waving his documents like a lottery winner. You hand over your tickets and passports to the check-in man (your lady has obviously gone off duty by now) who looks up at the clock. This is not a good sign.

You take the bull by the horns and tell him of your conversation with Margo. He sniffs. He is clearly senior to Margo who may or may not be a trainee or a work shadow. With some delight, he tells you that he can't allocate your seats as you are too late to check in and the best he can do is to put you on stand-by, but you may not get on the same plane and if you do you almost certainly won't sit together. And anyway, he doubts if your bags will travel with you. Delightful though it may have sounded, in other circumstances, to hear that an unsuspecting stranger will be seated next to your children, this is tempered by the fact that you are about to lose a day (if not more) of your holiday, whilst having to wear the clothes you stand up in for the foreseeable future. The *Old You* might have taken his chances and accepted the stand-by offer. The *New You* demands to see a supervisor. The line behind you is murmuring. The check-in man suddenly feels afraid, very afraid. He is more exposed than Davy Crockett at the Alamo. He hesitates, "The supervisor?" you repeat like a mantra. He turns to his computer again as if it has just been re-programmed and suddenly four seats

14

appear together as if by magic. You wait until the tickets are in your hands then, with your newborn confidence, ask him if the screen was telling him that the plane had suddenly got bigger.

He doesn't like the sarcasm and now looks at the weight of your luggage. "There is excess to pay on this," he says. "No, there is not. I weighed them last night," you say. "Then your scales are wrong," he says. "Let's see whose scales are wrong," you reply. "Try them on a different scale." The man has met his match and, giving up, tickets your baggage and reluctantly gives you the receipt and confirms it will not fly alone.

But what if the threat of the supervisor hadn't worked? What if there had been no seats, standby or otherwise? What if you had arrived at your destination twenty-four hours late? What if they had either demanded that you paid extra for your baggage (money which you did not have) or had taken revenge by deliberately losing your baggage?

Well, before all is revealed as to how to deal with that, let's see what lies in store for you in sunny Spain.

2

DREAM HOLIDAYS

Now, if you have booked from a brochure, it's fairly vital that you take the brochure with you to your destination. There is no point complaining about the lack of a jacuzzi if you can't remember whether or not there was supposed to be one there in the first place. So our intrepid travellers, you and your other half/better half/significant other/partner – I must be politically correct or you might complain to the publisher and bring my literary career to an even speedier conclusion than a lack of sales would achieve, arrive at your villa.

Check the time it takes to get from the airport. Almost every brochure will say, for example, "twenty minutes from Malaga". If it turns out to be an hour at 2 o'clock in the morning, when the only other traveller is a stray mule, then that is going in the letter too. Did I tell you that you were gathering material for your first complaint letter? In this case, they told you half-an-hour and it has taken nearly double that without the driver stopping even once, so that doesn't bode well. Make a note of the fare you give him and get a receipt.

The villa does at least look like its photos in the brochure, so that is promising. However, as the children run on ahead, their cries of disappointment don't bode well. "Daddy, the pool's empty!" Now, the brochure didn't promise a full pool but there was a photograph of a laughing, sun-baked couple lounging beside one, which appeared to have water in it and so, by implication, this was not an unreasonable expectation.

Before you phone the travel company, take a good look around. There may be other problems to add to the list. And – would you believe it – there are.

The kitchen is filthy, the cutlery dirty and unmatched. The bedrooms are unaired and one of the mattresses is stained. The fridge is old and noisy and, if you look out of the window, you find

16

the sea view obscured by a brand new hotel. Between you and the hotel is a dual carriageway and beyond the hotel is the sea, so it is not going to take Marco Polo to figure out that a journey to the beach is going to be somewhat hazardous.

Now, again, before you make the call, what do you want to achieve? As far as I am concerned, this question is the basis of all complaints. Sometimes there are grounds for just complaining without an end in view, but for the most part there has to be a game plan. Now, at this stage in your holiday, you don't want your money back, you don't want to go home and the agency can neither move the beach nor demolish the hotel.

The important thing, when making a complaint call, is not to lose your cool. The minute you begin to rant and rave, you lose the high moral ground and, quite frankly, having been on the receiving end of complaints (and, no, I am not going to tell you which hat I was wearing at the time, or whether they were justified), when someone starts to shout at you, then you simply entrench. You also believe that you are dealing with a loony and any justification for the complaint gets lost in the torrent of abuse. My simple remedy, when I was being yelled at, was to tell the yeller that I was putting the phone in the drawer and so was no longer listening. Quite often I returned to the drawer a few minutes later and the tirade was continuing, without the speaker having noticed that I had gone.

So, sarcasm is fine but a raised voice is not. And as to what you want to achieve, well, in this case, short-term, you want to be moved and, long-term, you are looking for compensation. At the same time as you make your call, if you have someone back home who can confirm your complaint in writing, so much the better.

Taking a deep breath and assuming that it is not two o'clock in the morning, you ask to speak to someone responsible at the agency and, with the brochure by your side, you reel off everything that is wrong. A little law doesn't go amiss so mention of the Trade Description Act and various other relevant statutes and murmurings about damages would be helpful. You tell them that you haven't unpacked, that you have no intention of unpacking and that unless they call you back within the hour (be reasonable about the time – telling them five minutes is absurd and gives them no opportunity to deal with anything) with the address of the alternative accommodation to which they will be moving you and confirmation they will be arranging (or at least paying for) a taxi to take you there, you will be mitigating your loss by booking into the best hotel in the vicinity and charging them for the privilege. Oh, by the way, if the pickup doesn't happen and there are no hotels available, then you will be decamping to their local office, unpacking there and staying there until something does happen.

Again, it doesn't hurt to mention the media and to give the impression (even if it is not a fact) that you know somebody at The Sun/Mirror/News of the World/BBC/local newspaper/central government/the Kremlin or the White House (whichever may be the most relevant). If the agency or tour company is genuine and bona fide then the last thing they will want is cameras and journalists at their local office cheerfully snapping away, interviewing a respectable family with young kids which has a genuine grievance and nowhere to stay.

Now, let's say the strategy works. You do get the call and you are moved. This time the accommodation is tolerable, it's clean, it has a pool (at worst, shared) and you have a twenty-minute walk to the beach and the shops. But when you get to the beach, the sea is polluted and there are all sorts of danger warnings advising anybody under the age of 16 to keep well away. However, you get on with your holiday and, once things have settled down, you find that the kids like to be by the communal pool rather than the beach, you get a lift from a neighbour when you need to stock up on provisions and the sun shines throughout.

You return tanned and fatter, rested and content, particularly as you have no hassle with the flights whatsoever. Is that it? Do you leave it there and simply decide that next time you will fly with a scheduled airline and book through a different travel company? Well, if you are that sort of person then hopefully you won't be after reading this book because to us professional complainants, this is where the fun really begins. Let's make no bones about it, you have been inconvenienced, you have suffered stress, it's probably taken you longer to unwind than would otherwise have been the case, so both the airline and the tour company are going to get no less than they deserve.

If you are going to complain on a regular basis it takes discipline, ruthlessness and a determined commitment to make the effort, but I promise you that nine times out of ten it will be worth it.

So, as soon as possible after you return, you write your complaint letter. Always address them to the Managing Director, unless you have the name of someone in a senior management capacity, in which case write to them personally with a copy to the Managing Director. Given the incidents I have described, this will be the sort of letter I have in mind as far as the airline is concerned:

Dear Sir,

On the [A] day of [B], my wife and I travelled with our two small children on your airline to Malaga with a view to staying in Marbella. We had booked our tickets directly with you on the [C] day of [D] and had paid for them. We were aware that we needed to check in two hours before the flight and, in fact, arrived at the airport and joined the queue three hours before the departure time, at [insert time] a.m. I enclose a copy of my car park ticket showing our arrival time at the airport.

It was quite clear to us that your ground staff were overwhelmed by the number of people travelling that day and there was no prioritisation of flights in departure order. This added to the chaos that duly faced us.

A few minutes before the two-hour deadline for take-off, I left my family and went to the head of the queue and spoke to Margo. I was told that everybody in the queue was waiting for my flight so I need not worry. I knew this was not the case, as the person in front of me was flying to Portugal on the evening flight, but I had no choice but to accept what she told me.

When we eventually reached the check-in desk, an hour or so before take-off, we were told by a different individual, Roger, that our seats had been re-allocated and that we were on standby. This caused great distress both to my family and myself and my previous conversation with Margo was totally contradicted. Basically, I was being called a liar in front of the people behind us in the queue, which was clearly defamatory.

It was only when I demanded to see a supervisor that four seats together magically appeared and we were grudgingly allowed to fly. Even then there was some argument over the weight of our luggage, when I had carefully checked the previous evening that this complied with the weight restrictions. Your staff were totally oblivious to and uncaring about the tearful condition of my children.

I should be grateful if you could look into this matter as soon as possible and I await hearing from you at your earliest convenience with a suitable offer of compensation.

Yours faithfully.

Then you diarise the matter for seven days and, assuming you have heard nothing, which is highly likely, you send a reminder. You may then get a standardised acknowledgement. Keep sending reminders until you get a substantive answer from someone in authority who will offer you more than an apology. In my view, an incident of this nature (which, joking apart, is fairly minor) is worth flight vouchers of at least the cost of one of your tickets. Don't get fobbed off with Duty Free vouchers that have to be used on that particular airline as you may never want to buy Duty Free. Always check the expiry date of any free tickets or vouchers anyway.

If you receive no response, then collect all your letters and acknowledgements together, copy them and send them by Recorded Delivery to the Managing Director. If that doesn't work, then repeat the process to the Chairman, but all the time upping the ante as far as your compensation package is concerned. If all else fails, then send everything to the Media, either a Watchdog type TV programme or a newspaper column in a tabloid that deals with reader's complaints or – even better – traveller's complaints. If you want to go to the ultimate level, then check out their advertisements and, if you feel that the service wasn't up to the standards promised by the adverts, then complain to the Advertising Standards Authority.

Now, all this over delays in check-in, a minor irritation, isn't it all rather an example of using a sledgehammer to crack a nut? Perhaps. But it is good training for the real challenges that lie ahead ... like your travel company.

Now let's run through the preliminaries one more time and maybe by the time you get to the end of this book you can make yourself an all-encompassing check list of all the things that can go wrong, in every sort of situation, and add a few more from your own experiences (feel free to share these with me at my website, www.howtocomplain.net or c/o the publisher if you like). It can be a little like those I-Spy books of your childhood, where you ticked off all the things you could see at the seaside or the zoo. Oh, such innocent days of yore!

1. Note travel time and ensure it accords with the brochure.
2. If you have pre-booked, numbered seats ensure you get them.
3. If you've got special dietary requirements make sure the airline provides them if they've been pre-booked.
4. Check the brochure (small print included) before you leave and don't forget to take it with you rather than relying on your memory.
5. If you have to expend anything unusual make a note and keep the receipt. For example, if a transfer to your hotel was included and the transportation didn't turn up, causing you to have to take a cab, then you're entitled to be reimbursed. If you have to buy a drink and a sandwich whilst you are kicking your heels and wasting your holiday time then you should get that back as well.
6. Ensure the accommodation is clean, including all the linen, towels, cutlery, china, etc. If it is not, insist someone is sent in to do it. And if they don't seek a refund.
7. Take photographs wherever possible.
8. Make sure the pool, if any, and its surrounds are up to scratch and that you can actually get a seat by the pool.
9. Check to see all facilities in the area are as promised. If the golf course is 5km away rather than 500 yards you need to complain. That's your holiday and your time and petrol that you're wasting.
10. If there's maid service make sure she comes, spends enough

time on the job and doesn't steal anything. Most people who do such a job are honest and badly paid, but inevitably there are going to be a few bad eggs. Reward the good eggs by leaving a generous tip and a thank-you note. That's another thing, always praise when things are good and always complain when they are bad.

11. If the views are not as promised then try to change your rooms or unit.

12. Complain at the time about noise or building works. You lose credibility if you wait to get back home. It may be tempting to wait so as not to interfere with the holiday but you have to make yourself do it.

13. If there's a gym, complain if the equipment isn't up to a decent standard.

14. Make a note of anything that was to be included and isn't. For example, if the brochure says there's a free cocktail hour and you turn up after twenty minutes to find all the drinks gone then you're entitled to complain. It didn't say "Free cocktails … unless the drinks run out".

3

TRAVELLING LIGHT

It's hardly surprising that so many travel companies go belly-up when they so often fail to deliver. As I've already suggested, it's not even a case of exceeding expectations, but merely fulfilling them. Our intrepid travellers, in the first two chapters, would not have been expecting the Ritz Carlton but they would have been expecting to return refreshed from a hard-earned holiday, feeling they had received their money's-worth. And that in a nutshell is the essence of when to complain. Whenever you feel you have not received value for money then that should be the green light to let loose the dogs of war ... or even just to write your first letter or make your first phone call.

I'm not a great fan of the telephone when it comes to complaining. It takes too long, you have to find the right person to address, and even then there is no guarantee that they will take down full notes or that you will not have forgotten something in the heat of the moment ... or the coolness of the half-hour it takes to be diverted past three call centres in the eastern hemisphere. There is no harm in a preliminary call, just to set the scene and for the sake of immediacy. If you can you should make that call whilst at the scene of the crime or what has passed for a hotel. It's never enough just to speak to the travel company's representative (assuming they have one) as you have no guarantee they will follow up with head office. Their time may be more fully occupied with keeping up with the heavier drinkers of your group or picking up (or being picked up by) the more attractive members. Even if they do give an accurate report of your complaint they may also say it's unjustified as they are hardly going to be impartial witnesses when any criticism you may be making of the holiday also reflects on them.

So, things have not gone to plan. You are back in England, frazzled, your blood pressure at its maximum and now you want some compensation. The travel company can't give you back your holiday time off work, but they sure as hell can give you some money to ensure that you are able to have a virtual cost-free holiday next year, or when you can next grab some time off work. And so, you write to them.

Dear Sirs,

I have just returned from a holiday booked through your company. We chose the resort because it seemed to be a family orientated resort, adjacent to the beach but with its own pool and a nearby golf course.

When we arrived, our room did not have the sea view, which we were promised in the brochure, but instead our balcony overlooked a building site where work commenced at 7 o'clock every morning and continued well into the early evening. This made the balcony unusable and the dust and dirt triggered off an asthma reaction in our youngest child.

We tried to sit by the pool and noticed that the surface was filthy and full of dead floating insects. Even if we had wished to continue to stay there no were no loungers available as these were "bagged" every day by German tourists with their towels, at some unearthly hour. Complaints to your representative on site were of no avail. We moved to the beach only to find warnings that bathing was dangerous as the water was polluted, a fact that you managed to omit in your brochure.

I decided to walk to the golf course, which you described as being a few hundred yards away. After carrying my clubs in the boiling heat for about a mile I actually asked for directions only to be told it was still another mile away.

The kitchen in our apartment was fly-ridden, the crockery chipped and dirty and the bath bore unmistakeable evidence of a previous occupier, a brunette, I would think from the hairs we discovered. All of our requests for the apartment to be cleaned from top to toe fell on deaf ears.

If I had wanted to holiday at a building site then I would have telephoned Barratt Homes to see where they were building their next development. If I had wanted to stay in a slum I would have tried to arrange an exchange visit with a high-rise inner-city council tenant.

I wanted to do neither and I must therefore insist on the return of my money and some suitable offer of compensation by way of damages for the holiday from hell, etc, etc.

I think you get the picture

Before you write, read through the booking conditions, as it helps if you can quote these in your letter; see above.

It may come as some shock to discover that the travel company is in the business of making money, which is made more difficult for them if they have to give you a reduced cost holiday, worse still a free one or, horror of horrors, actually have to give you any money back. So please don't think that upon receipt of your first letter they are going to roll over with their legs in the air begging you to tickle their tummies whilst somebody on their behalf empties their piggy banks into your eagerly outstretched hands.

The typical response scenario is as follows. First of all a delay, while they hope you will go away and forget all about it. Your carefully diarised reminder note to yourself will quickly disabuse them of that hope when you write your second letter. To this, you will probably get an acknowledgment that they are investigating the matter. This means that the recipient, if indeed it was ever read by the M.D, has passed it down the line. Somehow or other complaint letters never get passed up the line. It's one of life's little vagaries, like insurance policies never paying out the returns you were promised; see later chapter if this is of any interest. The investigation will often take longer than the police inquiry into the crimes of Jack the Ripper and will probably have the same result. The travel company will tell you that all your complaints were figments of your imagination and they are both hurt and puzzled by your ingratitude at the opportunity they gave you to frolic in the Spanish equivalent of Xanadu. In fact for a moment you may begin to doubt yourself and start to feel guilty about troubling such a busy company with something so insignificant as your ruined holiday. The moment will pass, believe me, the moment will pass. It is now the time not just to get angry, not just to get even, but to tip the scales in your favour.

So you write one more time. You rebut every single comment they have made (assuming they are unjustified) and you now provide photographs of the accommodation, together with written statements of the rest of your party and, indeed, anybody else who can support your version of events. At this stage it becomes quite important to copy the letters in to third parties and to ensure that the travel company is aware of this by you revealing this fact at the foot of your letter to them. Now there is no point in sending a copy to your Aunt Mabel in Cleethorpes, delighted though she may be to hear from you at a time other than Xmas. A solicitor's name is good. Just warn them in advance to expect to receive this and tell them to do nothing. At this stage they are just there as a warning and you don't want to incur costs. That's not to say you can't now tell the travel company that, if they want to settle with you, it's also going to be on a plus costs basis. I'm not suggesting you should try to defraud them but it's another negotiating string to your bow. In addition you should also copy in your own travel agent, if you didn't book directly. Travel companies rely on agents to send them business. That's why they pay commissions. If an agent is consistently getting bad feedback from holidays taken with a particular travel company then they will stop using them as they will want to preserve their own relationship with their clients. It's a very competitive market and your agent will have loads of alternative companies vying for their business. Finally, send a copy to that travel company's governing body, which will probably be either ABTA or IATA.

Most decent travel companies do have a complaints procedure anyway. It's important to follow the time scales set out in them as, whilst they can't remove your civil law rights, they may be able to force you into suing rather than going through any arbitration proceedings that are available to you under the booking conditions. They may say that you have 28 days from your return home to lodge your complaints, so never delay. Strike while the iron is hot and the nightmare is still fresh in your mind ... or probably etched there together with the sounds of your children's howls of disappointment and your wife's accusations that this was all your fault and she had really wanted to go to Blackpool or, more likely, taken a Caribbean cruise ... and I've really nothing against Blackpool, by the way.

This time round you may start to hit pay dirt. They accept your complaints, or at least some of them, but what do they offer you? My guess is that the first offer will be some vouchers or discounts for future holidays with them. It's not a good thing to say that you wouldn't holiday with them again even if they were the only travel company offering trips to the moon after a nuclear war had decimated the earth. One of the reasons they are offering you anything is to try and keep your custom. Without customers (even persistent buggers like you) they don't exist or if they do exist, they are posting horrendous losses year after year. So your response is to say that, while you might consider holidaying with them again now they have made an offer, you want to keep your options open. If they have offered you, say £200 in vouchers then go back to them and say that you would consider £1000 ... the five times multiple is always a good rule of thumb. They may come back and increase their voucher offer or they may make you a cash offer in addition, but whatever it is, you will suddenly realise that not only are they negotiating but you are negotiating as well. In fact you are enjoying it so much that it's almost better than a holiday and perhaps next year you will just spend your fortnight off negotiating.

Eventually you will hopefully get an acceptable offer. If it does consist of any kind of vouchers or discounts read the small print carefully. They are no good to you if they say they can't be used in school holidays, over bank holidays or have to be used within 12 months. What you want has to be open-ended and the equivalent of cash, though, in any event, cash is so much more preferable as you are not dependent upon the survival of the travel company until the date you want to book your holiday.

But before you accept the settlement, ask yourself if it is fair and if it's not then don't just give up because it's all becoming too much trouble. You've started, so you have to finish and surrender is never completion. If you are going to battle on then you generally have your choices ... litigation (either the county court or small claims), arbitration or media publicity. The last one of these, the Watchdog-type programmes on TV, I mentioned before, get swift results but only a few complaints get dealt with in this fashion. Litigation can be expensive, though small claims are dealt with by yourself but need commitment. Arbitration can be complicated and you may need legal advice. It's always better to get a result yourself through correspondence. Better and more satisfying. You are beginning to cut your teeth as a trainee complainant ... but there are bigger challenges ahead.

Just remember:

1. In your first letter be factual, though sarcasm is permitted and is even to be encouraged. It shows the enemy they are dealing with is a creature of some intelligence.
2. If they don't reply don't leave it. Diarise the matter for your follow-up letter.
3. If that doesn't result in correspondence then start firing off copies to anybody you think may be interested. Do refrain from making hysterical or defamatory comments. They can rebound on you and you could, in theory, find yourself as the defendant in the libel trial of the century. Don't forget that the opposition has a deeper pocket than you when it comes to both costs and resources so you need to be fighting them on your chosen patch.
4. Once you've started don't give up. Eventually you will get an answer from someone. As you'll see in later chapters in this book, persistence is my creed.

4

SHOPPING AND *****ING

Yes, there are times when the sheer frustration of shopping can reduce you to a helpless, swearing bundle of nerves. But no, this chapter is not about visiting the local shopping centre with your spouse. This is about the relationship between you and the retailer.

Like most things in life shopping is about relationships and like most relationships you have to work at it. It's a relationship between you and your regular shopping haunts and it's a relationship between you and the products you regularly buy. As with all relationships there are highs and lows, surprises and disappointments, all set against the background of your expectations.

It is not unreasonable to assume that customer loyalty arises from an expectation of a certain level of service and a certain standard of quality. There may be one or two occasions where there will be disappointment with either or both of these, but they will be forgiven if there have been enough times in the past when both service and quality have reached or exceeded the levels expected. It's a bit like going to a favourite restaurant and having one bad meal. It's almost inevitable, but generally you will go back to try again because you know it's just a glitch. I'd like to say it's also like your favourite football team. You don't stop watching and supporting them because of a bad result ... but if your team is like mine then you probably have to admit that this is probably one sector where you do keep coming back for more punishment. Though even in football there are limits and if a team continues to perform badly you can complain. You can ask for the manager, the Board, the Chairman, the kitman to be sacked and ultimately you can complain with your feet and simply desist from watching them until they improve. And so it is with your favourite store. You can simply stop shopping there because nowadays there are simply so many choices. Or you can complain and try and drag them up to the standards you expect. But why the effort? The fact is that we are creatures of habit. Just as we rarely change our football allegiances, so do we try at all costs to avoid changing our shopping habits. A very good friend of mine, Len, was and is a Marks & Spencer addict. He would spend so much there on a Friday on his way home that they gave him his own parking space. But he had one major problem. The plastic carrier bags kept giving way under the weight of his shopping. Mind you I think his plastic credit card was also in danger of giving way under the weight of his balances. He actually wrote to the Chairman of M&S to complain and not only received a reply but found to his delight that the bags were redesigned.

I also wrote to Marksies to complain about the lack of information on their bottles of wines as to whether or not they were vegetarian. I received a prompt and personal response and now if you bother to look you will see they are all labelled. What on earth is vegetarian wine do I hear you ask (and I will tell you a bit later) and who are these nutters who write to a total stranger in the shape of the Chairman of a Public Company asking him about the quality of his carrier bags and the ingredients of Chilean wine?

The point I am making is that you not only deserve satisfaction and near-perfection when you shop but are entitled to demand it. It would have been inconvenient for my friend to swap his customer loyalty from M&S to Waitrose, inconvenient for me to purchase wines online from one of the vegetarian/organic wine wholesalers. One polite letter to a receptive company and we were spared that inconvenience and, more importantly from the perspective of the company, they retained us as customers. Not only did they retain us but they had us singing their praises as we bored a countless succession of dinner parties with tales of our retail experiences. In fact, as someone to whom something inevitably happens whether travelling or shopping or, indeed, merely standing still and breathing very quietly, I have become something of a party piece as to my latest traveller's tale of disaster or high farce. Actually, I wonder why I've not been invited to too many dinner parties lately.

The other point I am making is that nothing is too trivial to complain about. If something in your life is making you unhappy and it is possible to make it better then there is no earthly reason why you shouldn't do something about it. There are, of course, far more serious things to complain about. And you have to be sensible and a little bit selective. There is no point in writing to Asda and telling them that their food-hall is not as good as Harrods. However, if you are shopping at the likes of Asda or Safeway then you are still entitled to value for money and a reasonably pleasant experience from the moment you get into the car park. Let's start with access and parking.

Supermarkets, in my opinion, have a moral, if not a legal duty, to enable their customers to park safely and easily. There is no pleasure in visiting a huge shopping mall on a busy day and having to drive around for an hour just looking for somewhere to park. So, if that happens to you, tell the company in charge of the mall and at the same time send a copy of your letter to the major stores in the shopping precinct. They may not even know how much of a nightmare it is to get to them and give them your money and they, certainly, have a vested interest in getting you and your wallet or purse inside their establishments. The car park operator (particularly where no charge is made) will probably have a more relaxed attitude. It's no skin off their nose if you give up at Bluewater and drive on to Thurrock. Actually, on the subject of car parks I really believe that it is the ultimate chutzpah for a charge to be made to shop. If that's the case then again you should try to persuade the shops, if they don't already, to give you a credit for the car park charges when you buy from them and, in any event, to give their potential customers some free parking time.

Mind you, I think hospitals have a similar obligation. Chase Farm Hospital in North London charges for its car park. Bit unfortunate if you're having a heart attack and can't find the odd fifty pence. But at least you can park if you have the wherewithal. My wife took her mother to a hospital in Essex, King George's and dropped her off at the entrance so she could park. By the time she had actually found a parking space the elderly lady had struggled along the corridors of the hospital, been seen by the doctor and was back at the front door waiting for her. And this is the National Health so you can imagine how long all that took.

Now as you know from bitter experience, there are all sorts of problems to overcome inside a supermarket. The lack of trolleys, the absence of any staff on the floor who have any idea where anything is, and most supermarkets seem to move their items around quite deliberately on a daily basis just to get you to spend longer with them; the bewildering choice and those confusing sell-by dates, not to mention a random provision of information on the labelling. Does anybody really know what e-472a is? Or even e-472b? Then there is the, "suitable for vegetarians," that is clearly stated on some products while others that look equally vegetarian, say nothing. Again, our old friend M & S is expert at this and it's only by writing and complaining to their head office that you get a list of their vegetarian products which, surprise, surprise, do include a whole load of items, such as biscuits, which are indeed animal-product free but do not have a large V for vegetarian on the label.

Not only are you entitled to know what you are eating (and by the way England is brilliant compared to the so-called health conscious Americans) but you are also entitled to know what's in what you are eating. Whilst we're on the subject of Americans I think I need to devote an entirely different book to the subject of How to Complain in America. It's not the same, as you'll see from some of my personal experiences scattered throughout this book. And just try and get them to commit anything to writing. I've just realised, as I check through this book, that I have virtually no letters whatsoever from any of my transatlantic complainees. My theory is that they are just so damned scared of being sued that they believe the less paper the better. My policy, as you will learn, is the exact opposite of that. The Yanks', "please let me know if there's anything we can do to help you," means "don't bother to ask for anything unless it's on the menu or we provide it as a norm." Whatever they may say, service in the States sucks, as does the very basic knowledge of food. I digress, but I sat in a restaurant in England listening to Americans refusing beef and asking the waiter to ensure that there was no beef in anything they were served lest they immediately race out of the restaurant mooing and lowing with mad cow disease. Meanwhile they happily ordered a New World wine that I knew had been strained through beef gelatine. I couldn't resist pointing this out to them and I don't think they even understood what I was saying as within twenty minutes they ordered another bottle. Mind you, by that stage I was beginning to think that their udders were looking distended. I'm not harping on the veggie theme, and believe me I'm not even a total vegetarian, but when you ask in the States if a cheese is vegetarian, they look at you as if you had taken leave of your senses and think that perhaps, in the UK, we have cheeses with four legs copulating with other cheeses to create small cheeses.

Back to our own trusty English establishments though. You have to know to whom to complain and how. There's no point in telling the lad on the check-out (whose focus is on the legs of the girl stacking the shelves) that you can't work out which biscuits contain animal fat or how you think it's a liberty that you've just paid fifty pence to park. If you want to make a complaint on the spot always ask for the store manager and never be fobbed off with the excuse that he's busy. Of course he's busy. He should be. Remind them that the customer not only comes first but also that the customer is always right. It's a great mantra, but you have to convince yourself to believe in it. When you get to see the manager (as I'm sure you will … I always do) be polite but firm. You need to come away with the feeling that something is going to be done about your complaints. This may be just an investigation without any guaranteed chance of success but it's where you have to start. Ask the manager to write to you to advise you of the outcome of his efforts and make a note for fourteen days on in case he hasn't. At that point you need to go over his head and write to the company's head office addressing your letter to the Managing Director. The result of this may well be to get the manager into trouble but you can't be committed to complaining and at the same time harbour any feelings of guilt. The two are incompatible and why should you feel guilty? Your complaint was justified in the first instance, you gave the store and the manager the chance to do something about it and he didn't. So, quite frankly, he deserves everything he gets from his bosses. Even if he had sent you a letter, saying that the parking was out of his control but the company had noted your complaint and would have the matter under constant review, that would have probably headed you off at the pass. If he had also said that goods had been moved around the store pursuant to a head office directive, to bring the store into line with the rest of the group, you might have accepted it. If they had apologised for the lack of ingredient details on individual products and sent you a list of their designated vegetarian products you would even have thought you had got a result. And so it goes on, as I have already said (and may well say again). If you get no response from the General Manager then you write to the Chief Executive and then you write to the Chairman. It's unlikely that you will fail to hear from any of them but in the event of total silence you now have a great paper trail, to use as appropriate.

Now, car-parking and ingredients are soft targets. What happens and what do you do if you buy some product that is defective? I have three favourite food stories. Many years ago I bought some apple turnovers from a now defunct baker (it's amazing how many companies who figure in this book are now defunct) and took them to the cinema with my mother. That will give you some idea of how long ago it was as I've been old enough to go to pictures on my own for nearly fifty years. However, looking back it was probably a watershed in my complaining career. We ate the turnovers in the dark and, whilst thinking they tasted odd and giving them a brief inspection which made us think they were blackberry turnovers (well, I was young and naïve), we carried on regardless. It was only when we got outside and saw the surviving turnover that we realised it was mouldy. Having a delicate constitution I was ill on the spot, which probably saved me a longer and more painful terminal fate. My mother, who came from good peasant stock, didn't turn a hair, but did suggest that perhaps I should tell the shop in case they actually poisoned an innocent customer. She was always the nice one in the family and fortunately or unfortunately I didn't inherit her caring genes. Without any of the lifetime of experience I have now gathered around me I stormed back into the shop and thrust the offending article over the counter. They were neither impressed nor surprised, suggested initially I had the wrong shop and then told me I must have bought them days ago. Finally and generously they offered to replace the two I had eaten! Not unsurprisingly I rejected the offer, went away and wrote them a letter of complaint and sent a copy (with the now increasingly unhappy turnover) to the then relevant officer at the local council. I seem to recall the baker sending me £50 (a huge sum in those

days) albeit probably smaller than the fine they received for actually selling the item in the first place (and probably loads of other
fines too for loads of other breaches of loads of other statutes and
bye-laws regarding cleanliness). All of which is probably why they
are now defunct.

Many years and what seemed like an eternity of complaints later
(my wife thinks that my name flashes up in huge red warning
letters whenever I enter a shop, plane or hotel) I bought some
dates from my favourite supermarket. Yes, you've guessed, Marks &
Spencer again. Actually I must make it clear that this book is not
intended as an ongoing tirade against the vicissitudes of M & S.
Most of my stories concerning food relate to them as I shop there
virtually exclusively (I do buy kosher products in Golders Green
but try complaining there. Now they make *you* feel guilty. It comes
from them all having Jewish mothers) In fact when Marksies
opened their new food store in my locality I went in there on the
first day of opening. I was asked at checkout how I had enjoyed my
experience. I think I rather shocked my questioner by saying that
I had loved it so much that I wanted to move my bed in, that when
I grew up I wanted to marry either Marks or Spencer and that I
couldn't see an M & S food delivery van pass by without wanting to
hi-jack it. Whenever I visited the store after that and went to queue
to pay, that checkout individual took one look at me, said something quietly to a colleague and then went off for his tea break.

But back to the dates. The dates clearly stated that they were
stoneless and carried no warning that this might not be the case.
How trusting of the store to rely on some bloke to remove the
stone from every date he lovingly packed. Whatever! I found a
stone in my box of dates. Not only did I find it but my tooth found
it and so did a filling. Was my first thought one of pain, an urgent
visit to the dentist and an ancient curse upon the date-stone
removing industry? Not a bit of it. My first rush of blood was to get
my thoughts into order as to how best to complain.

Clutching my jaw I immediately went back to the store, asked for
the duty manager, and showed him the stone. I asked him to
confirm he would send it to head office and I also asked him to
give me a written receipt and acknowledgment there and then. I
told him that I would be making an emergency appointment at my

dentist and that I would be writing a formal letter of complaint the next day. I actually dictated my letter before I went to the dentist to obtain the cathartic relief I knew it would bring and was then told by my dentist that I had merely badly bruised the tooth and that no filling would be necessary. I got a receipt for the visit and then sent that off to M & S as well. A week went by without response. I could only assume that they were treating the matter so seriously that they had despatched a senior board member to visit the date production and de-stoning factory. Anyway, I then wrote them a polite reminder and received back an offer of compensation that I considered derisory. The fact of the matter is that if you want to be a serious and competent complainant you have to regard every first offer as derisory even if it's not. Nobody ever believes that they are going to get out of trouble in the first round of negotiations so why should you shatter that belief? Another offer arrived, this time consisting of payment of my dental expenses and enough M & S vouchers to ease the pain. I was satisfied. However, if something like this happens to you and you are offered in-store vouchers, which are, of course, a much cheaper way of dealing with the matter from the store's point of view ... think about it. They are still making their profit on the item which they've either manufactured or bought wholesale and as you are being compensated in retail terms then only accept them if you do intend shopping at the offending store on an ongoing basis. Otherwise insist on cash and again, if you do accept the vouchers, notionally add on a figure to adjust the amount to reflect that saving to the offeror.

My third favourite food story (I bet you wish you could come to dinner-parties with me every night of the week) relates to spring rolls. Now it's really not fair to tell tales continually about Marks & Spencer so, although these were bought from M & S, let's imagine they weren't. Anyway, I decided on Sunday to cook the second meal I have ever cooked in my life. (Female readers please note that you should never, but never, let your daughters marry only children and particularly not only Jewish sons) This was going to consist of grilled Jerusalem artichokes, which was nothing if not ambitious for an amateur chef, and for some reason I decided to start with some vegetarian spring rolls. Fusion cooking I guess you might call it. I also decided to cheat by buying these in from the store that we are not calling M & S. So why don't we call it N & T? I got them home clearly marked in the packet as vegetarian spring rolls suitable for vegetarians and then spent hours chopping and preparing my artichokes before dumping the N & T rolls into bubbling oil. I got them cooked exactly right, nice and crispy and brown and put them on the plate. My wife, Marilyn (must remember now that I've named her not to divorce her before publication) who had been standing by, watching the devastation that Hurricane Mel was dealing to her kitchen, took a mouthful and spat it out. I looked on appalled. Was this a comment on my culinary skills?

"There's some kind of fish in there," she said. And there was. They were prawn spring rolls in the wrong packaging. Now to understand the full import of this I have to give you a quick lesson in kosher culinary matters. If we were really orthodox we wouldn't be buying anything from M & S or N & T, veggie or not. Truly religious Jews only buy things that are prepared under rabbinical supervision and which are certified as being kosher. My line is drawn in the sand if I am satisfied that what I am eating is vegetarian. This is truly confusing, as half of the civilised world thinks I am indeed vegetarian whilst in truth I am more than happy to eat meat as long as it's prepared in such a way as to make the poor animal look as if it never had a parent. You know what I mean, nice thin slices of chicken breast, steak burnt to a crisp, slivers of duck done Chinese-style in a pancake with onion and cucumber. However, apart from our quirky fall from grace when it comes to non-supervised veggie products, we do keep kosher at home – which fact is relevant when we come on to how to complain in restaurants and on planes.

What that means is that we keep two sets of crockery, one for milk and one for meat, two sets of cutlery, (for the same aforesaid purpose) and don't let either mix with each other (strict segregation) and obviously don't eat anything non-kosher off either. So, assuming you have all that straight (as if you were even mildly interested) you will understand how upset we were to discover that we had cooked prawns (which in case you didn't know and it's amazing how many people don't) are very much non-kosher. I recently flew back from Glasgow on British Midlands (no point in not naming guilty parties) when yet again my pre-ordered kosher meal didn't quite find its way on board. I have the feeling there is a parallel universe somewhere inhabited by socks I have lost between the dirty linen basket and the exit to the washing machine and kosher meals that have been promised to me on airplanes and never made an appearance. The stewardess solicitously offered me an egg and prawn sandwich and when I declined with less good grace than I should have, as I was bloody hungry, she offered to remove the prawn and give me the egg.

We too removed the prawn and, wrapping it in a see-through sandwich bag, I hastened back to N & T together with the product container.

"Excuse me," I said, "but can you tell me what sort of vegetable this is?" I pointed to the pinkish thing in the bag.

"A tomato?" ventured the N & T lady.

This was on a par with a British Airways stewardess telling Marilyn that the mould on an omelette was spinach, notwithstanding that the meal was about a year past its sell-by date (another complaint, another story, another chapter).

"No, It's not a tomato!" I replied, trying to keep my cool. It's all very well telling you and telling myself not to lose it but there are moments when it is very hard indeed. "Have another go." I encouraged her.

"It's too pink for a tomato, isn't it?" she said, by now entering into the spirit of the debate and showing a proprietary interest in the item which had emanated from her store.

"Yes, yes it is," I agreed.

"It looks a bit fishy," she said, without a hint of irony.

"Indeed, it is." I then gave her the lecture on kosher dietary habits, as above, watching for any hint of her eyes glazing over. There was none, just an occasional desperate glance around the store to see if there was anybody more senior who would assume responsibility for dealing with me.

Eventually we agreed that this was not only an affront to my religious sensibilities but could have been potentially fatal for someone else with a sea-food allergy. We parted on the basis that there would be a full inquiry and that I would get a phone call from Head Office in Baker Street the next day. Bit of a coincidence that, N & T having their head office in Baker Street just like Marks & Spencer. Clearly my complaint had been effective and I did get my call the next day, but just so that there should be no misunderstanding, and whilst the incident was fresh in my mind, I wrote a long letter setting out the facts. As a matter of experience it's always best to do that and eventually you will fall into the habit of carrying pen and paper or a memo dictating machine around with you just to make notes about events that have annoyed you sufficiently to complain about. The caller was very apologetic and told me they were putting in hand a full investigation. A week went by and I heard nothing. A week is generally sufficient time for a complaint to be dealt with and so I wrote again, this time to the Chief Executive. I received another phone call, even more apologetic than the first and then a letter enclosing some vouchers. I persisted. I had been forced to throw away the frying pan and also the plate so I felt, apart from the shock and inconvenience, that the least they could do for me was to ensure I could replace the pan and get myself a new set of matching crockery. After the third letter they caved in and justice was done.

Now you may feel that I was making a fuss over nothing, that it was all a prawn in a tea-cup. But the fact of the matter was that it was important to me. And that goes to the very heart of complaining. Something has gone wrong which is important to you but which may well be trivial to somebody else. Because it appears trivial to them they do not take it seriously enough and hackles rise on your side. Grounds for complaint are totally subjective and as long as you realise this and have the courage of your convictions to get yourself taken seriously, not only will it all be worthwhile but you, yourself, will feel much better about it. Never ever say, even to yourself, that what has happened is not worth complaining about. Trust me, it always is.

Just to get you started in stores here are a few things which I'd certainly complain about … no surprise to you, I'm sure.

1. Parking difficulties and unwarranted parking charges.
2. Surly service.
3. Poor labelling.

4. Sell-by dates passed with the item still for sale.
5. Constant moving around of items on display without good reason.
6. Long queues at checkout when there are not enough staff to man the counters.
7. Product doesn't accord with its description. If a food item is awful then the supermarket won't change or improve it unless customers complain.
8. Crummy carrier bags (that one is a tribute to my friend Len).
9. Complaints not responded to swiftly or sympathetically enough.
10. Derisory offer of compensation, or vouchers rather than cash.

5

SLOW TRAINS TO CHINA
(Or anywhere else for that matter)

In addition to the weather, Tim Henman at Wimbledon and the England football team, we in the UK have virtually no expectations from travel, particularly when it comes to trains. With 27 different train companies operating in the UK there are far too many organisations involved, not to mention chronic under-funding. In addition to these you have the Ministry of Transport, a rail regulator, a rail inspectorate, the Strategic Rail Authority and Network Rail, but, despite all of this, 1 in 5 trains are late in the UK. Virgin have just announced potential space travel, and although I probably have enough air miles with the compensation awards I get, there is hardly likely to be a queue for seats when they can't get the Euston to Manchester service to run on time.

So, with no guarantee of a seat, even for full-fare paying passengers, whilst at the same time having one of the most expensive rail services in Europe, that gallant band of rail-users must ensure they complain effectively with a view, not only to gaining maximum compensation, but equalling the sole achievement of Mussolini in making the trains run on time.

Let's get one of my favourite personal travel stories out of the way first, an incident that actually occurred in the salubrious and exotic surroundings of King's Cross Station, gateway to the North and the red light district of London. I wanted to travel to somewhere up North. The train was at the crack of dawn and I was told that if I didn't want to have to get to the station half an hour before the train departed then I had to collect my ticket the night before from Kings Cross. On asking why, as I thought I was travelling from the neighbouring St Pancras, I was told that the ticket was being sent down by train from a central booking office in York, and yes, I did need to collect it from King's Cross notwithstanding. Clearly the age of e-tickets had not dawned in the rail industry. Thus I found myself queuing at the ticket collection office at King's Cross at nine o'clock at night, having left my wife locked in the car outside with strict instructions not to speak to strange men (and to ensure that I got fifty percent of the takings if she did).

There was nobody serving at the first class counter, and the counter for pre-booked tickets was similarly deserted. I stood in the regular ticket booking line and waited, the clock ticking away, my wife doubtless thinking I had actually decided to travel that night and leave her to her fate. Eventually there was only one man in front of me but unfortunately he was Japanese and spoke no English. His booking therefore had to be conducted via a mobile phone (presumably back to an English-speaking friend in Tokyo) who eventually negotiated for his pal the right to travel on an English train. I bet there were recriminations about that when Japanese gentleman Number One wrote his diary about "Wot I Did On My Holiday In England". A whole chapter on a day spent staring out of a train window at a railway siding just outside Crewe no doubt.

I got to speak to a man finally and asked for my tickets (which by the way had already been charged to my credit card). The man then started to fumble through a whole pile of envelopes, none of which appeared to be in alphabetical order ... unless they had been rearranged in Japanese to accommodate the previous passenger, and finally told me they weren't there and suggested I should try across the road at St Pancras. I patiently told him that I had thought that was where logically they should be collected but had been told to come here. The man turned and began to go through the envelopes once again. I watched in increasing despair thinking that perhaps the tickets themselves had been sent down on a train that never arrived. By now the queue behind me had grown. The man looked at it, then casually put a closed notice at his counter. It was now almost ten and I had been there an hour.

"I'll go to St Pancras then," I said. The man shrugged. I raced across the road, pausing only to check on my wife's well being (no takers so far) and arrived at St Pancras only to find all the ticket windows closed notwithstanding the fact that the station was still open. I made my way to the Station Manager's office and knocked and entered. He, at least was still there, still on duty defending his station to the last man, which from the looks of it happened to be him anyway. I told him my story.

"The ticket will be in the ticket office then" he said.

"Good," I said, "so can we collect them?"

He shook his head sadly.

"It'll be locked."

"Yes, but you're the station manager. You must have a key."

Again a sad shake of the head.

"So what happens if there's a fire?" I asked.

"There won't be anybody in there so it can stay locked," he replied.

I was going to ask what would happen to my much-travelled ticket in the event of a night-time conflagration. Would I have to wait for the next train from York to bring me a duplicate? But then decided it was a waste of time.

"You need to get here half-an hour before your train leaves in the morning to collect it," the manager said.

I took a deep breath.

"So let me get this right. I was told I had to collect my ticket tonight to travel tomorrow if I didn't want to have to get here half an hour before the train departed but you can't give it to me, so having spent nearly an hour and a half here I still have to get up half an hour earlier tomorrow to get it."

The man nodded, seemingly pleased I had understood the situation.

"No," I said firmly. "This is what you do. You will be waiting by the platform ten minutes before my train departs and, if not you, then another man with a card with my name on it holding my tickets."

He wasn't there. Fortunately I was early and had time to go to the ticket window. I rapidly told the man behind the counter my sad story. He expressed no surprise but merely printed out another ticket. It was too early in the morning to ask why the man couldn't have done that the previous evening at King's Cross. I did write a long letter setting out the train (excuse the pun) of events and the result was an apology and travel vouchers which virtually equalled the cost of the fare. Oh, and a story that friends never cease to enjoy hearing (or at least they pretend to).

Now the moral of the story in complaining terms is obviously one of never give up, know when to be firm, know when to be sarcastic. You may enjoy that but it doesn't always get results unless used in moderation and upon people who will actually understand it. And know when you have the high moral ground and can press home your advantage. I'll be talking quite a lot about the high moral ground as you follow my adventures. Once seized it's vital to defend it.

Now, once you are on the train most train companies do have a charter which does guarantee you a rebate if the train is late by a certain amount of time. However, the amounts are pitiful and certainly may not reflect the damage done to you. If you are going for a job interview or have a first meeting with an important client the excuse that the train was late will cut no ice. So, remember what I said about subjectivity. How did the delay affect you? You have to be sensible about it. Complaining to a train company about a delay which was quite beyond their control is a waste of time and energy. If some bloke decides to drive his car off the road and onto the tracks then, short of sprouting wings, the train can't move. However, there does come a point when something can be done. Road transportation to your destination or another station beyond the accident could and should be provided after a reasonable period of time and, if it's not, then you are being perfectly reasonable in doing something about it. And the company is being perfectly unreasonable if they don't compensate you for failing to do anything about it.

Now full marks to Midland Mainline for responding and reacting to a trip I took recently. I think the correspondence speaks for itself, but this is exactly how a complaint letter should be answered and precisely the sort of outcome that should be sought.

Dear Sirs,

I had the misfortune to travel back first class from Stockport to London St. Pancras on the 16th March. I had travelled up on Virgin Trains from Euston but, having missed the 16.38, was encouraged by the guard to take the 16.59 to St. Pancras rather than wait for the 17.38 Virgin train as I was told it would be "a much more enjoyable journey".

The train itself had been restricted to five carriages and stopped immediately outside Stockport station as it was following a slow-moving train. There was no buffet car on board and, although in First Class, when coffee was brought round, there was no fresh milk.

I heard the attendant say that all the Midland Mainline stock consisted of trains that had been discarded by Virgin and I could well understand that. The windows were filthy, the curtains even dirtier. The train crawled its way to London, eventually arriving at 8.45 p.m.

I look forward to receiving some explanation, particularly given the fact that I had paid £280 for a return ticket.

Yours faithfully,

B MM 8 April 2004
Dear Mr Stein,

Thank you for writing to me on 01 April 2004 (I'd had to supply some more information) and enclosing a copy of your ticket.

For any delay of an hour or more, we will offer customers travel vouchers to cover the cost of the delayed part of their journey. Although the delay you experienced was less than an hour, by way of apology, I have ordered a cheque for £70.00, which will be sent in the next 7-10 days. This covers half the cost of your journey, and comes with our sincere apologies for the inconvenience caused.

Once again, please accept my apologies for the disappointing level of service provided by Midland Mainline and for the problems this caused you. Despite your recent experience, I hope you will use our services in the future.

Yours sincerely

All perfectly acceptable and I will travel on Midland Mainline again.

I was once stuck on a train half-way up the side of a mountain outside Vancouver. We needed to get back because we wanted to buy tickets for an ice-hockey game in the evening. Trains do break down, but on this occasion so did communication. We just sat there and nobody told us what was happening. The incredible thing was that none of the Canadian passengers on the train thought there was anything odd about it. I went in search of the train manager and told him that if this had happened in England then at least some complimentary refreshments would have been given to the passengers. It was, by the way, the one hot day of the year in Vancouver. He basically told me that this wasn't England and if I didn't return to my seat he'd phone the police and get me removed from the train. I replied that as long as they took me back to Vancouver and allowed my wife to come with me in the car then I was perfectly happy with that arrangement.

By now a few other passengers had overheard the altercation and joined in my demands for some drinks, etc. The train manager knew when he was beaten and arranged for them to be served. By now I'd really got the bit between my teeth and began to conduct a master class with my fellow travellers as to how we would deal with the matter when (and by this stage if) we got back to Vancouver; not only would we demand a refund on the fare but also some compensation, I said. As if by magic the train manager began to circulate and said exactly that, but, as I recall the $20 that was being offered was, in my view, not enough, particularly as I now knew I had no chance of getting to my ice-hockey match. Take it, I said, on account, but write in and ask for more. Whatever you do don't sign anything that says you accept it in full and final satisfaction. Oh, and by the way why aren't they sending buses up to get us down. I sought out my friend the train manager who seemed to be regretting not exercising the powers of arrest that he seemed to think he had. He declined to phone back to base, at which point I asked for the number so that I could call from my mobile and demand an explanation as to why we were still there. He made the call, but just as arrangements were in hand for the rescue operation, to an enormous cheer we began to move. Yes, I did miss the match, yes, I did get a fare refund *and* the $20 but when I wrote I also got an apology and another cheque. *Awkward bugger, moi?* Maybe. But what would have happened if, like everybody else, I'd sat around and accepted my fate?

There are just so may things that one can complain about in and on trains in this country that it's a bit of a soft target; soft and so large that you can hardly fail to hit it in some region on every journey. Indeed, I can hardly think of one train journey I've taken where there's not been something to complain about. I rarely travel on the tube but if I did on a regular basis I suspect they'd be chopping down whole rain forests to cope with the deluge of correspondence I'd be raining upon the heads of the bosses at London Transport. After my car had broken down for the umpteenth time (see chapter 21 for the whole story). I took a bus from my garage in Edgware to Kilburn intending to get a train the rest of the way to my office. Well, not quite all the way into the office of course, but as far as I could get without having to extend the underground tunnels and widen the doors of the building that contains my place of work. I think my complaint letter below tells its own sorry tale.

Penalty Fares Admin. Office,
London Underground Ltd.,
P.O. Box 4092,
LONDON SW1H 0BD.

Dear Sirs,

Re: Penalty fare Number XXX

I have just completed a Journey from Hell on the Underground, which has ended up costing me £11.20 to travel from Kilburn to Bond Street.

This morning the brakes on my car failed and I had to take it on an emergency basis to my garage in Edgware. I took a bus to Kilburn station and decided to travel by Underground from Kilburn to my office in Park Lane.

I had no idea how much the fare would cost or where I should change, not having travelled on the Underground for some ten years, and therefore joined a queue at the ticket window. After a ten minutes' wait, the queue had barely moved so I moved across to the automatic ticket machine. I checked to see that the single fare to Hyde Park Corner was £1.70 and I then pressed the £1.70 button on the machine. I inserted first of all a one pound coin, and then a 20 pence coin, at which point the machine delivered to me a £1.20 ticket. I then returned to the queue at the window to explain to your staff what had happened and to pay an extra 50 pence or to get them to endorse the ticket or change it. Again, I waited another ten minutes. There were clearly insufficient staff on duty, people were buying season tickets and making lengthy enquiries and I then decided I would pay at the other end.

I got to Bond Street Station, having travelled in what was the equivalent of a cattle truck, and asked the first London transport official where I should pay. She told me that I should pay at the window upstairs. I then went to the window and, to my astonishment, the staff member told me that I had to pay £10, as I had travelled with an invalid ticket. I tried to explain the situation, and went to the point of asking to see the Station Manager and was eventually told that, whilst staff accepted that the policy was absurd, I would have to pay and appeal. Reluctantly, therefore, I paid an extra £10, bringing the total cost of my fare to £11.20.

I am enclosing herewith my ticket and the penalty fare notice and await hearing from you with the return of my £9.50, and some kind of apology for the unnecessary delays caused to my journey as soon as possible.

Yours faithfully,

They cancelled the penalty and gave me some sort of apology. It could have been worse. They could have given me a free season ticket for life.

So what do we look for in respect of train complaints?

1. Ease of purchase of the ticket.
2. Punctuality.
3. Cleanliness of the train.
4. Comfort of the train.
5. Civility of the staff.
6. Cost of the journey.
7. Catering, both as to choice and quality.
8. Information on board as to reasons for delays.
9. Speed of dealing with complaints.
10. Level of compensation.

Each train company has its own passenger charter and you should obtain a copy from your train company. Keep evidence of all travel documents and if you have a complaint ensure you do not lose your ticket to a machine on exit and, in fact, to be on the safe side, ask a guard to let you through the barriers.

6

COME FLY WITH ME
(If the plane actually takes off)

I fly a lot (usually on a plane) so it is inevitable that I have garnered enough stories for a book totally dedicated to air travel. I once had cause to write to British Airways complaining about a flight to Israel.

Dear Sirs,

Further to my various telephone conversations with Jo at the Executive Club, I am writing to you to set out my anger and concern regarding the Journey from Hell that I and many other people were forced to undertake last week.

My wife, my son and I were, with many others, invited to a wedding in Jerusalem some months ago. The wedding was to take place on Sunday 6th February and, as the family had invited so many people from England, they had decided to organise an extended trip commencing with dinner for everybody on the night of Friday 4th February, a group breakfast and lunch on Saturday 5th and a party on the evening of Saturday 5th at the home of a friend who lived in Jerusalem. Our friends had organised a discount rated fare on El Al but, as a British Airways Executive Club member, I decided that I would prefer to fly BA as I had done so often in the past.

After discussions with various other individuals, I also dissuaded them from flying El Al and persuaded them that, although it would cost more money, British Airways was far more reliable and the flight would be a more enjoyable experience.

Having booked our own three flights (which cost us over £200 more than we would have spent on El Al), we drove to the airport on Thursday evening and checked in for 8 p.m. At the check-in, nobody mentioned to us that there was any problem with regard to the flight.

The first setback was when we experienced a very brusque reception at the Executive Club and were told that only one guest was allowed in. It took some persuasion for them to agree that my son (who was clearly part of our travelling party) could accompany us into the Lounge. We sat there for a couple of hours and again there was no indication that there was any problem. Shortly after 10.00 p.m., when we should have been boarding, my son went to the desk and, to his astonishment, was told that Tel Aviv airport was closed. He was then told, immediately, that the flight was cancelled.

We explained that we had to be in Jerusalem by sunset on Friday (i.e. prior to the commencement of the Jewish Sabbath). We were told there was another flight in the morning from Gatwick but that BA had already taken the decision to cancel that flight as well. At this point, all hell broke loose, both in the Executive Lounge and (I understand from other travelling companions) downstairs in the main hall. I asked if I could transfer on to the El Al flight which was leaving that evening and we were told that this was definitely not flying. Some people telephoned El Al and were told that everybody was on board and the doors were closed. Again I was told that El Al would not be flying as the airport was closed. People continued to telephone and then told British Airways that the El Al flight was in the air. When I relayed this to one of your representatives, I was virtually called a liar and told it was impossible. They then backtracked on this and admitted that the El Al flight was in the air but that it was flying to Ovda in Eilat. No explanation was given to me as to why British Airways could not have flown or at least commenced its flight in the direction of the Middle East and we were told that we could either go and stay in a hotel for the night or could simply go home.

I queued to try and re-book my flight to Israel and to see whether or not I could get out either via Rome or Paris or even possibly via Amman as I had a valid Jordanian visa in my passport. To say the staff were unhelpful is an understatement and I was told this was impossible. Very reluctantly, I re-booked the flight for Saturday night at 10.40 p.m. and was told that there was still an outside possibility that British Airways might fly in the morning and that I should phone very early. On that basis, because we were told that there was a "20% chance", we decided to stay over at the hotel.

We then sat on a bus outside the terminal for some 30 minutes, waiting to be bussed to the hotel and finally got to bed at 1 a.m.

I got up at 4 a.m. and telephoned British Airways. They told me that there was a 24-hour strike by baggage handlers at Tel Aviv airport and that the Gatwick flight had already been cancelled and would be flying on Friday night at 20.00 hours. Obviously this was totally unacceptable as far as I was concerned. I then telephoned our friends in Israel who told me, to my astonishment, that the El Al flight, which had departed from Heathrow on the night of the 3rd February, had landed virtually on time, that all the baggage had been unloaded and that the people on board had arrived safely at the hotel. I telephoned British Airways again and nobody had any comment to make.

Eventually, I decided to go home and accept the 10.40 p.m. Saturday night flight. We had no food at home as we had intended being away for the weekend and obviously had to purchase food for the Sabbath whereas otherwise we would have been the guests of our friends in Jerusalem at their expense.

Friends of ours who were travelling with us, Robby and Ros, had been willing to fly on Friday night. They had telephoned British Airways on Friday morning and been told that Economy was full but there were seats available on Business and First Class. Not unreasonably, they asked if it would be possible for them to have an upgrade and the lady to whom they spoke (in Newcastle) was extremely rude, refused to put them on the flight and virtually put the phone down on Robby. They did not even have a house to go back to as they had given it away to their daughter for the weekend and they had to come back and stay with us. Again, we entertained them at our expense.

We duly returned to the airport on Saturday night when, not

unreasonably, again at check-in I asked whether it would be possible to have an upgrade and this was met with a blank refusal. I was advised that there was a policy not to upgrade on this flight. On both check-ins I specifically asked for confirmation that my kosher meals were on board and was told in each case that they were available.

When we finally got on board the plane on Saturday night, there were in fact insufficient kosher meals and we therefore arrived at 5.30 a.m. in Tel Aviv without having eaten either supper or being supplied with any breakfast.

Having missed all of the pre-nuptial celebration, we arrived at the wedding absolutely exhausted which, as you can imagine, severely impaired our enjoyment of the same. The poor Wiltons had to return on the Monday and thus travelled to Israel for a little over 24 hours. We had to get up at 4.30 a.m. Israel time in order to catch a flight back from Tel Aviv. On this occasion we did receive a kosher meal on the flight but it was totally inedible and did not even have such basic ingredients as orange juice or milk.

Apart from the loss of enjoyment of the wedding (which can not be replaced), we have been put to a considerable amount of time, trouble and expense which could have been avoided had British Airways simply waited to see what was happening at Tel Aviv airport. Given that the strike was called off some two hours after BA aborted the flight (and well before the flight would have taken off from Gatwick), I find this utterly inexplicable and a harsh and thoughtless decision. One poor man on our flight was trying to get back for his mother's funeral (which had already been delayed a day) and another lady was trying to get back for a tombstone consecration (having already missed the funeral because of another strike).

As far as expense is concerned, we had to take a taxi from the hotel to the long-term car park, which cost us £10; I had an additional £11.40 parking at the long-term car park and spent over £150 on food for ourselves and our friends for the weekend. Had we arrived when we should have done on Friday morning, we would have been given a lift from Tel Aviv to Jerusalem but instead we had to rent a taxi. Of course, we had already paid for our hotel for the Thursday night (to guarantee us a room when we arrived early on Friday morning), Friday night and Saturday night, again at a cost of over £250 for us and £150 for our son.

When I spoke to Jo at the Executive Club on two occasions on Thursday, she did initially tell me that a supervisor would call me back and finally told me that I would be written to within the next five days. I did tell her that I would be writing myself and I must insist upon receiving some satisfactory offer of compensation and, indeed, a letter of explanation as to why BA took the extraordinary decision not to fly when other airlines (including Air 2000) flew and landed without any trouble whatsoever, and why we were so deliberately misled throughout Thursday night and Friday morning.

I await hearing from you.

I received no reply and wrote a reminder. This time I received a standard response enclosing a £25 travel voucher. I wrote again asking them to read my letter and reply. Another standard response but this time a £50 travel voucher. Both letters were signed by different individuals. Another letter; another travel voucher, this time back to £25. And I was hoping for double or quits! This one-way correspondence continued until I had assembled over £200 in travel vouchers and a whole host of new pen pals in the depths of British Airways. My wife, at least, got a Ferragamo bag, purchased in-flight with the vouchers even if I never got a satisfactory response to my letter. Just like M & S (though unlike them 'cos Marksies do respond eventually) BA will figure extensively in my book. Although I called it a day with my Israel trip complaint, my letters to them continued as, for a while I foolishly continued flying with them.

However, even my patience was stretched beyond endurance by a spate of flights between November 15th 2000 and March 2001. It all began with a flight I was due to take to Edinburgh for one meeting at lunchtime. I arrived early, checked in and saw that there was an earlier flight. I asked if I could change to that as I had no luggage and was told the flight was closed. I shrugged and made my way through security to the Executive Lounge (these were days when I still had a Silver Executive card ... yet another series of complaints when they took that away from me ... you would have thought they would have renewed it just to keep me quiet, wouldn't you?) To my astonishment the earlier flight was still shown on the screen as boarding. I asked at reception why I'd been told the flight was closed when it had palpably been open. I was told, rather unsympathetically, that it was closed now. So, I sat myself down and waited for my flight to be called. About fifteen minutes later we were told to go to the gate indicated on my ticket, but on arriving there we were then told the gate had changed. After a quick trot of about mile we arrived at the correct gate, only to find a scrimmage of unhappy people who had just been told that the flight was further delayed, as there was some fog. I asked if it was worth returning to the lounge and received a non-committal shrug. By now the complaint letter was forming in my mind, but far worse was to follow. Eventually we were boarded and again we just sat there for about forty-five minutes when we were told that we were, as I recall, 25th in line for take-off and we wouldn't be taking off for about another 45 minutes. My meeting was already looking like an impossibility and so I asked if I could, in the American parlance, (how I hate the word) deplane. I was told that wasn't possible, as the steps had been taken away. I politely asked if they could be brought back. Again a no-no. I looked around the cabin. A fair number of passengers seemed to be looking at their watches.

"Anyone else want to get off the plane?" I asked and saw some half a dozen hands go up.

"There are now seven of us who want to get off the plane" I said to the stewardess, "can we have the steps now?"

After a few phone calls back to base they finally arrived. The saga was not yet over. I tried to get my ticket back to get a rebate at the gate and was told this was impossible and I had to go to a ticket desk. I did and there I was asked to join a queue and eventually I left the airport and got back to my office some nine hours after I had rolled out of bed.

As you can imagine, I was not best pleased and notwithstanding the innumerable phone call, emails and correspondence that awaited me my first task was to do my complaint letter whilst the day's events were, not only fresh in my mind, but bitter on my tongue.

Dear Ms. X,

I have just returned to my office on Wednesday 15th November having wasted an entire morning, largely due to the incompetence of your airline.

I was booked to fly to Edinburgh on the 9 a.m. flight returning on the same day at 4.15.

I decided to get to the airport by 8.15 and, having ordered a car, was told that if I wanted to get there by that time, I needed to leave my home in North London by 6.30 a.m. This I did and, as luck would have it, I arrived at Heathrow at 7.15. I checked in (without bags) at the Executive Club desk in the main foyer and, at the same time, asked whether there was an earlier flight back as I only had a lunchtime meeting in Scotland. I was told there was a 3.15 flight and, if I wanted, I could change my ticket in the Executive Club. At no time was I told that there was, in fact, an earlier flight to Edinburgh, though one might have thought it would have been a logical piece of advice to proffer somebody who is clearly going to the city for only a few hours.

I asked whether or not my pre-ordered Kosher meal was on board and was told there was no record of any request for either a Kosher or a vegetarian meal and it might be too late to lay one on. I did point out that, as an Executive Club Silver member, my dietary requirements should be in my profile. For the last three flights, meals have not been available even though these had been pre-ordered by my travel agent.

When I arrived in the Executive Club, I asked them to check my profile and, at the same time, formally changed my flight from 4.15 p.m. to 3.15 p.m. Again there was no mention that there was an earlier outbound flight.

I went upstairs into the lounge, had a drink and, to my astonishment, then saw on the screen that there was an 8 o'clock Edinburgh flight. I went down to reception and was told that, yes, there were seats on board this but it had closed and that people were being bussed on to the plane. I accepted this information but, to my astonishment, when I went back upstairs, some ten minutes later I heard a call for the flight to which I had been denied access.

I left the lounge at about 8.40 as my ticket said I had to be at the gate by 8.50. I had been told to go to waiting area 5 where everybody else was waiting for their various flights. Notwithstanding the fact that many passengers (including myself) were unable to find a seat, British Airways staff, numbering some 8, happily sat on the seats, chatting, without any thought whatsoever for their customers. Eventually, at about 9 o'clock, we were told to go to Gate 76. On arrival there, I was told to take a seat because the flight was not boarding for another 10 minutes. This was fairly academic advice as there were no seats to be taken.

At no stage were we told that there were any substantial delays on the flight. Indeed, when I checked in, I had seen a note saying there might be some adjustments to schedules and I had specifically asked whether or not the Edinburgh flight was delayed. This was vital to me as I only had one meeting at lunchtime and needed to return on the same day. Again at check-in I was told there were no delays but there were some cancellations.

We were then boarded and at about 9.30 were finally told that there were going to be some more delays and it would take at least half-an-hour before we could take off. Some ten minutes later, that estimate was amended and we were told it would be another hour before we could take off. At this point, several passengers asked to leave the plane and initially were told this would not be possible as the steps had been removed. Eventually, the steps were brought back and I was finally de-planed.

I was then told that I needed to collect my voucher at the Customer Service Desk back at Gate 5 and when I arrived there, there was a long queue. When I finally reached the front of the queue, I was told that my vouchers were at Gate 76.

I made my feelings very clear to the Duty Manager, Jackie, who was extremely polite and as helpful as she could be and eventually she sent somebody up to the gate to collect my voucher and I finally left the airport and got on a train at 10.45 a.m., thus over four hours of travelling had taken me exactly nowhere.

I had spent £28 on a car getting to the airport, by the time I got to my office it was midday and I had thus wasted a half-day, quite apart from my failure to attend what was a very important business meeting in Edinburgh.

I really feel, in all the circumstances, that some of my problems could have been avoided had British Airways been more proactive and supplied more information. Presumably the 8 a.m. flight took off before the 9 a.m. flight even though it was delayed as well and might have made it possible for me to get to my meeting.

May I please hear from you as soon as possible with some explanation and a suitable offer of compensation?

Yours sincerely,

And thus began the most incredible saga of complaint correspondence I have ever experienced. By the 9th January I had not even received an acknowledgement of my letter of 15th November and yet, you may think somewhat foolhardily, my wife and I remained loyal to BA. We even trusted them to get us as far as Cape Town without mishap. A naivety which was to come back to haunt us for some time. Rather than set out the facts at length here's my complaint letter of the 9th January.

Customer Relations,
British Airways,
P.O. Box 5619 (S506),
Sudbury,
SUFFOLK CO10 2PG.

Dear Sirs,

Re: Executive Club No. XXX

Whilst I am still awaiting an acknowledgement (let alone a

reply) in respect of my letter to you regarding a flight to Edinburgh that I endeavoured to take on the 15th November 2000, I am writing to you again in respect of a flight undertaken by my wife and I to Cape Town, South Africa (BA58) on the 24th December and my return flight (BA59) from Cape Town to London on January 3rd.

On the outgoing flight, I was given some headphones, which, extraordinarily enough, were not compatible with the socket in my armrest. The lady sitting to my left had the same problem. It appeared that our respective armrest equipment had been changed but that no matching headphones had been put on board. I explained the problem to the steward who promptly brought me an identical pair of headphones, which of course were not compatible either. I then complained again and was told by the steward that he would find me another seat. That was approximately one hour into the flight and I did not see him again until he said goodbye to me some 11 hours later! Consequently, throughout the flight, I had no in-flight entertainment whatsoever, which might not have been quite so bad had I been able to move around the plane.

Given the recent health warning, I thought it essential to get some exercise but this proved virtually impossible during the flight as, for most of the time, the aisles were blocked with trolleys and equipment and long queues of people waiting to use the washrooms. The kosher meal was, inevitably, of poor quality and we were not even offered the opportunity of breaking the seal to satisfy ourselves that it was properly packaged and under supervision.

However, all of this pales into insignificance when it comes to our return flight. Whilst I was at least given the opportunity to break the seal on the kosher meal, nobody had thought fit to defrost the same and consequently the hors d'oeuvre was icy smoked salmon set amidst chunks of ice that passed for potato salad. The main course was cooked but had an odd taste (which I will deal with a little later in this letter). The orange juice was frozen and the dessert consisted of a slice of dry plain yellow cake.

On this occasion, there were no screens in the aisles, but

merely one big screen at the front of the compartment. This time my headphones worked but I simply could not see any of the screen and even the bits I could see were obliterated by the stewardesses and stewards walking up and down the aisles. I gave up on the entertainment and tried to get to sleep. At about 2.00 in the morning, I was awoken by very bad stomach cramps and my wife experienced the same. After passing a most uncomfortable night, for reasons that are quite beyond me, at 3 a.m. (some three hours before the proposed landing) all the cabin lights went on and we were served breakfast.

On opening the kosher breakfast, I noticed there was a yoghurt there and I thought this might settle my stomach. There were also some tinned peaches and a hot omelette. I chanced to look at the date on the yoghurt and saw that its Sell By date was the 12th November. Unfortunately, by then I had already consumed the orange juice and half a stale roll. The orange juice had the same date and when my wife opened her omelette and cut into it, it was green. She called over a stewardess who took it away and then returned it, saying that it was a "spinach omelette" and that she should eat it. Having suggested to the stewardess that she should try it first, I then asked to see the purser who came over and initially took a fairly aggressive approach and told me that BA was not responsible for the kosher meals served on board.

I then pointed out to her in no uncertain terms that I was an Executive Club member, that the only reason I was flying economy was because I had been unable to book a Club Class seat on the flights I wanted and that I was also a solicitor and was not impressed by her argument. At this point, her attitude changed and she became extremely apologetic, offered us some fruit and told us there would be a full investigation and took down my details.

My wife and I both felt so unwell when we got off the plane that, between visits to the toilet, we managed to leave a carrier bag of presents that we had purchased on the back of our trolley and which has gone missing. We both went home and went straight to bed and, several days later, my stomach is still feeling delicate.

I do feel that this is a matter that should be looked into most seriously and I do trust that I will receive a positive response at an early stage, rather than waiting the unreasonable amount of time that has elapsed since my previous letter to which I should be pleased to receive a reply in due course.

Yours faithfully,

Copy this form of letter or memorise it as a template. I would like to say it guarantees you instant success but then you've not, as yet, dealt with British Airways (or perhaps you have).

By the 26th February I had met (though probably not made) a whole host of new friends at BA Customer Relations including Alison, Dawn, Abigail and Julie. Each and every one of them had sent me a standard letter of semi-apology and none of them had addressed the main issues. I'd like to tell you that, as far as I was concerned, the story had a fairy-tale ending and BA and I rode off together into the sunset (even if we had I'm sure they would have put me on a horse going in the wrong direction). In fact they never did give me my silver executive card back, they did send me some vouchers/ and airmiles (so the persistence paid off there) but I vowed never to fly BA again save where I had absolutely no alternative.

So why have I told you at length about a series of complaints that were largely unsuccessful? Two reasons. One to demonstrate that you must never give up. At least persistence gives you the satisfaction of knowing that the company to whom you are complaining has to employ staff to deal (or not to deal as the case may be) with your correspondence. And finally to demonstrate that even after you have exhausted all the letters (and yourself) that there is the ultimate way to complain (other than litigation which you should always try to avoid at all costs) and that is to complain with your feet and your wallet and take your custom elsewhere. Which I did, and whilst doubtless Virgin and British Midlands may live to regret it, I am now a committed fan of both of them. Possibly (and indeed, probably) BA never even noticed the loss of my custom. I did later on tell them that I was responsible for deciding how all my staff flew and they didn't even bother to acknowledge that either.

What a way to run a company, but what glorious material for a book about complaints.

7

FURTHER ADVENTURES WHILST TRAVELLING
(But rarely arriving)

I've only just touched upon some of the problems one can experience by undertaking that good old English past-time ... travel. Travel not only broadens the mind, it can just as easily do the mind in. But only if you let it. What you have to understand, and may be beginning to understand from the previous chapters, is that every potential disaster is also a potential reward. The trick is to ensure the reward more than compensates for the disaster. To do this you have to put what has happened to you into perspective. A thirty minute delay on a train or a plane may well mean you have missed a vital meeting, but is unlikely to result in compensation, no matter how many calls you make or letters you write. On the other hand a day's delay, which may have meant virtually nothing to you other than the opportunity to sit around the airport and read that book you always promised yourself that you would, whilst drinking complimentary booze and eating free food, may well result in travel vouchers or cash. Just because you've not been greatly inconvenienced there is absolutely no reason why you shouldn't receive exactly the same treatment as those who have missed weddings, funerals or bankruptcy hearings. A court may well view it differently but, as you have probably gathered by now, this is not a handbook for those seeking a quick guide to the courts. Complaining is the thinking man's alternative to suing, far more enjoyable and likely to prove far more successful. As a solicitor I can say with some certainty that there are far more poor litigants than poverty-stricken lawyers.

So what else can happen (or not happen, as the case may be) on a plane that can give cause for complaint? Well, when I list them you will not be surprised to learn that most of them have happened to me. I've already dealt with delays, food problems, and entertainment systems not working. But then you also have to be wary of rude or indifferent service, seating problems, over-payment of a fare, lost luggage, noise and my pet-hate, the absolute belief of every airline in the world that their passengers would rather buy duty-free on board than do anything else … particularly sleep. The fact of the matter is that there are very few bargains to be had in the air nowadays. If you really insist on buying something that you don't really want (or worse still buying something for someone else that they don't really want) then at least take note of what you've paid and if you find it cheaper at the airport or indeed cheaper in the high street, then write and tell the airline and ask for the difference back. There's nothing more annoying than schlepping bottles and after-shave, etc, around with you from plane to plane only to discover that, to add insult to injury, you've paid some twenty percent more than if you'd walked up the road and bought it in your local supermarket. Happened to you? And what did you do? Nothing? I thought so. Again the airline may ignore you or try to fob you off by suggesting your lower price was only available as a special offer with 200 cornflake packet tops. But if they do and it wasn't, then persist. And if all else fails tell them you intend making their so-called duty free prices a matter of public record. That's not blackmail, that's your privilege. If you don't buy (and I hope you don't … you're thinking I'm a bit obsessive about this, I suspect) then you are also entitled to complain if you're woken or generally and persistently disturbed by such sales. On its own it's probably not worth a letter and won't win you any cigars but if there are other things that have gone wrong then it's something worth chucking in. There are those who believe that I think the kitchen sink is worth chucking in and they're right, but then we haven't got to builders or plumbers as yet.

As far as service is concerned no matter what you've paid for your ticket you are entitled to be treated like a human being. It goes without saying that service in First Class and Business is going to be better than economy. But by "better" I mean materially better and not in the way it's delivered. If you have paid £2000 for a one-way ticket to somewhere then you will have better food and nicer plates and real champagne and a wider choice of newspapers and films than someone who has bought a budget ticket for £199. There will be less of you and you should therefore have a more personal service. Yet, the service in all classes should be with a smile and ought to be accommodating. You have not abrogated all rights to membership of the human race by buying a cheap ticket. If you need a glass of water then by pressing your button you should receive one somewhat more speedily than a nano second before you expire from dehydration. And when it's brought to you then it should be served and not thrown at you or slammed down so that you are left with a few dregs at the bottom of the foul-tasting plastic container. Cabin crew do have an awful job. If you think about it they are glorified waiters and waitresses, or even nurses, who just get the chance to stay over in the occasional glamorous destination before they resume the day job. Yet, they chose it and they ought to do it cheerfully. The fact that they have an awkward passenger on board who is making their life a misery is no reason for them to take it out on you just because you asked for something to which you were entitled.

If you have an on-board problem then you should ask in the first instance for your cabin supervisor, but if you feel that you are not being taken seriously then you should ask for a comments form. With some airlines it may not be enough just to complete it and hand it to the supervisor, so you need to make a note of what you have said and, if you have not heard back from the airline within fourteen days, then you need to write in and ask why you have had no response, whilst at the same time reiterating your original grounds of complaint. And then the usual formula. Just keep writing and, however trivial your original complaint, e.g. the failure to bring one glass of water, it will be magnified with every epistle you send. That's part of the art of complaining when you do not receive an adequate response by return. Your original complaint tends to get submerged in your subsequent complaints about the delay in dealing with your complaint.

A complaint may arise from a casual conversation with the passenger in the seat next to yours. You say that you booked a scheduled ticket and paid full fare, say £2000. He will say that he has either been upgraded or that he booked his ticket through a bucket shop (don't ask, I've never understood either) and either he only paid £199 or else he paid half of what you paid for exactly the same seat, the same food, and the same service. Once you are on-board nobody from the crew actually asks what you paid to get there. Personally I think the whole pricing strategy on flights is outrageous but it won't be changed as long as people (or airlines) are making a profit from it. Don't get me wrong. I'm not against the capitalist philosophy and certainly don't believe property is theft. If I were, then you wouldn't have paid for this book or if you had, then the proceeds would have been donated to a socialist revolutionary cause. But there does have to be a balance and, again, if nobody complains the whole unfair irrational system will continue.

The thing to do is to write to the airline (and maybe to complain to your travel agent as well, who may be preferring to make as much out of you as possible rather than finding you the most competitive fares). The airline may well toss you back to your travel agent but once again (and sorry to be repetitive but you'll remember from your school days that it's the best way to learn) you have to keep writing and they may, just may, do something about it, like giving you some kind of discount on your next flight. The object is to shame them with your customer loyalty. It's an undeniable fact that it appears you can always get a cheaper flight on another airline. The thing to do is to convince the airline of your choice that you would rather fly with them than anybody else. I suspect that if the airline of your choice is BA then you are wasting your time, but you never know. Miracles do happen even in the world of international aviation.

So what else can happen? You've been delayed, your special meal hasn't turned up, you've suffered sleep deprivation, the bloke next to you paid half of what you paid and your entertainment system doesn't work on a long-haul flight that is absolutely full. Oh, and you are in first class but your bed won't lie flat. You stagger off the plane and wait at the carousel. You know your luggage will come off first; you saw them put the priority labels on it. Unfortunately the priority labels give another message. They tell any potential thief that you are rich enough to travel first class and therefore there may be rich pickings in your baggage. This has become even more of a problem since our American cousins in their wisdom stopped us locking our cases. Even with the case unlocked and unstolen I still get notes in my baggage from the American authorities telling me my bag has been subjected to a random search. And I have to tell you that although they search, their mummies didn't teach them how to repack, so your clothes reach their destination in a virtually unwearable state.

Let's assume someone (other than the Feds) has got to it before the baggage handlers and you wait and wait in vain, hoping against hope that it will fall from the chute. The last piece of cardboard wrapped luggage tumbles out and is claimed and still you wait. I have never actually met the person whose bag comes off the plane first but I have met all too many people whose bags never came off at all. Me included.

We all have our stories, all we weary war-veterans of travel. In our dotage we will sit in smoke-filled rooms and pass on our experiences to those raw recruits who have yet to go through what we have suffered at the hands of the ruthless and cunning airlines.

My tale was a journey back from the United States with a case-load of files that were needed for a court application later that day. I'd checked my bags through to London from my first airport and then changed planes. Of course I'd asked when I bade my bags a fond farewell if I would be sure of seeing them again and told the check-in counter that if there was any doubt I would like to take the somewhat heavy and cumbersome case on as hand-luggage. I was given that special wearisome look honed by all check-in staff that say silently "We know what we're doing. You don't. Trust us."

Now you may not realise it but when you hand over your bags to the care of an airline there is no guarantee that you will get back the full value of the cases and their contents should they be lost in transit. It was Laker Airlines of beloved memory who worked out that losing one's bags was one of the most stressful and traumatic things that can happen to an individual. Freddie Laker, bless him, even had someone standing by to supply you with all the bare necessities should his passengers' bags not arrive at the same time as his passengers. Were it ever so with every airline; but it's not. And although my bag with all my clothes turned up, my bag with the papers didn't. Now there was no way it could have been stolen or tampered with as the case itself was old (the travelling case, that is, not the court case) and nobody in their right minds would want to take a load of old files and papers when there were much richer pickings. So what was immediately clear was that this was down to the airline. The only question was, which one? I'd flown an internal flight in the States on one plane, changed to another airline for flight number two and yet another one (I think it may well have been BA but I can't swear to it) for my transatlantic journey.

This was many years ago and I was really just starting out on my career as a complainant, but given the circumstances and my inexperience I think I did then what I would have done now. I turned my wrath on those nearest to hand who were, of course, the operators of the flight from which I'd just deplaned. In fact, I think it was such a long time ago that I probably disembarked rather than deplaned. Such a different process and experience. Not withstanding the carriers' efforts to blame check-in staff and baggage handlers across the pond and then finally their suggestion that I waited for the next flight in as it was probably on board that, I stood my ground. If they were so sure it was going to be on the next flight then they could stand by the carousel and wait for it and then put it in a taxi to meet up with me. Meanwhile I too would take a taxi (I was now potentially late) at their expense and try to explain to our barrister why I had (metaphorically speaking) failed to bring home the bacon. The airline refused. They said I had to clear customs with my own bag. I pointed out I did not have a bag as they had lost it and if it were not on the next plane did they expect me to spend the rest of my life at the airport just in case my bag should ever turn up and require my assistance in clearing customs. There is a time and place for sarcasm when complaining and believe me this was both of them. They were unbudgeable. I then told them that if the case had to be adjourned they would have to pay the costs and the two taxis would be infinitely cheaper for them. I also asked to see the airline duty manager. As I said, early days, but I was already well on the way to success. He was more amenable, accepted that I was quite happy for my bag to be searched as it contained no contraband, albeit documents of equal or greater value to me and my client. I hopped into a taxi, the case was on the next plane and given that the case's driver took a better route than mine we arrived virtually simultaneously where there was heart-rending reconciliation between us.

I didn't leave it there, of course, I felt I had been unduly stressed (I had been) and I told the airline so in no uncertain terms. They, of course, said it wasn't their fault and after being shuttled between three airline companies where I made lots of new friends I did eventually get some air miles (again from memory enough to get me to New York and back). A result? Of sorts I suppose, but then if in fact my complaints got someone not only to acknowledge they were wrong, but also to do something about it, then my efforts were not in vain. My wife is convinced that my current high-blood pressure is due to my constant efforts to fight the corner of the little man, i.e. me!

The fact is that my consistent complaints about inconsistent services is a way of letting off steam rather than bottling it in and when you finally get a result which satisfies you the pleasure is indescribable.

And that is what happened with my mobile phone that was stolen at Johannesburg Airport on my way to see England get tonked in the 2003 Cricket World Cup. And would you believe it but the story once again includes, as one of its leading characters, our old friend British Airways. Lost bags are one thing (and I have another good lost bag story involving BA and my business associate later in this book), stolen items quite another and I felt I had uncovered a particularly insidious scam that was being worked not only at the airport but at the very heart of an airline. As to which airline that was you will have to read on.

My son and I flew from Heathrow to Johannesburg on Virgin. I switched to Virgin when I gave up on BA. I've had my ups and downs with them but the one thing you cannot complain about with any company run by Sir Richard Branson is the speed with which they deal with complaints. I do have a sheaf of complaint letters to them (mainly because there is so often a problem with my meals) but I also have a similar collection of response letters, often from Richard himself, and on every occasion, even without my asking, they have offered compensation the value of which usually exceeds the gravity of the complaint. On this occasion my son and I were up-graded with my Gold Card (thanks again Richard) to Upper Class and no problems. I wrote to them to thank them. That's another tip by the way. When something exceeds expectations always make a point of writing and telling the company or the individual. It also gives you the extremely high moral ground (yes, that again) when something goes wrong in your next meeting with them! From Jo'burg my son and I were due to fly BA to Cape Town. We sat and had a coffee in the Executive Lounge. They'd taken my card away by now but I managed to persuade them to let us in on the strength of my expired silver card and a certain amount of bluster and outrage as to why they had declined to send me a new card. I had with me a carry-on bag that I knew was standard size for overhead lockers on planes throughout the world. I dutifully turned off my phone and placed it in one of the pockets of my bag, knowing I wasn't going to use it on-board. We made our way to the steps of the plane and were there met by a gentleman who took one look at my bag and told me I had to put it in the hold. I told him I knew it would fit in the overhead and he then changed his story and said that the plane (and the overheads) were very full. He told me not to worry, that the bag would be waiting for me at the foot of the steps when we landed. And indeed it was. The only problem was that someone had tied a plastic security strap to the pocket which contained my phone. Or, as I found out, when I got someone to cut the strap (it was unbreakable by the way ... Nothing like security on an airline is there? And this was nothing like security) didn't contain my phone. It had been stolen between the door of the plane and the hold of the plane.

Now one didn't need to be Hercule Poirot, Inspector Morse or Sherlock Holmes to work out who had stolen it. I raced into the BA office at Cape Town airport who promptly told me they could do nothing without a police report. Nobody offered to accompany me to the airport police station and nobody even bothered to call Jo'burg to see who had been on duty planeside before we departed. The trail was getting cold, but I was hot in pursuit. Off I went to the police and, this being South Africa, they had a standard form to complete for a stolen phone and expressed neither any great surprise or any great interest in catching the thief. I returned clutching a small piece of paper that passed for the report and gave it to the BA office. My original point of contact had buggered off for the weekend and whilst I told the girl he'd left behind that they needed to arrange to replace my phone at their expense, as I needed it for work whilst I was in the country, I left without any great confidence that anything would be done. I was told they would phone me at my hotel the next day, but all I got was a fax telling me my phone had not been traced. *Quelle* surprise. I had little doubt it had been flogged at an airport bar before we had touched down at the Cape.

As it happened I had a remarkably quiet holiday (memo to me ... remember to have your phone stolen with regularity. I wonder if the bloke who stole it coped with the thirty people a day who usually interrupt my vacations. I suppose it's a bit like getting your credit card stolen. You just hope the thief will spend less than you). However, when I got back to England as you can imagine I was not slow to put pen to paper. To my astonishment BA didn't bother to respond until I sent them a reminder (or two) And then the saga began. It wasn't their fault because the carrier was Com-Air and not them so I had to pursue my claim with them. I pointed out I had never heard of them and had no idea how to contact them even if I wanted to. My ticket was booked with BA. BA told me that according to Aviation Regulations it's the carrier who's respon-sible. I told them, whilst I didn't accept this could be, that they at least should contact them for me as they were their sub-contracted carriers and eventually (albeit reluctantly) they did. Unfortunately Com-Air didn't fancy answering either. And when they did you will not be surprised to learn that they said it wasn't their responsibility either and perhaps I'd like to claim on my own insurance. (I'd already tried that and was told that mobile phones aren't covered. All you can insure against is the cost of calls made when the phone has been stolen before you put a stop on it.) Insurers and how to complain to them will be a later lesson. I needed to work up a real head of steam before I got to those thieving bastards. Give me a good honest phone thief in preference to an insurance company any day. Your phone goes and it's over. With insurers they steal from you for years, promise to give it back in spades, then steal not only the spades but the whole tool-shed.

But back to Com-Air. We embarked on a very interesting correspondence until finally, some eight months later, they hit on a brilliant loop-hole. Goodness knows how many lawyers I got them to instruct. I do hope it cost them plenty. The loop-hole was that for stolen items they would pay by weight and as my phone weighed next to nothing they owed me £2.47 or thereabouts. At this point I had had enough and hammered away at both BA and Com-Air with correspondence so vitriolic that the letters were probably tested for explosive substances. Finally, in November, some nine months later Com-Air gave in and offered to pay for the phone, albeit in dollars.

Now you may well think I had become obsessed with this incident. I don't call it obsession. I call it persistence and even at the end of the day I didn't get all my questions answered. Com-Air never told me whether or not they had instigated an investigation into the incident, certainly never told me the names of the man who had taken my bag or the baggage handlers on duty, and as far as I'm aware they are employed by Com-Air or Jo'burg Airport Authority to this day. All I can say to you is if anybody offers to put your bag in the hold of a plane (particularly BA or Com-Air) at Jo'burg say no to the offer, or if he persists make sure you leave nothing more valuable than a used tissue in it. And make a note of his name or better still take a photo of him. The likelihood is that you'll need it.

After reading all that, and with the advent of armed guards on planes, it will take a brave member of the public ever to fly again. But if you don't, just think what glorious opportunities to complain you will miss. As Marvin the depressive robot in the *Hitchhikers Guide to the Galaxy* might have said, "Air travel? Don't ask me about air-travel."

As you'll have gathered, there's so much potential material for complaints about air travel but here's a résumé of just a few issues that can give cause for complaint, a letter, and hopefully some free flights in the future.

1. Did you get full value for what you paid for the flight?
2. Was the in-flight service satisfactory? Were the seats, food, and entertainment acceptable?

3. If you asked for a special meal did you get it?
4. Were you interrupted in your sleep to be sold duty free?
5. Was the flight especially noisy?
6. Were there any drunk or abusive passengers on board, or perhaps any noisy children? If so how did the crew deal with them?
7. Did the flight take-off and land on time?
8. Were you helped to catch any connecting flight or just left to your own devices?
9. If there was a delay were you kept fully informed?
10. Was your baggage lost?
11. Was anything stolen from your baggage?
12. How quickly did you get your bags returned?
13. How sympathetic was the airline in dealing with the loss or trying to replace the necessities?
14. How did the airline react to your complaint letter and did they offer you adequate compensation?

If you've ticked more than one after a flight, or even just one important issue, then you should be complaining and you should be expecting some compensation. If you don't get it after some persistent correspondence then, as I've said, make the ultimate complaint and fly with some other airline in future. Believe me, there are a lot of them about and most of them will welcome you. Though, probably not me.

8

WHAT'S SIX MINUTES BETWEEN FRIENDS?

This chapter was never intended to go into the book but BMI (that's British Midland to the uninitiated) provided me with such glorious material in February 2004 that I felt I had to show my gratitude and give them a mention. Now, don't get me wrong. I rather like British Midland. There's something quite sweet and old-fashioned about them and it was to them I turned for my European short haul travel when I gave up on British Airways. I was somewhat impressed that they seemed able to conjure up a three course kosher meal on one-hour flights to Scotland, all of which were not only perfectly edible but, indeed, were at times mouth-watering. I say "seemed able" and choose those words quite deliberately because on a percentage basis of my flights with them the meals failed to appear. Indeed, in early 2004 they scored a hat-trick of non-appearances, not even making the subs' bench.

BMI say they want forty-eight hours' notice to supply special meals of any kind. Fair enough, I say, it's their airline, their rules, but really, were they cooking the meals themselves? Did they have a little Jewish grandmother sweating over a bowl of chicken soup and a roaster demanding that she be given two days to prepare her delicacies. I don't think so. All they needed to do was phone the kosher caterer at Heathrow and call up a meal. But what's quite obvious is that after their 48 hour deadline passes they just don't bother. It's easier to say no. For the three flights mentioned above I did give them their required notice, but the food must have been cooking on a very low light because as I said, in each and every case, it wasn't ready by the time I got on-board. They did, however, unlike BA react positively to my complaint letters, initially sending me Marks & Spencer vouchers and latterly even giving me the phone number of someone to call when I was taking a flight with them.

I got the impression they really wanted me on board and would be heart-broken if they lost my custom.

The disillusion really began to set in on a snowy day in January 2004, when I sat in the BMI Business Lounge at Heathrow for over four hours whilst they delayed and delayed a flight to Edinburgh. Now, I know, I can't blame them for the English winters, but I can blame them for closing their lounge fifteen minutes after the airport closed for the night and then making an announcement that they would have to call the police if we didn't all go home like good sheep and return in the morning. The police? What were they going to do? Baton charge us weary travellers? Tear-gas us? Had all those announcements that the plane was only delayed for half an hour been part of a psychological war campaign to ensure we were no opposition to this police charge. I, like most of the other business passengers in the lounge, had paid well over £200 for my ticket and was desperately trying to make some arrangements for my own long journey home. It was at that point that they actually turned off the lights, and before the heavy mob in blue could come bursting through the door firing in all directions, I decided it was prudent to sweep the bits and pieces of my mobile office into my bag and head for the tube. The right thing to have done was to offer the people the chance to stay in the lounge overnight or to have helped them with some local accommodation. But no, it was just a question of coming back the next day and hoping for the best. Even BA could not have been less helpful.

So why couldn't I have made an effective complaint then, you may ask? How dare you get us to buy a book demonstrating the art of complaining when you went meekly into the snow and ice saying "I may be gone some time" or words to that effect.

Well, the fact of the matter is that when some fifty or so angry individuals are scrimmaging around the desk besieging two very harassed ladies who were only obeying orders, and when the person ultimately responsible for those orders was probably not even at the airport, what would have been accomplished? And as I have tried to hammer home the point of complaining is not to create, or add to, a scene, but to accomplish something material. Yelling and shouting to be heard above everybody else would have just been counter-productive.

It was with some hesitation that I decided to fly BMI again to Glasgow two weeks later. My wife is convinced I have a woman in Glasgow despite my protestations that I only go there on football business. I do adhere to the Bill Shankly philosophy that football is not a matter of life and death, but is far more important than that. Mind you, he's dead so it's easy for him to say. Consequently, faced with the choice of a night out on the town with a beautiful Glaswegian or 90 minutes at Celtic Park or Ibrox it's no contest as far as I'm concerned.

Anyway, on this trip to Glasgow they did have my kosher meal on the way up (though who on earth wants to eat chicken … yes, it had been cooked all the way through by then … at eleven o'clock in the morning?). Nothing on the way back though so I assume the Jewish grandma had gone on strike so another letter and more Marks & Spencer vouchers. Clearly they knew about my special relationship. I could now afford to buy a whole barrow-load of vegetarian spring-rolls containing prawns and stone-less dates with stones in the middle.

I persevered. At the end of February I was Glasgow bound again. (Wife, please note, more football business.) My travel agent booked the tickets on Tuesday morning for me to fly up Wednesday night and back on Thursday lunchtime. I really do get around, Glasgow twice in a fortnight. Ain't foreign travel just glamorous? I realised we hadn't given forty-eight hours notice for the outward bound flight but we'd certainly given it for the return journey. At 7.30 pm on a cold winter's night at the end of a long London day's work (sounds like the start of a Dickensian ghost story that … I must remember to stop being so literary, this is a book about complaints, not *War and Peace*, though I appreciate that for some of you it may be beginning to feel like it).

I sat in Row 12 of the Business Class section of the plane. Trust me, that snippet of information is relevant. Immediately behind me, divided only by a curtain, I heard passengers being offered a choice of meals accompanied by the sound and scent of pouring coffee. Peering down the aisle of my section it was clear that, with a good pair of binoculars and twenty-twenty vision, I might just have been able to see a trolley in the distance quite possibly loaded with food and drink. Twenty drinkless and foodless minutes passed. The trolley inched nearer. It was now gone eight and we were due to land in twenty-five minutes. I was encouraged by hearing a voice asking:

"Chicken and mushroom or vegetarian?" Maybe the vegetarian meal might be truly veggie.

Eventually the trolley reached me.

"Would you like chicken and mushroom?" I was asked.

"Er, no," I replied, thinking this wasn't perhaps the moment to go into the detailed requirements of a kosher diet. "What's the vegetarian?"

"It was spicy vegetarian curry," I was informed.

"Was? Has it died?" I enquired with some concern.

"We've sort of run out," the lady said, "But you've got your box there, and it's got apple and chocolate in it."

I looked inside the box. There was a bag with little cold slices of a rapidly browning apple. Perhaps it, like the curry, was also dying. Close inspection of the ingredients of the chocolate bar revealed glycerine and a whole plethora of non-vegetarian additives and no indication anywhere on the label that it was suitable for vegetarians. It was going to be another dieting flight.

I had my meetings in Glasgow and arrived back at the airport shortly after 11.30 am in good time for a 1.00 pm flight. I called my travel agent. Her name is Lee if you are interested ... I can give you her phone number as well if you like. If she can deal with me she can deal with anybody. Yes, she said, she had ordered my special meal, yes it was more than 48 hours in advance ... but on looking at her computer screen she could now see that she had received a message back from BMI stating they had not received enough notice. I was not happy. I wasn't in a complaining mood that day (that's a sort of a quote from *Richard III* by the way in case you didn't get the Shakespearian reference ... I told you this was getting to be real literature). I went into the business lounge, looked enviously at the Gold Card door that was barred to me, wondering just how often you had to fly to get in there, and spoke to a very nice lady. I will call her Michelle, mainly because that was the name on her badge, though for all I know she may have borrowed it or picked up the wrong badge in the dark, though I'm sure she'll know who I mean if she ever reads this.

Michelle began an investigation on my behalf. If she ever decides to follow an alternative career with the CID I'll give her a reference, though I think CID in my personal circumstances stands for the Cases of Invisible Dinners. Michelle at first couldn't find my request for a special meal on her screen. Perhaps my travel agent had made a mistake, she suggested. I phoned the indomitable Lee. No problem there, of course, as she quoted chapter and verse and promised to send me all the documentation she had on screen. Michelle, who, by now was heading for her own role in the Number One Ladies Detective Agency, phoned check-in. The lady there was dealing with two queues, all doubtless consisting of people checking up on the existence of their specially pre-ordered meals. Michelle, my little private eye, persisted. She came back triumphantly with my booking. According to her information this had been made at 12.54 pm on Tuesday.

"There you are," she said, "the flight's at 12.55 pm. So it's less than 48 hours."

"By one minute," I pointed out, "but, in any event the flight is scheduled for 1.00 pm so we are in hand by six minutes."

"Ah," Michelle explained, "but it was less than 48 hours before your first flight."

"Yes, but I'm flying back now. Forty-eight hours and six minutes later." I decided to leave the Jewish grandma out of it. She would only confuse the issue. I was, however, growing quite fond of those magical six minutes. They were moments I was going to treasure on my death bed.

"But they only look at your first flight," Michelle said, with a look on her face that told me she knew this wasn't going to be the end of the conversation or the matter, though for her the case was closed.

"So if I booked a flight on Monday, departed on Tuesday, stayed a week in sunny Glasgow (now that would arouse my wife's suspicions) and then flew back they still wouldn't be able to get me a special meal on my return flight?"

Michelle and her companion, who was by now warming to the situation as a way of relieving the boredom of a virtually empty lounge (I wonder why that might be?) nodded and agreed with the absurdity notwithstanding that her pension might well be at risk. I would be writing another complaint letter. But we weren't done yet, not by a long sandwich.

I got on board to find my seat broken.

"It's the Velcro," the stewardess explained, "It comes unstuck," she added, hastily putting it back together. I just hoped the plane itself was kept together by something more substantial than Velcro and a crew member's technical talents.

She came round with the food. There was no point in asking for my non-existent kosher meal.

"What have you got that's vegetarian?" I asked. I might as well have a recorded message for those words.

"We've got cheese and vegetables and tuna and sweetcorn sandwiches."

I didn't comment as to the tuna's vegetarian antecedents, but asked if the bread was vegetarian. The young lady, whose name was Alicia and about whom I promised to write nice things in this book because she was really helpful, showed me the ingredients. There were loads of additives in both, many of which I knew were not usually of vegetarian origin. The brie cheese wasn't described as vegetarian though the labels on both proudly claimed they were suitable for vegetarians. I wasn't convinced. Alicia gave me a banana. She said she would go in search of more fruit. She gave me another banana. I felt as if I might be expected to swing from one overhead locker to another along the length of the plane. Still, the bananas did complement nicely the slices of apples I'd had the previous evening. Alicia promised to put in a report. She also promised to order a copy of this book so she could show her mother.

"I always knew I'd be famous one day, "she said. And there you go, Alicia, you are.

With nothing to eat and nothing much else to do on the flight, except replace the seat Velcro occasionally, I wrote this chapter. It would make the complaint letter that would follow just that much easier to compose.

Dear Madam,

Further to my previous correspondence, it must appear as if I am forever complaining but I have to write to you again regarding problems I have experienced on two BMI flights.

On the evening of February 25th, I travelled to Glasgow, intending to return on the 1 p.m. flight on Thursday 26th. The flights were booked on Tuesday morning, a clear 48 hours before my return.

I was aware that I was not going to get a kosher meal on the journey out but I would have hoped that, at least, there would be a suitable vegetarian option. I was seated in row 12 of the Business section on the 7.30 p.m. flight. Within 10 minutes of us taking off, I could hear, immediately behind me, those fortunate individuals seated in Economy being served food and coffee. It took some 25 minutes for me to be served anything at all, at which point I asked if there were any vegetarian options and was handed a box and told that this contained suitable items for a vegetarian and that a hot dish would be served later. Within the box were some very aged apple slices and a chocolate bar which contained, amongst other items, glycerine and other additives which certainly proved it was not vegetarian.

It was after 8 before the food trolley reached me, by which time the stewardess asked me if I would like chicken and mushroom. I asked if she had any vegetarian alternatives and was advised that she had just given the last one away.

Matters got even worse on my return journey. I arrived at the airport shortly after 11.30 a.m. and telephoned my travel agent (Parador Travel) to confirm that they have given 48 hours notice of my requirement for kosher food. Again, I was told that the order had been placed on Tuesday morning and it was more than 48 hours. However, my travel agent then told me that she had heard from BMI advising her that not enough notice had been given.

I then proceeded to the Lounge and, after a very helpful lady made some enquiries, I was told that my reservation had been confirmed at 12.54 p.m. on the 24th February, i.e. 48 hours and 6 minutes before my return flight. To my astonishment, I was then also told that, because my outward journey had been booked less than 48 hours before my departure, you could not arrange the food for my return journey. I pointed out the absurdity of this, giving the example of my booking a flight on the Monday, flying on a Tuesday, staying for a week in Glasgow, and then returning 8 days after making my booking and still being unable to get my kosher meal because the initial booking was less than 48 hours from the time of my departure.

When I got on-board, again I asked if there were any vegetarian options and I was offered either a tuna and sweetcorn sandwich (quite how tuna can be classified as vegetarian, I am not sure) or a cheese and vegetable sandwich. I asked if the bread contained only ingredients suitable for vegetarians and I was shown the sandwiches and read the labels giving the ingredients. The cheese used in the sandwich was Brie, but no information was given as to whether it was made with vegetarian rennet, the bread contained all sorts of additives which are not normally vegetarian and the stewardess (who was extremely helpful) could not confirm one way or the other even though the sandwich did say "suitable for vegetarians." She then offered me a flapjack biscuit which contained margarine and we finally settled on two bananas! She promised to file a report but I think you will agree that it is unacceptable that, having paid nearly £500 for a return flight, all I should have to eat, on a cumulative basis, is one tiny packet of apple slices and two bananas.

You have responded in the past by sending me a Marks & Spencer's voucher. Quite frankly, I regard these as a token, as all I really want is to get my meals on-board and, if my special meals aren't on-board, to know that vegetarian (and I don't just mean non-meat and non-fish-based) options are available.

I look forward to hearing from you at your earliest convenience.

Yours sincerely,

Again, they responded positively. I now have the name of a lady and a gentleman (as you'll see in time I have the names of lots of such individuals) who are to be told when I am flying and they will personally arrange my culinary delights. Hurrah, for BMI. Until the next flight, anyway.

9

A GOOD NIGHT'S SLEEP
(The jacket which refused to die)

You've ended your long day's journey into night or perhaps your long night's journey into day, depending on which way round the world you're going. The nightmare (or daymare) of air travel is behind you and you've arrived at your hotel. The odds are that you're either late (because your plane landed late) or very early (because your plane landed so late that it's now the next day). Either way you want your room, shower and a bed. What you don't want is to be told that the room is not ready because the previous occupant left late. How many, of you have ever asked for and received a late check-out? Not many, I'll warrant. How many of you have asked for a late checkout and been refused? Quite a lot, I'll warrant. So how is it invariably when you arrive that your predecessor has enjoyed a late checkout? Maybe the law of averages is the reason you don't get it ... because the previous occupant of your designated room always does.

The hotel may think it's enough to offer to put your bags in storage and point you in the general direction of its restaurant or coffee shop, or both, in the hope that you will spend some money with them whilst you wait to spend money with them for a room. But it's not enough. Even if you've arrived before your appointed check-in time it's not unreasonable to ask for access to your room provided a reasonable enough time has elapsed since the official check-out time. If they don't have your room ready then you are perfectly entitled to ask for another room either on a permanent or temporary basis. And it's also reasonable for you to be offered a complimentary drink whilst they busy themselves trying to meet your requirements. And if they don't or won't meet your requirements then you need to complain. Ask for the duty manager and, if he's not available, the general manager and if you still have no luck, then ask when he'll be on duty. Sometimes the mere fact that the matter may go to a higher authority is enough for you to get satisfaction. If they don't satisfy you then, assuming it's not a peak holiday season, ask for the phone and start calling other hotels to check the availability of rooms. The odds are that the hotel won't want to lose your business when it's running at considerably less than capacity. Much of the art of complaining is bluff and double-bluff and knowing that, if they call your bluff you can fold with dignity. If you can play a decent game of poker then you can certainly succeed at the art of complaining. And an art form it definitely is.

When you finally get to your room always remember that the moment to complain about its size or position is before you unpack. There's little point or effect in writing to the hotel when you get home saying that the price they charged for a monastic cell was outrageous. It may make you feel better but it won't have made your stay more pleasurable. Even if they offer you a reduced rate for future stays you are unlikely to want to go back there with the unpleasant memories of your first stay embedded in your mind. There are, of course, always things that will come to light during your stay. The proximity to the lift or laundry room, the defective air-conditioning, the permanently flushing toilet (a favourite of mine). In fact I'm sure that I'm followed around the world by the flushing fairy who has the power to produce water 24/7 from a seemingly fully-drained cistern.

And let me tell you that the fairies do not answer letters of complaint. But hotels do. Or at least they should. Inevitably, I have my own personal hotel stories. Why do you think I decided to write this book in the first place? To help you? Well yes in part, but this is also about revenge, which is better in the written word than eaten cold. So, step up to the rostrum to get the Gold Award for things to complain about ... Loew's Hotel in Miami Beach. I arrived there one evening, straight off a flight from Tallahassee. (Tallahasee is a place to complain about generally, but more of that later.) I had a meeting at 8.30pm with a restaurant owner who had actually booked me into Loew's.

On my arrival I told the lady on reception I was in a hurry. She asked for my credit card. I told her the room had already been guaranteed on my credit card and the hotel had all the details. She continued to show her feminine curiosity by persisting in her request to see the aforementioned card. I looked at my watch to see how late I was and then fumbled in my wallet before triumphantly producing a credit card. I showed it to the lady. She examined it as if the whole concept of English plastic was new to her. She was clearly finding it hard to believe that anybody but Americans could produce credit cards. She then told me that as they were holding my reservation on a different credit card she would have to re-process the booking. By now I was feeling that everything around me was happening in slow motion. I looked at my watch again. Time was not moving slowly, that was for sure. I was even later.

I dashed up to the room I was finally, and benevolently, granted and realised my luggage had lagged behind. Maybe it knew in advance that the temperature in the room was sub-zero, as the air-conditioning was pumping out cold air with considerable enthusiasm. I looked around for the means to adjust it, or even turn it off, but found nothing. After five minutes I rang down to enquire about the well-being or, indeed, location of my case. It was on its way up, I was told. Presumably under its own steam, I replied, but Americans just don't get sarcasm or irony. A few minutes later I rang again. It would be with me before I could stride across my room, I was told. I can't stride across the room, I said, it's too bloody cold. That, too, would be dealt with, I was assured. My bag and a reasonable climate, what else could I want for my money? The Floridian clock ticked on. At home my loved ones were sleeping and that was exactly what I wanted to be doing. Only first of all I had to have my meeting and before I could get to my meeting I needed my bag and before I could contemplate sleep I needed some reassurance that I wouldn't be getting frost-bite during the course of the night. Still no bag. Striding across the room? I could have strode across the entire North American continent by now. Did the woman on the front desk think I possessed the genes of a snail? Just when I was about to stride across the city to another hotel there was a knock on the door and my bag arrived. I pointed out to its bearer that if it was left there on its own whilst I was out I might well have to chip the ice off it to get it open when I returned. I have never understood the American obsession with air-conditioning any more than I understand their need to fill every glass with lumps of ice until whatever liquid it contains becomes steadily more unrecognisable (and undrinkable) as the ice melts. I have a ready-made knee jerk complaint for American bartenders.

The man who brought my bag told me that the air conditioning would be dealt with by the time I got back. Just before I left (I was now so late it didn't seem to matter if I was just a little bit later) I had one more look round to see how I might be able to adjust the Eskimo effect but still couldn't find any readily apparent internal unit. Still, the man had told me it would be dealt with, but as I went to my meeting full of apologies I didn't have a lot of faith that there would be a fruitful and warmer resolution to my problem.

I returned to the hotel at about midnight. The temperature in my room seemed to have dropped by several degrees if, indeed, that were possible. The thought of ringing down and waiting for a maintenance man had to be balanced against the possibility of my demolishing walls in search of the air-conditioning adjustor, which in turn had to be weighed against the desirability and need for bed. As I'd not seen my bed for about eighteen hours I chose to renew my acquaintance with it and pulling on a jumper rather than pyjamas, I snuggled beneath the bedclothes. Actually, although I know you are not really interested and it has little or nothing to do with a book about complaints, I wear t-shirts and shorts to bed rather than pyjamas. I don't want to paint the picture of a grumpy old man in striped flannel jim-jams and a nightcap clambering into his four-poster with difficulty. Mind you, on this occasion I could have done with a nightcap as I shivered my way through the night just hoping I wasn't going to have an asthma attack or get a chest infection.

I found myself with nothing to do the next day and a flight that didn't leave until early evening. As, by then, I'd spent less than seven hours in the hotel and most of them in Antarctic conditions, I didn't think it unreasonable to request a late check-out. I should have known better than to ask for anything in a hotel where everybody tells you to have a nice day as long as they are not required to do anything by way of a contribution to making it nice. A late checkout was impossible as the hotel was full, I was told, but I was welcome to use the hotel facilities for the rest of the day and they would be happy to store my luggage. I asked if they would provide anywhere for me to change before I went to the airport, or maybe even a room in which to have a shower? This caused great consternation and as I had obviously exceeded the boundaries of what constituted a nice day I decided to drop my request. My complaint letter was already being drafted in my head. Once that happens you almost always will find more things to go wrong just to make sure it's a real cracker of a missive and this place already seemed to have huge potential for that.

After breakfast, at which nobody could tell me if the bread was vegetarian because they bought it in rather than baking their own (well, what else would you expect from Miami's Premier Hotel?) I went back upstairs to pack up my things. By 10.30 am I was all ready and a porter came to take it away, including the jacket in which I intended travelling home and which I specifically asked them to hang up for me. I was now homeless and for a few hours' use of their virtually uninhabitable room I was being charged a King's Ransom.

An hour or so later as I stood in the lobby a man came in from the street, asked for a room and one was magically found for him. Perhaps there is a room fairy operating in Miami. Or perhaps it was the room into which I theoretically could have moved if the hotel had not been full, as the receptionist had claimed. Maybe they have a different definition of full in Florida. Was the hotel half-empty or half-full? In any event I just sat by the pool the rest of the day, tried to have lunch and failed when they didn't know the ingredients of their own menu. I began the countdown to the moment I could leave the hotel, which by now had intrusive music blaring across the swimming pool which was filled with even noisier children. I've had children. Well, not literally, I mean my wife had them. I had the responsibility for them. They're now people. I really don't need other people's children until they, too, become people. Although with my luck they will probably turn into the sort of people who delay me with demands for spare credit cards, have an inability to adjust air-conditioning and then lie to me about availability of rooms. I do realise there is not a lot one can do about children, although I do think that airlines and theatres which permit them in without anaesthetic deserve a complaint letter. More about the theatre later and how I, myself, learned a salutary lesson in complaining.

At 3.00pm having been driven inside by the noise to more violent air-conditioning, I asked for access to my luggage so I could change for my flight (probably in one of the toilets it seemed to me). They took me into the baggage storage room where I was appalled to see that my expensive Jaeger jacket (not name-dropping or advertising, but merely to underline the gravity of the hotel's offence) was stuffed through the narrow handle of my case like an old rag. I lovingly removed it and shook it. It didn't wake up and it didn't really shake either. It sort of stayed concertinaed and hung sulkily and half-comatose in my hand. For almost the first time in my life I was lost for words. I was almost lost for words in the 1976 League Cup Final when Asa Hartford scored the winning goal for Manchester City against my beloved Newcastle, and was stuttering a bit when my own client Chris Waddle blasted his penalty over the bar in the 1990 World Cup Semi-Final against Germany. So, if my seemingly ruined jacket struck me dumb and made me think of these other major traumas in my life you can imagine how I felt. I pulled myself together even if I couldn't pull the jacket together.

"Right," I said, in my best English clipped tones that the Americans so love and fear, "you've twenty minutes to get that jacket back looking like a jacket. And then we'll talk about compensation."

The man in charge shook his head as if inspecting the engine of an irreparable car.

"Can't be done. Can we send it on to you?"

I shook my head. Even if I hadn't wanted to travel in the jacket the track record of this bunch of clowns gave me no confidence that my jacket and I would ever be reunited.

"No, I'm heading back to England." I wanted to add 'and to civilisation' but restrained myself. "Get me an iron and I'll do it myself." I didn't tell him that I'd never ironed anything in my life. I just wanted to demonstrate just how much of a waste of space they were. It was my ultimate bluff. As I said never, ever, believe an American when he says, "Can I help you? Can I be of service? Is there anything I can do for you today to make your day better?" and such other platitudes as may be spouted by them from time to time. They don't mean it and will be horrified if you try to take them up on the offer, which isn't an offer at all but merely a comment in the same vein as the ubiquitous "Have a Nice Day."

However, before my offer on the ironing could be taken up a young Aussie came to the rescue, calmed me down and took away my pathetic jacket. It returned nineteen minutes later, but it was only when I was on the plane that I noticed the sleeve had been pressed so badly that a completely new crease had been created that bore no resemblance in size or position to its opposite number on the other sleeve. I got back to the office and set to work.

Dear Sir/Madam,

I am writing in relation to my stay in your hotel on the night of Wednesday 18th June.

I have never stayed at your hotel previously but it was recommended to me by the proprietors of Yuca Restaurant, with whom I had a meeting that night, as being convenient for their establishment.

I arrived at the hotel at 8.30 p.m. and I can only describe the greeting at check-in as hostile. I presented a credit card different from that with which I had made my reservation and the young lady complained that, if I gave her that one, she would have to redo her paperwork. I was in a hurry and late for my meeting so I did not bother to argue and simply handed over the appropriate credit card.

When I got up to my room it was absolutely freezing and I telephoned down to ask for the air conditioning to be adjusted whilst I was out. I then dashed out to my meeting as I was late and when I returned nothing whatsoever had been done as far as the air conditioning was concerned. I simply wanted to try to get to bed and tried to find out how to adjust it myself but without success. I am asthmatic and find it very difficult to sleep in air-conditioned rooms anyway and slept extremely badly.

In the morning, having only had a few hours in the hotel, I

requested a late checkout as I was not being collected until 3.45 p.m. by my car from Virgin to take me to the airport. I was told this was not possible as the hotel was full. However, when standing in reception a little later, I distinctly heard rooms being allocated to people who did not have reservations.

At 11 o'clock, I duly vacated my room and my bag was collected to be put into storage, together with my jacket which I requested be hung up. When I went to collect my bag at 3 o'clock to change for the airport, I was appalled to find that my very expensive Jaeger jacket had been shoved through the tiny handle of my case, making it look like a dishrag.

I requested that this be pressed immediately and was told that this would not be possible as I only had 20 minutes until my car arrived. The gentleman in charge of the luggage suggested that I leave a forwarding address so that the jacket could be sent on to me. I then advised him that I was returning to England, at which point a very helpful young Australian attendant came to my rescue, took the jacket away and returned with it, pressed, some 20 minutes later. Unfortunately, the pressing was done in such a manner that the crease by the cuff of one sleeve is now out of alignment and I am having to see what can be done to rectify it and a mark has been left on the jacket by a label which was stuck on it by a member of your staff.

Given that it took three people to get my bag to my car, i.e. one to bring the bag down, one to take it from baggage and a third to load into the car (three gratuities), I think I deserve better service and, given my brief sojourn in the room and the cost of the same, I think you will understand exactly how I feel.

On the subject of diet, I am vegetarian (a bit of literary license there) and did ask whether or not the bread /croissant at breakfast was suitable for vegetarians (i.e. contained no meat-based additives) and similarly, at lunch, asked whether the cheese used in your cooking was made with vegetable rennet. Incredibly enough, nobody could give me a satisfactory answer.

I look forward to hearing from you in due course once you have had the chance to investigate these matters.

Yours faithfully,

No response.

Dear Sir/Madam,

I am absolutely astonished not to have received a response from you to my letter of the 23rd June, a copy of which is enclosed herewith for ease of reference.

Yours faithfully,

No response

I wrote to Loew's Head Office. No response. I spoke to the restaurateur who'd booked me in there. She went in to complain and was told they had written to me with an apology and some vouchers. I told her that unless they were Jaeger vouchers of sufficient value to buy me a new jacket I really wasn't interested. I wrote again. No reply. This was becoming a real challenge. I contemplated a law suit, which is always a last resort and quite frankly means that one's complaints have been a bit of a failure. It was then that, as chance would have it, I met the Director of Tourism for the Miami area in the lobby of one of the few perfect hotels in which I've ever stayed, namely the Ritz-Carlton in Coconut Grove. You see, I don't always complain and indeed whenever I've had the pleasure of staying there I've always written to the Hotel Manager and told him what a great establishment he's running. I've just realised that I'm starting to sound like Michael Winner.

Anyway, not for the first time and probably not for the last, I digress, so back to the Director of Tourism. I told him all about my stay at Loew's and he asked me to send him the correspondence.

At least I felt I was making progress as I despatched the by now bulky package of correspondence with strict instructions to my PA not to spare the postage. And guess what? Yip. No reply. The great American malaise!

I never did hear from the Director of Tourism. He was probably too scared to write to me in case Loew's sued him. Or else he was too busy telling everybody how they could have a nice day in sunny Florida. Actually it generally rains there, or at least it does whenever I go, just in case you were thinking of gracing them with your presence. Go to New Zealand, it's much more pleasant. However, I did hear eventually from Loew's in the shape of a most charming lady called Heather. I seem to collect these nice young women. The Manager finally deigned to write to me and gave me Heather's name in case I couldn't get through to him. The letter which was addressed to my company as "Unlimited!" came to the correct address. It referred to all my letters which had been safely received and enclosed what purported to be an answer (to letter number 3 in the sequence, I think). They were very sorry they'd fallen short of their normal standards, they were sorry I'd had a bad experience and to compensate they were enclosing a voucher (room only ... whew that's a relief ... I might have had to try to eat there again) for a one night's stay to be taken before December 2004. They enclosed a letter they'd sent with a duplicate certificate which had been sent to an address in City Road EC2 which was, in fact, the registered office of my travel agents. It was little wonder the letter and its delightful enclosure had not reached me. They also produced a copy of a fax they had sent to the restaurant in Miami Beach, with which I have no connection whatsoever, enclosing a copy certificate.

I decided to cut out the middle-man in the shape of the Royal Mail (whom I had already made rich beyond their wildest dreams) and to phone the Manager. I got put through to Heather. She knew all about it and it soon became quite clear that the Manager of Loew's Hotel had decided to keep the width of the Atlantic Ocean and an entire Continent of land between me and him. I explained to her that I didn't want a certificate, that hell would probably reduce to the average temperature of their bedrooms before I set foot in their establishment again. I told her that I just wanted my jacket replaced and that surprisingly and, doubtless somewhat unreasonably, Jaeger's in Regent Street, London would not accept a gift certificate from Loew's Hotel, Miami Beach, in part exchange for a top quality cotton jacket to the value of some £250. Heather was very loyal, both to her employers and to the State of Florida. She tried to tell me what a great hotel she worked for and how nice Florida could be. I remained somewhat unimpressed, but did tell her she would get a nice mention in this book. It's a shame I'm married because I've just realised what a great chat-up line that is. If only I'd known that thirty-six years ago. In case you wonder why I choose thirty-six it's because I met my wife thirty-six years ago, which was also coincidentally (or not) the last year that my football team, Newcastle United, actually won anything of note. And please don't suggest I complain to them. I've tried. It doesn't work. Heather, bless her little Floridian socks, did take my phone numbers (I told you it was a great chat-up line) and agreed to re-read the file and call me.

And you know what? She did. The very next day. For the first time I felt as though I were actually getting through to Loew's Hotel. She had read my letters. She had some answers, or at least what passed for answers. They'd sent the certificate to the address on the computer. Quite why it was on the computer she couldn't say. They had faxed a copy to the restaurant because they thought I was back in Miami. Quite why they had thought that or done that she didn't know. She suggested the reason my letters hadn't been answered was because they thought my problem had been resolved. I asked her why they hadn't written back to say that and she said she didn't know. Heather was brutally honest. She pointed out to me I'd never said how much the jacket cost. She was right. I told her. She didn't flinch. She was obviously a woman who mixed with men who wore expensive clothes. Actually on reflection £250 is not a lot nowadays for a jacket; about $500. That's the room rate for a night at a five star hotel. Like Loew's, I suspect. Now I knew she would speak to the manager. She liked my letters. She told me I could write. I liked Heather. I told her a little more about this book and its title. Is it all about Florida? She asked. Not quite, I replied. But almost, I thought. I've never been to England, she said, wistfully. I almost felt as if I should invite her to stay. Maybe I'll send her a gift certificate for a night's accommodation Chez Stein (excluding food, of course). I awaited Heather's next call with eager anticipation.

But when it came it was a bit of a disappointment. Just as the Promised Land of a settlement had hove into sight it had disappeared again. Heather had passed the matter over to Scott, who was head of their security department. He was in charge of insurance claims. We had a repetition of earlier conversations. Could I speak to the Manager? No, that wasn't possible. He had delegated this matter to Heather. She was obviously very proud of the responsibility. Now it was being delegated again to Scott. Did this mean that this was the end of a beautiful relationship between myself and Heather? It would appear so. Would Scott be calling me? He would.

He did. He sounded very business-like but, in fact wasn't living in the real world. He wanted me to send him a receipt for the jacket and a copy of the credit card statement showing I had paid for it. I asked him if he was suggesting I had stolen it. No, but they needed some information for their insurance claim. And he also wanted me to send him the jacket. I told him that the best I could do for him was to go to Jaeger and get something from them to prove what a replacement jacket would cost. He seemed quite happy with that and when I went into Jaeger they were happy to oblige. It seems they do this all the time for insurance claims. I asked if many of their customers stayed at Loew's Hotel in Miami Beach and had their jackets ironed there. It appeared not, but there was nothing like spreading the good word about the hotel. Scott also wanted me to send the jacket. I asked him for his size. He sounded big on the phone and I doubted it would fit him. Like most Americans, Scott did not appear to have a sense of humour. I asked if he would reimburse me the postage and he said that he would supply the hotel's Fedex number. My poor jacket was to return to the scene of the crime.

I was at a wedding and told somebody about this book and the Loew's story.

"Is it really worth it?" she asked, "you must have spent far more time on it than the jacket actually cost."

I shook my head sadly. She just didn't get it. It doesn't matter how much time you spend on a complaint. If a complaint is worth making then it's worth making well and once you set out on the rocky road you have to travel its whole length, however long that might take.

I did get a valuation from Jaeger. I did fax it to Loew's. I did send the jacket by Fedex (or at least, my PA spent most of an afternoon filling in the forms in quinduplicate, including details of the fabric make-up) and now Loew's had no excuse but to compensate me. Or so one would think. Instead, enter Maria. There had to be very few of Loew's staff that I hadn't met by now. She phoned through to introduce herself and tell me she was Scott's assistant and he had asked her to call because they had mislaid the fax with the Jaeger valuation. Given their track record it would not have surprised me if they mislaid the jacket when it finally arrived. We faxed it through again. Astonishingly a few days later Maria called again. Scott, her boss, knew he had the valuation somewhere, but he couldn't lay his hands on it right that minute. I pointed out that I'd now faxed it to her twice. I asked her if she had received the much-travelled jacket. She said she had. I told her that the original valuation was inside. "Oh," she said. That seemed to satisfy her. Mind you, by the time I had originally finished writing this chapter a month or so later I'd heard nothing more from anyone at Loew's. But I did feel fairly confident I would, so confident that I went out and bought a new cotton jacket at Jaeger. I wasn't too sure when I would hear from Loew's and there wouldn't be much point in buying a cotton jacket for the English winter. I then got a phone call from the UPS despatch company saying they were trying to deliver a package for me from Loew's Hotel, Miami but hadn't been able to do so as nobody at the Florida end had bothered to tell them the name of my company. That sounded par for the course for Loew's.

The parcel arrived. It contained my jacket. It also contained the only letter I ever received from Loew's.

Dear Mr Stein

Thank you for your patience in resolving the incident with your sport coat. We appreciate your effort in helping us to resolve this situation.

We have had the opportunity to examine your sport coat at length to inspect the damage you indicated. We took this opportunity to have this garment examined and professionally dry-cleaned by a Company here in Miami. It is the opinion of this company and our opinion also that this garment was not permanently damaged. We have had your sport coat cleaned and pressed and have found it to be in excellent condition considering normal wear. We do not feel that reimbursement for replacement of this garment is reasonable.

Again I thank you for your patience in resolution of this matter.

Sincerely

Most people would have leapt out of the nearest window on reading that. I have to admit that the air did turn blue around me, particularly when I removed the creased and crumpled jacket and saw that they had replicated the damage to the sleeve about which I'd been complaining, on the previously undamaged sleeve! But as luck would have it, I was having a little altercation with Jaeger at the time and suddenly, as has happened to me so often, everything fell into place. We now need to take a small diversion. I bet you're pleased about that, particularly if I don't mention either Loew's or my damaged jacket for a few paragraphs.

I had bought a jacket and some trousers at Jaeger in Regent Street on June 22nd. This was the jacket to replace the one of which we will not speak. Everywhere else in the West End seemed to be starting their summer sales. I asked when their sale started and was told in a couple of weeks. I specifically asked if this jacket would be in the sale and was told categorically not. I had to go into Jaeger's on July 7th to collect something for my wife. The sale was just starting. Whilst I was waiting for Marilyn's garment I went downstairs to look at the menswear. I bought a shirt to go with my new jacket, which I happened to be wearing for the first time. In passing I said:

"I hope this jacket isn't in the sale," and from the expression on the salesman's face I knew it was. I began to tell the story of its purchase when a manager overheard and said it was quite impossible that I'd been told that, as none of "his team" would do that. I repeated what I'd been told and the bloke got quite stroppy with me. I pointed out that he was calling me a liar and that he had just earned himself a chapter in my book on complaints. He didn't take kindly to that and said I was threatening him. I said I wasn't threatening him as I was just telling him what I was going to do.

I went back upstairs and collected my wife's garment and then returned to the fray below. The manager had obviously had a few moments to ponder his impending notoriety and was now quite conciliatory. He asked me for my details and said that if I brought in the receipt so that he could see who had sold the jacket to me then he would reconsider.

I did take in the receipt on the morning of the receipt of my battered jacket from Loew's. The salesman was called Mahmoud. I've been dealing with him for over twenty years. To his great credit he didn't hesitate in confirming that, in all good faith, he'd told me the jacket wouldn't be in the sale. The manager was contrite and Jaeger's couldn't do enough for me. They gave me a credit for £75, being the difference in the sale price at which point I produced the Loew's jacket. Sorry, but I do have to get back to it at this stage.

"What on earth have they done to it?" they asked. "It's ruined."

"I know," I said. "Can you give me a written report to that effect?"

"We think they've washed it as well," they opined and seemed very happy to give me the report that would, I hoped, finally sink Loew's to the bottom of the Atlantic Ocean.

I wrote to Scott again and, just for kicks, sent a copy of the letter to the President of the company, in New York. Suddenly I struck paydirt. The President, a guy called Jonathan Tisch, responded. He was horrified by what had happened. We had a long chat. I not only got a check for the full £500 by return but also an invitation to stay at the Regency Hotel. I arranged for him to get membership of the Soho House in New York and he is now my new best friend. I was thinking of having the words "sponsored by Regency Hotel" emblazoned on the back of my new jacket, but that might have been over-egging the omelette. However, if you do stay at Loew's Hotel in Miami Beach, it might be as well to deny all knowledge of me. The fact of the matter is that I've made about half a dozen trips to Florida since the incident. If they had behaved properly I probably would have stayed with them each and every time. Perhaps, they too can learn something from reading this book. Not just how to complain, but the price you pay for not responding positively to a justified complaint. Actually, that's not a bad idea for a follow-up. How to deal with complaints? The poacher may yet turn gamekeeper. If you're anxious for a hotel check-list regarding potential areas of complaints, then you'll just have to restrain yourself because they come at the end of the next chapter. Just hold the thought of Loew's and my troublesome jacket for a few more pages if you will, please.

10

SOMEBODY'S GHOST FLUSHED MY TOILET

If the Loew's story is about how to complain to a hotel with no immediate results, then the Stanhope Park Hyatt New York adventure is more of a success story. With hotel chains like the Hyatt you usually get what you expect, no more and no less. If you like the brand then staying at a Hyatt, a Hilton or a Marriott around the world should always give you the same sort of experience. But the Park Hyatt in New York was a little different. It used to be The Stanhope, a fairly typical, sniffy, Upper East Side hotel which had an enormous client loyalty of its own. Then the Hyatt bought it and it never quite decided what it's meant to be … part of a chain or an individualistic boutique hotel. It did have a charm all of its own compared to the typical Manhattan skyscraper with five hundred rooms and its location, right opposite the Met in Museum Mile, with great views of the park, was to die for.

I'd had my problems there in the past, but I still went back there. Why? Because when I complained they accepted responsibility and tried to make it up to me. That, after all, is the *raison d'etre* for making a complaint in the first place. There is no point in complaining just for the sake of complaining. That's moaning. I certainly don't want to be a moaning old git, though both my children think I am. MOB they call me. Miserable Old Bugger. And that's in their more affectionate moments. We complain about our children. We complain to them to try and make them behave better and we complain about them to our friends so that we can swap experiences. And so it is with hotels, or so it should be. Complain to make them better, not just for yourself, but for others who may follow after. There, doesn't that sound heroic? Don't use the form that's left in your bedroom as a bookmark or something to stick under a table leg to stop it wobbling. Fill it in and, if you don't get an acknowledgment or response within a month, then send the hotel an e-mail or letter addressed to the

General Manager (unless it's him who you were complaining about, in which case send the letter to the Chairman or Managing Director of the Company which owns the hotel). It may be that you criticised the member of staff to whom you handed in the form or who got hold of it first and they simply didn't pass it on. The reality is that you are more likely to get more compensation in return for your complaint if your complaint didn't reach the ears of the appropriate authority first time around.

But to return to The Stanhope. And I would have returned there but some philistine at the Hyatt's head office has decided to sell it off for condominiums. We arrived too early to get our room, but the hotel was very nice about it and I could live with that, as it was a lovely day for a walk through Central Park to my favourite vegetarian restaurant in Manhattan (despite it having the worst service of almost anywhere in the world, but we'll get to restaurants eventually, don't worry). We'd ordered kosher meals for the weekend and actually, on reflection, if I didn't travel so much and request either vegetarian or kosher food I'm not even sure I'd have ever been inspired to write this book.

The Stanhope, bless them, through their Food and Beverage Manager, had confirmed everything to Lee, my travel agent, who is even longer-suffering than my spouse. I'm sure Lee could write her own complaint book about clients like me who are forever changing their travel plans. Anyway, I was delighted to learn from The Stanhope on checking in, without even having to ask, that they had our special food order. (Note, "order" rather than "ordered". It may give you a clue to the dénouement of this tale). However, on the basis of the information received our walk in the Manhattan sunshine was made just that little bit more stress free as we had one less thing to worry about.

We returned to the hotel and got our room. Has anybody out there noticed the American propensity to give you a huge bed, which takes up most of the room, very little cupboard space and a bathroom that barely gives you enough space to swing your wash-bag. Perhaps it's because so many Americans are so obese that they need the big beds, but goodness know how some of them actually manoeuvre into the bathrooms.

This small bathroom contained a toilet, I suppose it would have to really, and this particular toilet began to flush during our first night, perhaps from embarrassment at the size of the room in which it found itself. We asked for it to be mended and a nice little man arrived with an impressive array of tools. As somebody who can't even change a plug or a lightbulb, I'm always impressed by anybody who owns a tool-kit. Perhaps I shouldn't have been so impressed by the hotel's little man because, within an hour of his departure, the toilet began to flush again. As we left on Thursday morning for the Macy's Thanksgiving Parade (I've never had any cause to complain about them so why not give them a plug?) we asked the hotel to ask the little man, or any other men, big or little, who might be working over Thanksgiving, to have another go at it. When we arrived back that night it was still merrily flushing. It was too late to summon anybody back to the room and we decided to try to sleep through it, even though we'd failed to do so the night before.

Two sleepless nights later, at Friday morning breakfast, I asked the hotel to confirm all was well with our Friday night and Saturday lunch kosher meals. Now if you want to eat kosher, New York is the place to do it. You have everything there from Chinese kosher, through to Italian kosher to kosher sushi. Which reminds me about the worst kosher restaurant I ever visited (it's long closed. I suspect the chef fell on his sword.). It was called, wait for it ... Shalom Japan and if I mention that the menu contained an item called Karate Chopped Liver you will get a feel for it. They had a floor show with a delightful young New Yorker looking for all the world like a well-fed Madame Butterfly (more like Mrs Fegelstein, actually) singing Yiddish songs. They even asked diners to come up on stage and sing themselves and after several shots of saki (one of the few edible, or drinkable, items on the menu) I gave out with a few verses of Blaydon Races. Incredibly enough, to anybody who has ever heard me sing, nobody complained. My Zimbabwean friend Dickie Israel gave them a twenty minute rendition of an African tribal war song, including much clapping (not from the audience) and foot-stomping and still nobody left the place. We reckoned that the food had rooted them to their seats. Anyway, the one thing that the Stanhope should have had no problem providing was our kosher meals. However, what I was told at breakfast was that the chef wasn't in yet. I couldn't see the relevance of that as he wouldn't be cooking our meals alongside the hotel's no doubt excellent Steak Diane, but as they were happy that all was well then so was I and off we went for a day's sightseeing.

We arrived back just before the start of the Sabbath and I asked for our meal to be served in our room at 7.00 pm and saw a look of alarm pass across the face of the receptionist at the front desk. A more noticeable look of alarm passed across the face of my wife when we returned to our room and found, and heard, that the toilet was still flushing. We went downstairs to the delightful lounge/library that the Stanhope possesses. A man was on his mobile phone shattering the peace and tranquillity. After ten minutes I knew his life-story. I would have liked to help him sort out his problems but he wouldn't get off the phone. Instead the noise level gradually grew in intensity, supported by a couple of typically American kids who decided to use the lounge as a playroom, vaulting over chairs and emptying out the chess set in, a Dadaistic gesture. Drinks came; tea came. Nothing went. The room began to resemble a Hogarthian kitchen. The man was still on the phone. The children were clearly from another planet as their energy grew, rather than faded. Dirty cups rattled; empty glasses shook. Then Lissa (yes, with two 's's) entered my life.

Lissa was the Hotel's Food and Beverage Manager's assistant, but with all her problems she wasn't going to let us see her panicking. She'd read the Company Handbook and knew how to play it strictly according to the rules. She asked for my "take" on the situation. I wasn't quite sure why she wanted it but I was prepared to give it to her anyway. It was quite simple. If they had our meals they would have served them. They hadn't served them. They had served up poor Lissa on a plate as an appetiser. It therefore followed, ergo, that they did not have our meals and as it was already a couple of hours into the Sabbath and all the kosher caterers would be at home tucking into their gefilte fish, chopped liver (karate or otherwise) and chicken soup they were not going to get them delivered now. Lissa was not to be stopped in full flow. She gave me a quick résumé and told me she was making a phone call. I enquired politely as to whom she might be calling. New

Zealand or Australia, perhaps where the Sabbath was already finished. Lissa wasn't letting on. That wasn't in the handbook. It was clearly a corporate secret. But in so far as she was able to reveal what was going on she would keep us posted. Thirty minutes later she returned, picking her way through the increasing debris in the lounge. There was a clear union division of tasks. Whoever brought the drinks belonged to a different union to anybody who might eventually remove them. Lissa had made the call and she was waiting for a reply. I suspected she had made more than one call and was desperately phoning every hotel in New York, and probably beyond, to see if they had anything that approximated to kosher food in their freezers. I made no mention of this to Lissa. She had the glazed, determined look of a woman on a mission in her eyes and I didn't want to be the one who got in her way.

Another thirty minutes and she was back again. Incredibly the man was still talking on his mobile phone. I made a mental note to ask him where he bought his batteries, as they were so much better than mine. The children's parents showed no sign of coming to collect them. I could understand why. Lissa had good news. The meals were on their way. She'd had an E.T.A. Yes, she actually said that. She had obviously been a pilot in another life. Forty-five minutes; I was getting hungry. I considered eating the children. I considered eating the man's mobile. I considered eating the man. An hour passed. The man and the children disappeared. I began to miss them. Lissa returned with a triumphant expression on her face as one giving the news of a famous victory. Our meals were here. Would my wife like to inspect them?

"I'd rather eat them," I muttered, but then realised I was being selfish and spoiling Lissa's moment of glory.

By now we were back in our room. The toilet was still flushing. My wife departed and returned looking grave. Instead of four meals, for Friday night and Saturday lunch, they had delivered just two. She hadn't liked what she'd seen of the two either but, like the girl guide leader she had once been, she had used her initiative and made the best of what she had by dividing the meals into four. Oh, and by the way the Manager would like to talk to me tomorrow. I wanted to talk to him too, but realised, as is always the case with complaining, that timing is everything. I had the feeling that this drama still had some way to run. And I was right. We sat down to eat the half meal One and it was dire.

Saturday morning. The Manager would like to talk to me later. I asked if something could please be done to stop the toilet flushing as it was now almost permanently embarrassed. Half meal Two arrived at 1.00 pm. At that moment the toilet had had enough and overflowed. Water began to flood into the room. It seeped under the door and into the corridor. The Manager decided to bring our meeting forward and came rushing to the scene. Personally, splashing through the steadily rising water, he escorted us up to another room, whilst emergency works continued apace amidst the flood. I could have sworn I heard a voice from above advising me to start building an Ark as soon as the Sabbath was over. The Manager asked us if we wanted anything else (yes, my room back please) said he would leave us to our lunch and that we would talk later. I got the impression that this was not a conversation he was anticipating with any great pleasure.

And talk we did. Normally, I might have waited to write my letter, but this was a moment to complain on the spot. There needed to be some immediate pay-back, and how. I complained about the toilet. I complained about the meals (or lack of) I complained about the unwillingness to clear dirty cups and glasses. I even complained about the man on the phone and the children from hell, who even now were probably at the police station whilst a world-wide search was being instituted by Interpol for their parents. The Manager listened and nodded and agreed. I was rational and reasonable. I didn't threaten to walk out or sue like any American would have done. And I praised Lissa with her two 's's and her ability against all odds, and my increasing scepticism and sarcasm, to conjure up Kosher meals on a Friday night in Manhattan. A bit like getting a cab on Yom Kippur in the rain in Barkingside (with apologies to Blackadder).

By way of an immediate apology the hotel laid on a limo to take us to the theatre. They gave us free breakfasts. They gave us an apology and almost royal treatment from then on. And when I arrived back in England I got an e-mail from the F&B Manager (Lissa's boss) to say it was all her fault as she had forgotten to order the meals and there would be no charge for what we had received.

And they hoped we'd forgive them and come back. I have been back several times; on each occasion they upgraded me. I know they were trying harder because I had complained justifiably and they want to keep my custom (goodness only knows why). But then I think I might have become a challenge for them, just as I've become a challenge for Virgin and, I suppose, Marks & Spencer. And that's the art of persistent complaining. If the complainee has any pride at all in their services or products (and obviously Hyatt, Virgin and Marks & Spencer do) then they will rise to the challenge and actually welcome it. No big corporation wants to make mistakes, but it is one of life's certainties that they will and if they are decent they will want to know about them so they are not repeated. Just remember you are not necessarily complaining for yourself but to make it better for others, and indeed the companies themselves. Who knows? These favourite targets of complaints may even be using me as an example in their staff training. The hotel guest from hell and how to deal with him short of manslaughter. How do you deal with him? Very easily. You give him no cause for justifiable complaint and if that leads him to look for unjustified complaints then you are justified in not wanting to keep his custom. To get to heaven you need to stay on the side of the angels. Oh, and I may even visit the Condominiums they built on the site of the Stanhope – just to see if the toilet is still flushing.

It's time for a bit of revision for all the examinations of life that are awaiting you in the real world. Believe me, there are times when I feel that reality is not a place I inhabit. As someone once said to me, "Why is it that everything always happens to you?" If I had the answer to that question then I truly think that I would have the keys to the universe. So, from what's happened to me it's possible, nay advisable, to create some kind of travel check-list. Whether you are obsessive enough actually to write this down or whether you keep it in your head is entirely up to you. Whichever is the case, when you arrive, during your stay and when you leave, it's worth ticking off the items and, as I've mentioned before and make no apologies for mentioning again, if there are more than a couple of them giving you negative vibes then you should be complaining. I've mentioned those forms they leave in hotel rooms, well fill them in and if there are negative items in them, then chase for a response. But do you know, of the hundreds of forms I've completed (often containing what I believe to be constructive criticism) the only hotel from which I ever received a first time response was the Marriott in Glasgow. So, hurrah for them!

Just to save you going back these are some of the things that should put you on complaint alert:

1. Unfriendly check-in or refusal to give early check-in after a long flight when you can tell the hotel isn't full.
2. Nobody bothering to help you with your bags.
3. Room smaller than you expected or with an awful view of a building site, etc.
4. Room dirty; always check the bathroom.
5. Curtains dirty or dusty.
6. Windows failing to open.
7. Ineffective (or too effective) air conditioning system.
8. Bed uncomfortable.
9. Linen or duvet grimy.
10. Furniture old, chipped or dusty.
11. Poor TV reception.
12. No fridge, safe or free water.
13. No hangers, or just a few old wire ones (don't you just hate it when they mark your trousers ... still it's better than having your jacket ironed at Loew's).
14. Delay in delivering baggage to the room.
15. Insufficient, or paper thin, towels.
16. Crummy soap and lack of shampoo, bath and shower gel, etc; or worse still such poor quality products that they bring you out in a rash. Part of the pleasure of going to a decent hotel is in bringing home the freebies (even if it just proves to the wife that you've really been where you've said you've been). If any husbands need some washing things by way of alibis I have a whole cupboard full of them.
17. Undue noise, either from the neighbouring room, the adjacent lift or hotel staff. Even outside noise such as early morning refuse collections or building works are worth putting on the agenda.

18. Room service (or lack of it) both in respect of delivery of food or finding you an iron when you are in a hurry to get to an important business meeting.

19. Poor service at breakfast, or bad food. I've always found that the cleanliness of the cutlery is in direct proportion to the quality of the food. If it sparkles then so does the menu. And how annoying is it when you are in a sunny climate and they give you tinned fruit in the buffet? And when they don't bother to change the hot food for hours, as it just lies there simmering? There are laws about that in England but they don't seem to apply anywhere else.

20. Unreasonable telephone charges or lack of Internet access, or absurd charges for the privilege of logging on.

21. Broken or dirty equipment in the gym.

22. Maids knocking at your door at an unearthly hour just because they want to get on and clean the room (which you've paid for until midday).

23. Lack of choice of foods both by way of room service and in the restaurant. Not everybody wants a burger at 2.00 am. And some eccentrics like me actually want veggie food that really is vegetarian.

24. Dirty or crowded swimming pools. Loud music blaring over tannoys, no special hours for kids, lack of loungers, people "bagging" seats with towels. Trust me, it's not just the Germans who do that.

25. Nowhere to sit in the public areas. Nowhere to read quietly. Nowhere to escape smokers.

26. Uncooperative concierges; rude staff.

27. Missing items from your room. Don't jump to conclusions that stuff has been stolen, check carefully, make sure you didn't leave it at home in the first place, but once you are sure then go for the jugular. It may be flattering to your tastes that someone has nicked your t-shirt, perfume, after-shave or belt, but it's still bloody annoying.

28. Things don't work in the room e.g. toilets, phones, TVs, kettles, baths, showers and lights and worse still, they don't get fixed. Not a lot worse than having a kettle but no coffee or tea. How many phone calls does it take to get these items

supplied? Phone calls are a bit hard when the phone doesn't work either. You can always go down to the front desk (sod's law you are on the 27th floor and the lift is out of action) but try getting anything out of the front-desk after midnight.

29. Wake-up calls that don't come.
30. Hidden extras.
31. Mistakes on the bill.
32. Churlish goodbyes, even though you may be only too glad to say goodbye.
33. And finally, and probably the most important, the overall value. Did you get what you paid for or do you feel cheated?

As I said, take any one of these items individually (other than grand larceny) and you can whinge but probably not complain. Take any combination of three and it's worth a letter (or an on-the-spot complaint if appropriate) and you should receive something back in return. Whether it's something off your bill, a complimentary bottle of champagne or a free night at a hotel you wouldn't want to revisit until hell freezes over, will depend. I have no crystal ball, nor magic wand. But hopefully I can teach you how to light the touch-paper and retreat. Maybe the flame will fizzle out, maybe you'll just get an explosion, but hope upon hope, and you may just get a firework display to beat all firework displays.

11

BANKERS OR *ANKERS?

When it comes to banks, aiming complaints is a bit like shooting fish in a barrel. You can't help but hit your target and you almost feel sorry for the dead creature with its cold eyes and wet skin floating to the surface. Dead creatures with cold eyes and wet skin just about sums up your average bank manager. If indeed you have one. Do you remember those good old days of yore when you had a bank manager for life. He was a comfortable well-padded, middle-aged, round-faced gentleman who never seemed to grow any older as he peered at you over half-mooned spectacles and listened carefully to what you had to say and what you required. You sent him a bottle of port at Xmas or a food hamper if he'd been particularly helpful. Though I do know of one bank manager who received so many gifts in the shape of microwaves, fridges and portable TVs that his office wasn't accessible from December 1st right through to New Year. Mind you, he was forced to take an early pension, though I suspect he could afford it.

In those halcyon days quite often the bank even remembered your birthday (now they don't even remember your name and woe betide you if you don't remember all your security codes and passwords). If you were overdrawn by a little you received either a polite telephone call to see if there was a problem or an even politer letter asking you if you minded finding a few moments of your valuable time to pop in to discuss your requirements as to a slightly larger overdraft to tide you over your short-term difficulties. What you didn't get was your cheques bouncing and an unauthorised overdraft charge as a win bonus. What you didn't get was the computer saying "no".

If your recollection of banking is the same as mine then you are probably over fifty. If you think I'm painting a portrait of Banking in Disneyworld then you're not. That's how much things have changed and yet, so often, we all feel this sense of helplessness, of futility at the inability to do anything about it. Banks have just become another huge, amorphous entity, without shape or substance. When the Royal Bank of Scotland posts record profits of some six billion pounds (at today's rate of exchange for the few American readers I haven't offended and who have got this far that's about eleven billion dollars) you have to take a deep breath. And that's just one banking group. But I suppose if you've rid yourself of all those nice plump bank managers and just have a load of dead fish it's really not that difficult to get to those figures.

If you want to make a complaint nowadays (and as I've said, just so many people take what the world and the banks throw at them on the chin and don't bother) you're struggling to find somebody to address it to. Your branch? You probably don't even have one. You may have a local banking office into which you pay your money. It may even have a manager (or two) but unless you are a Premier or Favoured, or whatever Posh Name the bank may give to customers who either have a barrowful of money or else a huge overdraft that pays the bank loads of fees (must be loads to get to six billion profit), then the likelihood is that they won't even know your name. Go tell them you're not a number, that you're a human being. All you will do is howl at a huge office building made of steel, concrete and dark sexy glass.

Your local bank certainly won't have a phone number. Try getting the number of your High Street branch nowadays from directory enquiries. Mind you, try finding directory enquiries, but space and time do not permit a guide on how to complain to them. Even if you get the number try calling it. If you do then there's a strong possibility of you making a new friend in Singapore or Malaysia, or perhaps even somewhere which doesn't yet have any material for a philatelist's collection. The person to whom you speak will invariably introduce themselves by name (first name only) but don't even write it down as the chances of you ever speaking to them again are remote. I wouldn't bother asking for extension numbers either. I've tried to call back and ask for extension 7149 only to be told that no such extension exists as since yesterday morning all extension numbers are prefixed by 444 followed by a three digit number to which you are obviously not privy. Doubtless if you call back an hour later in this

Kafkaesque world then they would have changed again. They probably employ somebody with the sole task of changing extension numbers.

Now banks may think that the introduction of the Banking Ombudsman solved everything. Now you, the innocent, naïve customer had somebody to look after you, somebody who would deal with your complaints and make it all better. But if you've gone marginally overdrawn, and the bank has failed to honour a cheque, then making a written complaint to the Ombudsman is a total waste of time. By the time he's sent you the daunting forms, you've completed them and sent them back, he's adjudicated and written back to you telling you that you were in the wrong for failing to keep within your overdraft limits – by that time your creditworthiness could have been shot to pieces. That is if you are still alive. In my Banking Disneyworld you would have asked your nice bank manager to find out which of his clerks had failed to look at your account on a monthly basis, to satisfy himself that it always came back into credit when your salary arrived and he would have done so, reprimanded him, and written you a letter of apology whilst inviting you to lunch at a restaurant of your choice. The fact of the matter is that, in this world of techno-madness nobody even looks at your account, just at the balance every thirty seconds and if anybody can tell the exact balance on their accounts on even a weekly basis without going to a hole in the wall and punching out a slip or dialling up on line then they are a better man than I, Gunga-Din.

So, there's all the problems, but are we beaten, are we going to give up on this one? Arc we, hell, no as John Wayne might have said; flawed individual that he was he was never scared of battling against overwhelming odds. When it comes to banks nowadays then, in my view, the pre-emptive complaint is the best way to deal with things. If you open an account at a new branch ask them who is going to be your personal manager and if they say it's not possible to allocate one to you then take your business elsewhere. Once you've done that write a letter of complaint to the Chairman of the bank and tell him exactly why he has lost your business. He may not care but if everybody wrote to him then he may just start to show a little concern. The banking industry is a highly competitive market and nobody likes to feel they are losing out on even a tiny part of it.

Assuming you've got a result and have the name of your new manager then also ask for a number you can call in case of need. These requests may seem to be very basic but trust me, nothing is what it seems in the twenty-first century world of banking. It's quite extraordinary that many managers no longer have direct lines, but mobiles instead. I assume that the call-centre system doesn't provide for the manager to have an outside line in their office. In any event, grab what you can get, take the mobile number and don't hesitate to use it; for anything. They've installed the system to gain access to the managers, but you never know, they may just change it. The fact of the matter is that even when you call the mobile number the person to whom it's allocated rarely answers. You still get somebody asking for your details and seeing if they can help you with a view to cutting you off at the pass on your way to talk to the one person who knows your history ... or should. Even more annoying is the recorded message, which tells you that your manager is busy but will get back to you because you are important to him as a customer. That's almost as bad as the Americans telling you to have a nice day. If you make several of those calls note what they cost you. It's all going to go into your complaint letter. If your call is not returned and you don't get to speak to anybody else who could have helped you and you were only phoning to get a very temporary new limit on your account, then there can be all sorts of repercussions. The cheque you've drawn in anticipation of funds coming through (and which do come through) gets bounced, the international transfer takes a day or so longer than you thought, or a cheque you've paid in takes three days to clear and all through those three days the bank is sitting on and using your money. In all those cases the bank does something that causes you grief with the third party to whom you've drawn your cheque and charges you as well just in case you've not learned your lesson. But you've done your best to get through and at that moment you really do need to start firing off complaints.

It may seem to be Catch 22 but if you do have a manager and a number (isn't that where we came in?) start off by ringing the number and leaving a message. Note the time you called and then also write to the name. The letter may just reach him even if it has to make its way via the Far East or the Galapagos Islands. Even if you are a preferred client and have a personal manager allocated don't think that you're home and dry. If he's any good he'll fast track his way to some head office position, wherever it is that they have head offices nowadays. In the Wonderland that's the world of high street banking, and it wouldn't surprise me if they had managers commuting from Lahore to the City on a daily basis.

I actually had a manager's card in front of me the other day. Name: Branch: Phone number: Fax Number. I needed to speak to her. I called. A nice lady answered and asked me which branch I wanted. I've just called the branch. I said. No, you've got through to me, she replied. I'll call the branch for you. Now which branch did you want? King's Road, I said. That was the address on the card. Which city might that be, the nice lady asked. London, I replied grimly. I'm not getting anything she said as I looked at my watch. But it's on the card in front of me, I said between clenched teeth, trying very hard to obey my own maxim of never losing your cool. Can you give me the full address? King's Road, Chelsea, I said. Do you want me to spell it for you? Oh, Chelsea she said, obviously relieved that I'd given her the name of place she recognised. So can you put me through now? I asked more in hope than anticipation. Can you give me your account number and sort code she asked? Oddly, this was not information I knew off by heart. No, I said. This presented a problem. Well, she said, still as nice as pie (but then I suppose I had relieved the boredom of her day, wherever she was, which was patently not in the branch of the bank I wanted to contact) I'll put you through this time. Silly me, I'd tried to call my bank manager without having my account details to hand. Well, that's one mistake I won't make again. The phone rang. My dialogue with the mysterious nice lady was at an end. Somebody answered the phone. Progress! Once again I was making lots of new friends and acquaintances. As you've probably gathered from reading this book I do have an uncanny knack of widening my Xmas card list almost without trying. I asked to speak to my bank manager. What's your account number I was asked. I resisted the temptation to scream or throw my phone (with me attached) out of the window; I don't know I replied, by now feeling extremely guilty that I was putting the bank to so much trouble. It's a bit difficult without the number, I was told. Why? I asked. I've told you who I want to speak to, I've told you my name, those are the usual two pre-requisites to start a conversation, what's the big deal? I need your account number, she persisted. She'd read the same training manual as Lissa. Look, I said, why not just take my name and ask the bank manager to call me back. She's in a meeting right now (it was 9.55 am. It had been about 9.00 am when I'd started my first call). She should be free at five past ten. I was impressed by the precision but said nothing. I'll send her an email to tell her you called. What happened to all those telephone pads we used to have where the receptionist took a message, wrote down a number and your secretary brought it in to you together with your tea and shortbread biscuits?

By one o'clock I'd heard nothing. I had no great confidence that my message had even been passed on. I thought I'd phone back but then decided I couldn't face the obstacle course of the call centre again. I had a fax number. I would use it. I faxed and complained. Two hours later the manager called me. It had taken some six hours to get to the point of a conversation. But ... with my complaint letter in front of her she did feel guilty enough to give me what I wanted without hesitation. So, I suppose you could say I got a result. My complaint had succeeded. But I couldn't leave it there. I needed to store up some more moral points for a rainy (or poverty) day. And so I wrote and set it all out just as I've told it to you. If the bank manager buys the book she may have a complaint in so far as she can honestly say she's read part of it before. I've yet to cash in my points, but when I do I feel that all my efforts will have been worth it. And it made me feel better. That's all part of the psychology of complaining, to allow you to vent not only your spleen but also your frustration.

Astonishingly, I recently had a credit request at a bank refused. It was a bank with whom I had enjoyed a relationship for some thirty odd years. It was merely a temporary facility I was seeking and it came at the recommendation of my personal bank manager over a lunch. I queried the reason for the refusal. It appears they have to tell you. It seemed that they didn't like my business accounts. I didn't like them either. In fact I disliked them so much that I didn't have any. I wrote to them complaining and received an apology. I suppose I could have pushed it a little further and asked for some damages, as the credit department had effectively defamed me to my own bank manager, but as she gave me what I wanted by way of a simple overdraft top-up I thought that might have been gilding the lily. I do now have some credit stored with my bank and not of the kind you can visibly see on bank statements. I've also been rather nice and not named and shamed them either so they owe me big time.

It may seem that I have severe financial problems (not the case but I hope my finances are going to improve with the sales of this book anyway) but I was called at home just on the day I was putting this text to bed finally. So, nice timing from Lloyds TSB Collection Department in Sussex. A bloke called me and asked for my name, date of birth and postal code. He was from Lloyds. You would have thought that as he was calling me he might just have had that information. He told me my account was overdrawn. I told him I'd been getting letters to tell me exactly that but I'd done nothing about it as I knew that monthly funds came in to put the account substantially back into credit. I told him that if he bothered to look at the account he'd see precisely that. He wasn't going to be bothered, that was for sure. He'd just been told to tell me that my cards had been cancelled. The fact was, that I'd never used my cards and truth be told didn't really know where they were. That wasn't the point. I told him he had a bloody nerve doing that and asked him for his name, as I wanted to put the episode in my book. Do you know, he wouldn't tell me? I pointed out that I didn't take kindly to an anonymous phone call cancelling my bank cards. He told me he was a "human being" albeit one who didn't seem to have a name. I asked to speak to his superior; he did have a name, Darren. He explained that it was an automated system that took no notice of the pattern of my account and there was nothing my manager could do about it. We'll see about that, I thought, as I slammed the phone down on Darren and his shy buddy.

I called my Privilege Manager, Danielle, on the number she'd given me. And do you know it all started again. I spoke to a

Geordie girl called Lianne. What branch do you want? What's your account number? Can't you tell me as I'm here to help you? Somehow I didn't think she could. Eventually I spoke to Maria at the branch as Danielle wasn't there. I pointed out that just a fortnight earlier I'd been dragged down to the bank on a wild goose chase when I'd had another phone call asking me to come in to see the manager. The result of that was that they seemed so pleased to have our accounts that they offered us a Platinum Card! Now two weeks later my account was with collection for over £500 and my cards were in notional shreds. She couldn't explain. She had no idea how the balance had come to go to collection. She would speak to Rebecca, the manager, who would call me. She didn't. It got worse.

When they told me they were stopping my bank cards they didn't bother to tell me they were also stopping credit cards. I found out when I tried to pay with one in a garage in Italy. They also didn't tell me they were stopping my wife's debit card. Marilyn doesn't believe in borrowing money. She always has her account in credit and, indeed, the balance in her account far exceeded the tiny overdraft which had triggered off the cataclysmic sequence of events. She only found out about this when she tried to buy a bag in duty free at Rome airport. To say she was unhappy is an understatement. To say I was unhappy when my last card was taken from me in public, in Ralph Lauren in Bond Street, whilst buying my son a birthday present, would be like suggesting the flood was a passing cloud.

Letters began to whirl off the presses

20th July 2004

By post and fax
Privilege Manager
Lloyds TSB
Kings Road Branch
33-38 Kings Road
Chelsea
London SW3 4LX
Dear Danielle,

I do trust that, by the time you receive this letter, we will have spoken on the telephone.

On Friday the 9th July, I was working at home, completing my latest book, when I received a telephone call from a gentleman who did not introduce himself but who claimed to be from Lloyds TSB. He asked me for my date of birth and then asked me for my postal address. I supplied both though, with hind-sight, I probably should have checked his credentials.

He then told me that, as my account was £600 overdrawn, the bank was "cancelling my cards". I told him that I did not use my cheque card or my debit card anyway and that, in any event, all he needed to do was to check with my branch, see the pattern of the account, and to realise that regular sums of money came in and would wash away any overdraft. He told me that it had nothing to do with the branch and the matter had "automati-cally" gone to Collections.

I found this very hard to believe, given the length of time I had banked with Lloyds and at that point I was so annoyed I once again asked him for his name and told him I was writing a book about complaints (which included a chapter on banks) and, as far as I was concerned, this incident was going into it. He then declined to give me his name, whereupon I asked for his superior. He did give me that person's name, and confirmed that my cards had been invalidated. Again I asked if he had bothered to check with you at my branch but he said that this was not necessary. At that point, I told him that I was going to talk to you and put the phone down.

I then called you, you were not available and I was told by a lady called Maria that the Manager, Rebecca, would call me. She did not. I then went on holiday.

I attempted to use my Lloyds TSM Gold card (which has nearly £7,500 worth of unused credit on it) and this was declined. My wife used her debit card on her personal account. This was declined on three occasions. Her account has always been in credit, continued to be in credit and, indeed, has several thousand pounds in it.

She was so outraged that she asked me to consult a solicitor,

David Swede, who tried to telephone you yesterday. His call has not been returned. I telephoned myself at lunch time to speak to you or the Manager. I gave a brief summary of the circumstances of the situation and, again, my call was not returned.

We did finally speak when I called you again and you told me you had not received my message. You acknowledged that this should have crossed your desk before it went to Collections, when a simple phone call would have enabled my wife to transfer funds from her account. The fact of the matter is that your bank has denied my wife access to her money and that is just not acceptable. Nor is it acceptable for it to take four days to replace our cards.

You have told me that the senior branch manager will call me but have offered no explanation as to why the mysterious "Rebecca" chose not to call.

You really must resolve this issue to my satisfaction and in particular to the satisfaction of my wife, bearing in mind that she has received an enforcement notice under Section 761 of the Consumer Credit Act 1974 containing a formal demand for £660.44 which has, in any event, now been paid as our joint account is back in credit and her account always had a credit balance in excess of the total overdraft including the facility!

I await hearing from you.

Yours sincerely,

Eventually I did get a call from the manager who did offer a sort of apology. I did also get a small Credit in my account from the bank. My wife is still outraged and even considered moving her account from Lloyds. The ultimate complaint.

Neither you nor I need to invent the wheel to be able to complain to our bank but here are a few suggestions. Each and every one creates a cause for complaint:

1. Cheques dishonoured with no warning.
2. Unexplained exorbitant charges.
3. Unauthorised overdraft charges when you weren't truly overdrawn.
4. Misleading and confusing debits and credits.

5. Calls unreturned (even if you can actually get through).
6. Call centres.
7. Failure to provide a new cheque book.
8. Unjustified credit refusals.
9. Absence of any designated bank manager.
10. Delays in replacing lost, stolen or damaged credit or debit cards.

A machine in a wall recently swallowed my son Nicky's, debit card. He reported it and was told it would be replaced. He gave them all his details. After ten days he was still unable to draw any cash. He called again and they had the nerve to tell him they were waiting for him to make a formal request for a new card. They said they could send it by courier but it would take three days. Obviously the courier was travelling via one of the far-flung call centres. You can imagine his reply. He is his father's son.

12

DEMOLITION OF BUILDING SOCIETIES AND INSURANCE UNCOVERED

I thought of combining Building Societies with banks but finally decided to lump them together with insurance companies as they sort of deserve each other. They both chunder out numbers which make no sense to the layman, both try and confuse their clients as to how much they are paying or earning and, as Building Societies love to sell insurance, it seems to me to be a marriage made in heaven.

Building Societies used to be places where you saved your surplus income, when we had surplus income. You built up a savings account so you could have a deposit on a house, show an ability to repay your borrowings-to-be and to develop a relationship with the company from whom you would borrow when you came to make your first time purchase. Just to put things into perspective (and this is for the benefit of younger readers) the way it used to work was that you might have saved £5000 by the time you got married (yes, amazingly enough people did get married before they bought something). You'd find a house for £50,000 ... do I hear the sound of everybody under forty lying on their backs, kicking their legs in the air and dissolving into hysterical laughter? You'd use your savings to put down your ten per cent deposit ... no 95% mortgages on £300,000 first time purchases then ... and you took out an endowment insurance policy which, with profits, would pay off the £45,000 you owed and leave you enough money to treat yourself and whoever you might be living with twenty years on, to a round the world holiday.

Just as was the case with your friendly neighbourhood bank manager, you would go to see your building society manager when you found your dream house, he'd help you fill in the application forms, and tell you he'd lend you twice (or if you were a favoured client or very pretty) thrice your joint income. Nowadays Building Societies are like supermarkets. They sell everything and you leave the premises with a load of things in your basket that you never wanted in the first place and most of which you could have got cheaper at the even bigger supermarket down the road.

Building Societies used to attract the same sort of loyalty as banks. Once they got you then you were theirs for life. Funnily enough, and it may not appear so from these pages, I'm a loyal sort of guy. I've been with the same bank for about thirty years (the one I refrained from naming), had a million insurance policies with the Royal, even went out of my way to buy my evening paper from the same lady until she gave up her pitch to have a baby. And so it was with Building Societies. I opened an account with the Alliance & Leicester when they still had a branch in Regent Street near my old office (from the roof of which, by the way, I saw The Beatles concert on the top of the Apple Building in Saville Row). I even encouraged my wife and indeed my sons to open accounts with them. Now, as I mentioned in the previous chapter, my wife is not a woman who believes in credit. If her lead were to be followed the Chairman of every credit card company in the land would leap, lemming-like, off cliffs as their businesses crumbled around them. However, Marilyn does believe in savings (the planet, me and money are amongst her collections) She also believes that it is nobody's business but hers as to how much money she has in the Building Society. Indeed, all I know myself is that she has more than me. Well, somebody has to spend money to get the material for a book complaining about all the things it's been spent on. So, she was somewhat miffed when she went into the Alliance & Leicester branch in Cockfosters, North London and had some young man behind the counter call out her balance in front of other customers. Do Building Societies have customers, or clients, or savers, or just mug punters? Whatever! Actually, I've had more complaints about my throwaway phrase, *whatever,* than anything else in my life. It may just be acceptable for a teenager, I am told, annoying, but acceptable, but it doesn't sit well in the mouth of a man of my advanced, and even more rapidly advancing, years. Whatever!

She was not a happy lady. My wife has a certain expression, which I call "the shopping face". Turned upon any unsuspecting shop assistant, this can freeze them in their tracks. She is not a woman to be trifled with, although oddly she is not the world's best complainer and, as you may have gathered from past chapters, she very often has an inclination to be swallowed by a convenient piece of earth when I am in full complaining vein. On this occasion she needed little encouragement to write and we did, simply setting out the sequence of events and gently inquiring as to whether or not the Alliance & Leicester wanted to retain our family's business.

We heard nothing so we threatened to remove all of our accounts. At this point we got a phone call and an apology. To my astonishment I then got a letter telling me I'd failed to attend an appointment to discuss some investments. I don't know who they made the appointment with, but it certainly wasn't me. This time I meant it when I said we were going to switch our allegiances.

Dear Ms. X,

Re: Premium Plus Account No. XXX

Thank you for your letter of the 29th April which completely perplexes me.

No appointment was made for me to see you on the 28th April. Could you please let me know who allegedly made this appointment, when and how?

I am astonished that you expect me to read newspapers to ascertain best available investments within your company.

You mention that you enclose a "list of the requirements" but these were not enclosed, which seems fairly in keeping with your approach to my family's accounts, as previously indicated. I simply do not have the time to get in to see you so would you please post to me the appropriate information regarding the various options open to me to obtain a better rate of interest than that now being received on our current account.

I note that you have been "serving your customers for 150 years." May I suggest you still have a considerable amount to learn in relation to customer service?

Yours sincerely,

We received an abject apology. Would we like to come in so they could apologise in person? We did. We met a young man called Mohammed who gave us excellent advice and the relationship was restored. The Alliance & Leicester is situated very near a road in Cockfosters called Mount Pleasant and I did comment that as Mount Pleasant wouldn't come to us we would have to go to Mount Pleasant and Mohammed.

Now, the object of that lesson is sometimes one's need to complain even though there is going to be no material benefit at the end of the day. I didn't expect Alliance & Leicester to give us an extra percent on our investments or to offer us a cash compensation payment. But I liked being with them, I wanted to stay with them and felt it was worth the effort to tell them what was wrong with their service so we would be happy in our ongoing relationship.

One company with whom I'm certainly not going to have an ongoing relationship is Sun Life Financial of Canada. They didn't use to be called that. They were Confederation Life. Now as far as I am concerned SLFC and Conlife as I shall call them ... mainly because I can't be bothered to keep on typing out their names in full) are the Jekyll and Hyde of the insurance industry. I heard a radio programme the other day which said that the three industries which attracted the most complaints were the motor trade, banking and insurance. I wonder why. What was even more interesting (as you can see it doesn't take a lot to interest me) was the fact that only one out of ten people who were dissatisfied with anything ever bothered to complain. Which is why I suppose companies think they can continue to get away with sub-standard service and if you want to know who sets the standard then the answer is, you.

In 1993 I took out a ten year policy with Conlife recommended by my good friend (and still good friend, Frank). Unlike many insurance salesmen, or Financial Advisers as they like to be called, Frank was totally honest and truly believed, when he was selling Conlife products, that they represented one of the best opportunities in the market place. My policy was quite simple. Pay £50 a month for ten years and we will guarantee you £4500 if you die or when the policy matures in 2003. But it should produce in excess of £8000 and maybe as much as £10,000. I cheerfully paid the premiums and received encouraging letters to tell me how well my investment was doing. Then suddenly Conlife ceased to exist and they became SLFC (in case you have forgotten they are Sun Life Financial of Canada ... I wouldn't want you to forget that).

In May 2000 I was told the surrender value of the policy was £4545. I was told I couldn't increase the premiums (well, thank heavens for small mercies). Nothing was said as to that surrender figure ever going down and as there were still nearly three years' premiums to pay I was hopeful we could still obtain a reasonable return. This hope was supported when, in June 2000, I was told by letter that my policy would be worth £7350 on maturity if there was 4% growth, £7730 if there was 6% growth and £8120 if there was 8% growth, I suppose they might have told me it would be worth £40,000 if there was to be 40% growth as well because none of these projections were really sustainable. With hindsight it was interesting that they didn't bother to tell me what would happen if there was 1% growth or 0% growth or a 5% decline.

I got out my abacus and worked out that in ten years they would have had £6000 of my money. At 5% per annum, non-accumulative I could have got the figure up to £9000 and here were these supposed experts falling woefully short of that target.

I left them to get on with making me fortunes and waited patiently until March 2003. I'd heard nothing so I wrote to Frank enclosing a copy of his June letter and sat back to wait for my cheque which I thought would be at least £7350, particularly as, since May 2000, my friends at SLFC had had another £1700 of my money. £4545 plus £1700 plus a bit of interest should have got us to £7350 without any problem.

I heard nothing and so I tried to phone Frank only to find out that he and SLFC had parted company. I tracked him down and discovered it had neither been a voluntary or happy departure but he would see what he could do to help. He phoned me back to say that SLFC had overlooked the matter and would be sending me a cheque within seven to ten days. He also told me that, in view of the poor performance of the policy they would also be writing to me with various alternatives to taking out the money. I pointed out that the money had to be made available before one could even dream of taking it out and that still seemed some way off as far as I was concerned. I could not have envisaged then how far away it actually was.

April Fool's Day came and went and SLFC couldn't even be bothered to send me an unsigned cheque by way of a rib-tickling joke. On the afternoon of Friday April 11th, having nothing better to do other than some work for important clients, I phoned SLFC who some time earlier had had the gall to send a letter which said … And I quote:

"We are pleased to advise you that Sun Life Financial of Canada is introducing a new Customer Careline which will be able to handle all your policy related queries and changes.

From premium payment questions to maturity values, whatever your reason just telephone 0870 161 3333. (If you have a few hours to spend and want to save the money from dialling a premium chat-line you may want to give them a call … Ask for Julie … she's good for at least half an hour of entertainment.)…… Our intention is to provide a constantly improving level of service and we hope you will agree that our Customer Careline achieves its aim."

Well, I don't and it didn't. Were they having a laugh in sending out a letter like that? It's a bit like the thought of Sunderland ever qualifying for Europe again.

I did spend my thirty minutes on the phone to Julie. I can't tell you if she's prepared to talk dirty but I came off the phone feeling very aroused albeit not in a sexy kind of way. Amongst other things, she told me that my cheque had been drawn and was being sent to me and that I would get it the following Tuesday or Wednesday. I pointed out that I should have had it on March 10th and that if Michelangelo were drawing it then it wouldn't have taken so long. I suspect the ceiling of the Sistine Chapel would have been well under way in over a month and that was done with him up a ladder. She didn't even acknowledge the sarcasm. Here was another lady with her rulebook in front of her. By the Spring of 2003 SLFC weren't writing any new business and she was just in charge in dealing with the rump of their portfolio (including me) and her career prospects weren't good within the company. In any event I told her in very plain English (even though she was working for a Canadian company) that this was not acceptable and that I wanted either a banker's draft to be delivered to me on Monday or a telegraphic transfer to be made into my account, so that my account could be credited with the sum on Monday. Julie told me that as the cheque had already been drawn that wasn't possible and neither could she accept my invitation to tea when she could deliver the cheque personally.

I then asked for the maturity figure. She told me that this would be £4955.57. I was, to say the least, unimpressed. However, I knew from complaints I had made on behalf of my wife regarding Clerical Medical, where she too had seen a surrender value fall whilst her ongoing premiums fell into a bottomless pit, that I was not on a winner. However, I had gone through the process of complaining to the Financial Ombudsman Service so I was able to tell Julie that, unless she got her rapidly disappearing company to do something about my already disappeared money, I would be making a formal complaint to the Ombudsman once again.

I pointed out to Julie that whilst my money had been retained the stock markets had enjoyed their best run for many a long month and, as I assumed my money had still been invested, I should have enjoyed the benefit of that. If I had received my money I could have invested it into shares and got the benefit that way. I also told her I was entitled to interest and she agreed to speak to the directors. I think by this time she would have agreed to speak to anybody just to get me off the phone.

Astonishingly, by the 14th April I had still received nothing and so I wrote a complaint letter to the Ombudsman.

Dear Sirs,

Re: Sun Life Financial of Canada – Policy No. XXX

I wish to make a formal complaint regarding Sun Life Financial of Canada (formerly Confederation Life).

I enclose herewith a copy of a policy that I had with them which, as you will see, matured on the 10th March this year. As you will also see, I have had this policy for 10 years and have paid £6,000 in premiums over that period of time.

I heard nothing from Confederation Life or their successors, Sun Life Financial of Canada, with regard to the policy's maturity and wrote them a letter asking what was happening. I received no reply to that letter. I then wrote directly to their former employee, who had dealt with the matter on my behalf, Frank, and he duly telephoned them and was told that they had overlooked the matter and would be sending me a cheque within seven to ten days. He also told me that, in view of the poor performance of this policy, they would also be writing to me with various alternatives to taking the money out at this stage.

By the 11th April, as you will appreciate, I was somewhat angry that I had received no money or any direct communication from this company, even though my policy had matured over a month earlier. I therefore telephoned them on the afternoon of Friday 11th April and spent some 30 minutes on the telephone with a lady called Julie in Customer Services. She told me that a cheque had now been drawn and was being sent to me. She told me that I would get that the following Tuesday or Wednesday. I told her that this was not acceptable and that I wanted either a banker's draft to be delivered to me on Monday or a telegraphic transfer to be made so that the money could be in my account on Monday. She told me this was not possible.

I then asked for the maturity figure. She told me that this would be £4,955.57. I pointed out to her that whilst my money had been retained, the market had substantially improved and that therefore the figure should be recalculated on the date that I was actually being paid, rather than the date of maturity. She told me that was not possible.

I then told her that, in addition to that, I believed I was entitled to interest. This had not been calculated and she said that she would speak to the directors and see whether they were prepared to pay this.

I do firmly believe that, in all the circumstances, I should be entitled to compensation and whilst I have told them to proceed to send me the cheque in order to mitigate my loss, I also feel that I should be entitled to avail myself of the various options that would have been open to me had the matter been dealt with in a competent manner.

I await hearing from you in due course.

Yours sincerely,

On the 15th April I received a letter from SLFC.

"I write with reference to the maturity of the above numbered policy and your recent telephone call to our customer careline. (No mention of the deep and meaningful bond I had forged with our Julie.)

Firstly may I apologise for the service you have received from our company, with regard to the way your maturity was dealt with. Please be ensured (I thought I was insured, not ensured … what does that mean? Did they intend to say assured? Who knows? Whatever!) that this is not the usual high standard of customer service that Sun Life Financial of Canada prides itself on (you see, even they had to set out their name in full so I couldn't forget it). The delay in your proceeds being issued was a completely manual administration error and for this I accept full responsibility (how nice of him … Or her … to fall on their sword, I thought. Manual error … And I though we were living in a world of technology).

I can confirm that the maturity proceeds were sent first class post yesterday (so I've not even received my money yet).

Secondly, (is there such a word? I don't think so) by way of an apology (silly me, I though this letter was it) please find enclosed a cheque totalling (totalling? Does it contain several amounts?) £50 as gesture (they missed out the "a") of goodwill, hopefully (they missed out the "and") this can go someway (thought that was two words) towards the inconvenience you have been caused.

I trust this is to your satisfaction, however (should have started new sentence there) if you require further information please contact me on the above telephone number."

That may have been difficult as whoever was apologising, whoever had committed hari-kari, whoever was asking me to call them, whoever couldn't write a letter to save his, or her life, had scrawled a signature that was totally illegible and had not typed their name underneath.

My response was to write again to the Ombudsman:

Dear Sirs,

Re: Sun Life Financial of Canada – Policy No. XXX

I refer to my earlier letter of the 14th April.

I now enclose a copy of the settlement letter I finally received from Sun Life Financial of Canada. As you see, this letter was dated the 12th April, but I also enclose a copy of the envelope, from which you will see that it was not posted until the 14th April and I did not receive it until the 15th April. By the time the cheque is paid into my account and cleared, bearing in mind the intervening Easter holidays, it will probably not be until the 22nd April.

As you will see, they have not seen fit to apologise, offer any explanation or, indeed, offer any compensation by way of interest.

I await hearing from you with regard to my complaint in due course.

Yours faithfully,

On the 17th April I got two letters. One was from the Ombudsman enclosing his complaint form to complete. I liked that. Here was a man who understood the need to complain. The other (incorrectly addressed) was from SLFC. This time it was signed by a man in their Complaints Support Dept. My letter had now been registered as a complaint (well, at least they had understood that much) and an investigation was being undertaken by one of their Client Service Advisers. Once again I seemed to be meeting lots of exciting people at a company and although I had yet to be introduced to the writer of the anonymous letter, my Christmas card list was expanding at a rate of knots.

On 22nd April I returned the complaint form to the Ombudsman. I then received another anonymous letter from SLFC. I was getting worried. How long before they started to demand money from me with menaces? How long before incriminating photos of me with my cat appeared on the web? This time they just wanted to classify me as a client. That was easy. Discontented.

The Ombudman acknowledged receipt of my complaint on 23rd April. He would reply as soon as he could. I understood. If SLFC were anything to go by he was getting more mail than Santa Claus. He was clearly on my case though, as on 24th April he sent me an identical letter. I was impressed. Then on 28th April he told me that before they could consider a complaint the firm concerned had to be given the chance to put things right. I was not impressed. I had little confidence in the ability of SLFC to put anything right, even the syntax, grammar and spelling in their correspondence. However, the Ombudsman was obviously more confident because he sent me all my papers back.

On the 9th May Christina, the Complaints Adjudicator at SLFC (doubtless another busy lady, though how she was going to be employed by them and adjudicate on my complaint I found hard to understand) wrote me a three page letter. This is slightly less impressive than might appear at first sight as the first page was merely a rehash of my complaint letter and my relationship with Julie and the third page tailed off in the top third of the sheet of paper. In between, Christina (I feel I can refer to all these people by their first names now) told me they were installing (no, sorry, in the process of installing) a new system to "administer your plans more effectively" It appeared that they should have had a daily list of the plans that were maturing together with a letter to me." Regrettably" (Yip, I'll drink to that … or would if I could afford to buy some decent malt whisky) they'd experienced some problems with the system. "Although a letter is evident it does not appear to have been produced and sent to you. Additionally your plan did not appear on the relevant list" Ah, ha! Was this the famous manual error of which my anonymous friend had told me?

They had noted my conversation with Angela on the Customer Careline. I haven't told you (or my wife) about Angela. I had her (well, not in the biblical sense) on the same day I spoke to Julie. So many names, so few faces, just one company. It was all so confusing for a man of my age. It wasn't just my policy that was maturing. I was ageing by the minute.

The letter from Christina got really boring at this stage as she went all technical on me and tried to give me a lecture on how my policy had worked, or in my case failed to work.

She then dealt with Mr (or Mrs or for all I knew Ms) Anonymous. Wait for this gem.

"A decision was taken by the Company to use a universal signature on all of our letters. However, this is being monitored and your comments have been noted." Well, noted at least to the extent that Christina and Mr S had been bold enough to introduce themselves and now I knew Angela's last name as well. If they tried to threaten me I would respond in spades and name and shame (which I suppose is what I'm doing right now).

Then came the final rub.

"I understand that a cheque and a letter of apology was sent by our Client Services Dept on 15th April (that would have been Mr X I guess and I'm not so sure about the apology bit). This offer was made by our Client Service Dept and not as a final response to your complaint. However, after due consideration of your complaint I feel that this offer was appropriate and would have covered any loss of interest on the maturity proceeds."

Whoa, Christina, hold it right there. What about my time? What about the fact you buggered up my investments in the first place. And don't you work alongside Mr S and Mr X and Angela and Julie and the like, so how come you are my independent adjudicator?

I wrote back again on 20th May.

Re: Plan Number XXX

Thank you for your letter of the 9th May, the contents of which I note and which are, quite frankly, exactly what I would have expected from your company.

In fact, what I was told by my original agent was not that I would be "offered various alternatives to taking the money" but that, in view of the poor performance, I might well be advised to reinvest rather than take the monies. In fact, I was never given any opportunity to reinvest, nor, indeed, given any choices whatsoever other than the late payment of my monies.

The fact that you have now introduced a new system does not

help me at all, nor does it in any way compensate me. I enclose a copy of the letter that I wrote to your company and to which I did not receive the courtesy of a reply.

Given that the delay in payment was entirely your fault, I find it quite astonishing that you still maintain that you would have sought to charge me £20 for making a telegraphic transfer so I could have received the monies into my account a few days earlier than was in fact the case.

I note that once a maximum investment plan reaches its maturity date, the plan will cancel automatically. However, payment should have been made automatically and this was not the case. It is open to you, as a company, to do what you want as far as your investments and customers are concerned and you seem quite unable and unwilling to do this on my behalf even though you accept that I am due an apology.

As far as the telephone call to yourselves was concerned, I understand that this was in fact made by Frank's daughter, Tanya, and the fact that you have no record of the same seems in keeping with your chaotic method of recording information and dealing with your clients.

As a practising solicitor, I have spent several hours now trying to rectify this matter and an offer of compensation of £50 when my chargeable time is something in the region of £250 an hour is, to say the least, insulting.

I have therefore sent a copy of my response to your letter to the FOS and trust that they, at least, will deal with this matter in a fair and equitable manner.

Yours sincerely,

I had heard from the company and as it had not been satisfactory I went back to the Ombudsman on the same day. I sent him Christina's letter and my reply and asked him to adjudicate given that, as far as I was aware, unlike Christina, he didn't work for SLFC. On 23rd May he acknowledged and said he would reply as soon as he could. He was obviously still very busy. On 27th May he wrote again and asked me to send him a complaint form. On 3rd June I told him I'd already done that and I was beginning to wonder who you complained to about the Ombudsman! We sparred a bit in several letters though every time I wrote to him I got my standard letter telling me he would reply as soon as he could. I was beginning to wonder if he was employing the same staff as British Airways. Finally on 10th July I capitulated and sent him the form back. Lo and behold on 14th July Christina woke up and wrote to me again.

She started off on the right foot.

"Please accept my sincere apologies (I liked that) for the delay with this matter. Regrettably (they like that word a lot down at SLFC but presumably they have much to regret) your letter arrived whilst I was on holiday and then got caught up in my subsequent work-load. This is not intended as an excuse but an explanation for the delay."

I hoped she had experienced an enjoyable holiday and was contemplating offering her my services to help write a complaint letter just in case she hadn't.

On and on Christina went in similar vein. I won't bore you because you may already be bored enough by this saga. She apologised again about the system to the point where I was almost feeling guilty for raising the issue in the first place. She apologised about the fact that they should have transferred the monies to my account telegraphically and hadn't and that they should have borne the cost ... but to do so they would have required written instructions from me. (That was new. Nice one, Christina, change the line of your bowling.)

She appreciated I was unhappy with the goodwill payment. She had got that one right and "after further consideration I feel it appropriate to offer interest on the maturity proceeds and a further payment ... for the distress and inconvenience caused by this error."

The payment was acceptable. I had made my point and won. But how many others would have persisted as I did. I was not put off by taking on a big company. I used the tools and weapons available to me and I did not have to resort to the law. That is really the point of this example. The compensation did not make me rich, it didn't even achieve the levels the policy should have got to. But I got something I would not have got otherwise and I hope that SLFC will not take such a cavalier attitude in future. The only disappointment is that I still don't know the identity of Mr X. If he should read this book perhaps he would like to write to me c/o the publishers and perhaps he could take some care over his universal signature so I can read it this time.

Complaining about insurance companies does need some pre-planning as you do need to keep papers that may go back some twenty-five years. But assuming you have here's what to look out for:

1. What were you told when you bought the policy?
2. Were any promises or guarantees made or was it just sales puff?
3. Were you given comparisons with other products in the market?
4. Were you kept fully advised of the progress of the policy over the years?
5. Did you have, or were you given, the chance to have regular meetings with your financial adviser?
6. Was your financial adviser fully independent or was he tied to the company whose policy you bought?
7. Were you given the chance to change the type of policy or increase or decrease the premiums?
8. Did the insurance company change its bonus policy at any time during the policy?
9. Did they pay out promptly?
10. Were you satisfied with the results of your investment?
11. Would you have done better with any other kind of savings plan?
12. Did it pay off your mortgage as intended?
13. Did it provide you with an adequate pension as intended?

As far as building societies are concerned again you need to pose some hypothetical questions to see whether or not you have the basis for complaints:

1. Is your investment what you were seeking? By that I mean in terms of its returns and risk.

2. Were you told about alternate investments?
3. How competitive is your Building Society with other Building Societies?
4. Were you able to get a mortgage easily because of your customer loyalty?
5. Was the rate of the mortgage as good as, or better than, that of other lenders?
6. Has the Society been supportive of you if you have had problems? This can't just be a one-way relationship.
7. Have they tried to sell you all sorts of other products that you didn't want?
8. Have they treated your account confidentially?
9. Have they always been available to give you prompt and up-to-date advice?
10. Have they kept you up to date with new products and advised you to change your investments if appropriate and not just so they can earn more commission?

Those of us who had accounts with Building Societies back in the 80s mainly benefited when they went public and probably still have their shares today to prove it. But now the market is tighter, meaner, leaner and it's the same with insurance companies. There are no longer any totally safe investments and a failure to complain today can mean a financial disaster tomorrow. If you do nothing, if you simply bin all the correspondence you get from insurers or Building Societies, then you have only yourselves to blame and don't complain to me. I warned you.

13

STORIES ABOUT DINING OUT ON
WHICH TO DINE OUT

Food, glorious food. Oh, if only it were. It seems so easy for every-body else I know just to go out for a meal, eat, enjoy and pay. Only when you get talking to them, really talking to them, analysing the experience, there is, in fact, always something they didn't enjoy, something for which they begrudged paying mainly because they didn't feel as if they had received value for money. But when I asked them what they did about it, the answer is usually a shrug and a mumbled, slightly embarrassed, "Nothing."

How many times, I wonder, have you gone to a restaurant, eaten a meal and left, not just dissatisfied, but with the vow of "never again" ringing in the air and mingling with your indigestion. Now, it may seem odd, but apart from praise, the thing a restauranteur most wants to hear is criticism. Not criticism for the sake of it, but constructive criticism so that he can do something about it and retain the goodwill of you, the customer.

I've been involved in both sides of the restaurant business for some years and I can assure you that if a decent restaurant receives a complaint they'll not only investigate it, but will invite you back on a complimentary basis to make sure they'll get it right next time. They know that if they do there'll be a next time and a next time and they are guaranteed not only your loyalty but also your recommendation. Of course, there's always the odd person who'll try it on just to avoid paying the bill.

If you have a genuine complaint, the soup is cold, the fish is undercooked, the meat is too salty, the meringue is too tough, then tell the waiter as the meal progresses or ask to speak to the manager. But do it politely and discretely so as not to be over-heard. There's plenty of time for that if the manager does nothing about it. Believe me, there's not a restaurant in the country outside of Fawlty Towers (though despite its gourmet night ambitions I

136

think it was more of a hotel than a restaurant), which wants to have a slanging match with a justifiably outraged customer in full view and hearing of the rest of its clientele.

If you are too embarrassed to complain at the time then, as you pay, simply tell the manager that it hasn't been a rewarding experience and you'll be writing to them to tell them exactly why. Similarly, if you get ill after dining somewhere, then for heaven's sake let them know. They may have merely poisoned you but next time they may actually go one step further and kill somebody. Trust me, no restaurant wants you to leave and never return, though my wife maintains that both before and after I write this book there are many establishments around the world who would move, leave no forwarding address and change their names as failsafes, just to ensure that I never favour them with my custom ever again.

So why don't we look at some of the places in my personal hall of restaurant infamy, examine what went wrong, how I dealt with it and what sort of results I achieved. And perhaps, at the same time, ask yourself whether you would have done the same in similar circumstances or whether or not I was justified in my actions. My wife, who unlike *moi*, is a nice person, never thinks I'm justified. I could be lying on the floor, under a table, foaming at the mouth, suffering from extreme food poisoning, the ambulance sirens growing ever louder and she will be apologising for my behaviour. But, as I said, she's nice and I'm not. After thirty-three years of marriage she's generally known in our neighbourhood as the Saint of Southgate amongst our friends (or at least those who are still talking to me) and I genuinely believe she could write her own three volume book of complaints (with several sequels in the pipeline for which I've little doubt she would receive massive advances) just about her life with me. As she often says, "Well, at least I'm not related to him". Harsh, but true.

To begin with something trivial. A coffee experience gone wrong. Here's my letter to Starbucks:

13th May 2004
The Chief Executive
Starbucks Coffee Company UK Ltd
11 Heathmans Road
London, SW6 4TJ

Dear Sir/Madam

On the morning of Wednesday 12th May I went to a meeting in Queen Anne Street, London W.1. and, with our corporate accountant, visited your Starbucks in Upper Regent Street for a coffee.

I ordered a regular black coffee and my accountant had a latte. There were no empty tables upstairs and therefore we tried to take a seat at the window. The wooden counter was covered with dirty coffee cups, coffee cup stains and discarded newspapers. I asked somebody to clean this for us so we could actually sit down, and removed the cups myself and placed them on the serving counter.

I was then told that there were tables available downstairs. We then went downstairs and a similar scene of devastation met our eyes. Tables were covered with dirty crockery, the carpet was dirty and, when I visited the WC, this was filthy as well and there was a roll of toilet paper between the wash basins, presumably to be used to dry one's hands after washing.

My coffee was thin and quite undrinkable and the latte was all milk and no coffee. We abandoned these and, as I left, I saw that the paint was peeling off the walls and the general impression was one of neglect and decay.

I have visited other Starbucks in the past and I must say this is the worst experience I have ever had.

I await your comments in due course.

Yours faithfully,

And here's their reply:

27 May 2004

Dear Mr Stein

Thank you very much for taking the time to contact Starbucks Coffee Company, as it is always a pleasure to receive feedback from our valued customers.

I am extremely sorry to hear about the in-store appearance of our Regent St W1 – Espirit store. Providing a clean and comfortable environment, in which you can relax and enjoy your favourite beverage, is a high priority at Starbucks, so your comments are of great concern to me.

All our Partners (employees) attend a training day, where the 'Starbucks Experience' is clearly explained and one-to-one coaching enables partners to consistently deliver prompt and professional service. To work toward this aim and address the situation directly, I have shared your concerns with the Store Management Team so that the store will be brought up to the required standard immediately.

I sincerely hope that we may encourage you to return to Starbucks and am pleased to enclose some beverage vouchers for you to enjoy on your next visit with our compliments.

Once again, thank you very much for sharing your feedback with us and for giving us the opportunity to improve our operations. We hope to welcome you back to Starbucks again soon.

Yours sincerely,

Easy isn't it? Until you get to America. (OK, I know Starbucks are an American company.)

I know it must appear as if I'm always picking on the Yanks but back to one of my nightmare restaurant experiences. There was this place in Tallahassee, Florida, run by a very nice lady called Judy. A place which, sadly, no longer exists.

I had asked my hotel where they thought I might be able to get some decent vegetarian food in Tallahassee. After they had rolled around laughing for a few moments, and suggested Martha Winthrop's vegetable patch in her back yard which produced the best tomatoes in the Florida Panhandle, they told me to go and see Judy. I did. I was eating with another lawyer who called and spoke to Judy. She was really looking forward to meeting with me, I was told. After visiting her establishment I could understand that. She would be looking forward to meeting anybody, even the Florida equivalent of Environmental Health. She must get very lonely.

We needn't have booked. The sole occupants of the restaurant were two men seated in a corner, Judy herself (a lady of indeterminate age) and a very nervy young man who seemed to be rocking and rolling to a tune audible only to his ears. We sat down. Judy was not just pleased to meet me, she was ecstatic. She loved my accent. She knew I was after a veggie meal. She had so much to offer she could hardly wait to share it with me. Once I was in on the secret then I would be as excited as she was. I could hardly contain my excitement. Would we like a drink? Judy asked, coming over all professional. We would, but then so would the dying plants dotted around the room. Do you have any vegetarian or organic wine, I asked, much encouraged by her enthusiasm. Judy looked at me blankly. I gave her my usual explanatory lecture with which I have bored barmen and restaurateurs around the world. Judy, however, seemed very interested. She had a child-like thirst for knowledge. I just had a thirst. I gave her the names of some Californian wines (Bonterra, in case you are interested). She would look into it, but, as for right now, she could not offer that which I sought. (Yes, she actually spoke just like that.) No problemo, I said. I'd not really had any prior expectations so I wasn't disappointed.

"I'll have a screwdriver," I said.

Judy looked slightly more puzzled. Perhaps she was related to Basil Fawlty as well.

"Vodka and orange" I prompted.

"Oh," she said, much relieved. I waited.

"We don't have a permit to sell spirits right now."

"I'll have a coke ... Presuming you have permit to sell that. And please go easy on the ice. "

140

I've told you about my problem with the great American obsession with ice. It's something I've never understood. Having any kind of cold drink in the States is a little like enduring the Titanic's collision with the iceberg, but without the Titanic.

The coke came in a warm glass. I didn't like to ask for more ice. I already felt I might be making a nuisance of myself. Judy showed us the menu which was printed out on a tatty sheet of paper. Every starter (well, all two of them) that seemed to be vegetarian contained cheese. Judy knew as little, if not less, about vegetarian cheese than she did about vegetarian wine. The two men finished their meals, loosened their belts, burped and left, doubtless to saddle up their horses and ride off into the night. We were alone with Judy, the bopping waiter and an elderly, somewhat desiccated lady, who had appeared from hibernation in the kitchen. In terms of staff-customer service ratio we were in danger of being overwhelmed.

I explained patiently to Judy about the cheese. This was her day for further education. Eventually, to Judy's delight, I ordered a plain salad. It was a wonderful choice, she thought. It was my only choice, I thought. Judy decided that our company was so fascinating that she couldn't waste the opportunity of getting to know us better. She pulled up a chair and sat down with us whilst her chef, doubtless, went on a raiding party to Martha's vegetable patch. She began to talk and I soon realised it was going to be a case of us getting to know Judy better. She was divorced, but that was good, because it had made her a better, stronger person and helped her to "Find Jesus". I imagined he'd taken every precaution to hide himself from her, but she was a born-again Christian for all that. She was into holistic remedies, yoga, and, even though, as yet, she had done nothing to provide any evidence to that effect, she was also into vegetarian food.

After thirty minutes my salad arrived. It consisted of cucumber, tomato and onion. Judy gave it an admiring glance as if I had just been presented with a hand crafted ethnic work of art, but did not pause for breath. She asked me how I was enjoying it as if she had cooked it herself. We had a long discussion as to what I might eat as a main course. We (that is Judy and I) decided on a pasta dish with a tomato sauce but no cheese. Whilst I waited Judy's life continued to unfold before my ears. I now knew all about her ex, her church and her therapist. I was beginning to need both mental and spiritual counselling myself. My companion's steak arrived as did my pasta liberally covered with lumps of tomato and ... cheese.

"I did say I couldn't eat the cheese, Judy." I said. We were now on first name terms and soon we might be making holiday plans for her to come and stay with me in England.

"I'll have it removed," she offered.

"'Fraid not, Judy, it's been cooked in it."

"I'll have it done again," she said a little accusingly and I felt guilty again as this was clearly going to make a substantial dent in her night's profits. Maybe that was the loss that tilted her balance over the edge, so perhaps I should be having feelings of guilt.

"I'll wait," I replied.

My companion finished his steak. The frail lady emerged from the kitchen and had the temerity to interrupt Judy in full flow.

"Shall we proceed?" she asked.

I wondered what was going on in the kitchen. Where they conducting illegal operations? Autopsies even? Maybe the whole restaurant was a front for a drug ring.

"No," Judy replied, scarcely listening, "don't proceed"

This, although I did not realise it at the time, was a pivotal moment in our relationship. However, not knowing what they were talking about, I breathed a sigh of relief. No procedures today. Hurrah!

At last Judy rose to go.

"I'm sorry to leave you. I have to go home. It's been great talking to you. I've learned so much. Bless you both."

"Talking to me, Judy," I thought, "more like talking at me," but I said nothing. As I said way back, she was a nice lady and I felt rather sorry for her. I also felt very hungry.

The young waiter hovered around with nothing to do.

"You're not really a waiter, are you?" I asked, giving him the lead so that he could tell me he was a neuro-surgeon researching reaction times amongst diners in Florida.

"How did you guess?" he asked.

"Just a wild stab in the dark," I replied. It wasn't very original, but it seemed appropriate, as did the Blackadder thought that this was exactly what he was going to get if he didn't produce any food for me.

"I'm a musician," he informed me.

Now, I don't know why I said what I said, but I did and certainly lived to regret it, though my survival was, by now, under threat from malnutrition.

What I said was, "Oh, my son's a music lawyer."

"Gee, maybe he'd like to hear where I'm at." And maybe not, but before I could say that for my part I'd just like to eat in the here and now and not the hereafter he was off and running, returning with a stack of CDs all of which contained his own, original work. I have to say he handled them more professionally than he'd been handling the plates. He put on the first selection, which I assumed he thought was the best and I shuddered at what might follow if that was, indeed, the case.

Could I finish the meal before the first CD came to an end? Could I even finish the meal before the last CD came to an end? Could I finish the meal before the world came to an end? Who knew? I listened as politely as I could to the first track. The waiter (whose name blessedly I can't recall) shut his eyes and bounced up and down to the approximation of the tune that was his composition.

"Er, very nice," I said, "but do you think I could have my food now?"

That stopped him dead in his tracks even if it didn't stop his track.

"I thought you weren't going to bother. Judy told us not to proceed."

I shook my head in disbelief. The woman had been so busy talking that she'd not been listening. If she had been within distance I was so hungry I might just have been tempted to take a bite out of her.

"Look, we could, maybe, make it for you special like. But chef will have to start from scratch so it'll take about 40 minutes."

More disbelief on my part.

"But it was only pasta."

"Yeah, but the chef likes to make everything fresh, like."

"But it was only pasta ..." I repeated, still in shock.

"Yeah ..." the waiter's words trailed away to nothing.

"He doesn't make the pasta does he? You know, fresh like." I was slipping into the vernacular. It seemed the best way to communicate.

"No ..." he trailed off again.

"Look," I said, with a wild-eyed desperation, "I'll leave it. I'll just go straight to dessert. You do have desserts, don't you?"

He immediately regained his confidence, remembering all he'd been taught in training by Judy.

"Oh sure. Judy specialises in desserts. She has great desserts."

"Like she specialises in vegetarian dishes?" I enquired, but the sarcasm was wasted.

"So, desserts. Which are vegetarian?" Why do I bother, you ask? Well, at least it gets me material for the book.

We examined the menu closely. They had nothing. There was an obsession with gelatine, margarine and cochineal (that's made from crushed beetles by the way).

"I think I'll just go," I said, wondering whether it was too late to find somewhere open that would sell me a packet of crisps and a kit-kat, or potato chips and whatever passed for a kit-kat. Have you ever tried ordering a meal in the States? You ask for chips and you get crisps, you ask for aubergine and they have no idea what you are talking about (eggplant as far as they are concerned ... Not that I order aubergine or eggplant 'cos I hate it/them) you ask for a tomato salad or tomato sauce with basil and they need a translator, you ask for biscuits and they have to translate it to cookies. And they think they speak English. They probably have a different word for "complain".

"Don't go," the young waiter pleaded as if his whole life depended on it. "Judy will be very upset. I'll call her now."

I slumped back in my chair. We'd been there for over two hours and all I'd had was the salad and the coke and for someone who was writing a book about the art of complaining I wasn't doing too well.

The waiter returned beaming.

"Judy says her chocolate meringue is fine for you. She baked it herself. We've been eating it all day. It's really good."

This was clearly the secret of her staff loyalty and obedience. She just fed them chocolate meringue she'd made herself. She probably put sedatives in it.

I knew when to admit temporary defeat.

"OK. The chocolate meringue it is."

It wasn't. Well, it was chocolate and there was meringue on top. But it wasn't edible either as a whole or in part. The chocolate was that baby-mush of a dessert they used to serve at kiddies' parties in England. And I couldn't cut the meringue either with a spoon or a knife.

"Excuse me," I said, lifting the meringue and stretching it almost to the width of my spread hands, "this meringue is elastic."

Regrettably I never did meet the chef though I thought I may have seen a shadowy figure sneaking out a side door whilst we were discussing the dessert.

But we weren't done yet. My companion who had watched the evening's performance with the amused, world-weary cynical look of an American lawyer, who until then had believed there was nothing new under the sun, suddenly cracked up and suggested we have coffee. I wanted anything that could be taken into my blood-stream, but even more than that I wanted to be out of there. No more customers had entered and we were on to the third CD of the waiter's music. I decided to have coffee too. Why bring a magical evening to an early conclusion? The waiter brought it and it was translucent. There's a lot wrong with America and Americans but one of the good things out there is the coffee. It's always fresh and hot and strong, unlike the tea which bears little or no resemblance to what we perceive to be our national beverage. I discovered recently that this is because no-one possesses a kettle and they heat the water up in the microwave until they think it's boiled. They really are a very sad race when it comes to tea-time. I held Judy's coffee up to the light as if inspecting a fine wine.

"I can see right through this coffee," I said.

The waiter hung his head. His CD ground to a halt.

"Hold it there, I'll be right back," he said and changed the CD. He returned.

"I know," he apologised, "it was the end of the pot and there wasn't enough for two cups and I knew you'd been very patient so I added a load of hot water." Hot water, note, not boiling. And probably heated in the micro-wave.

I nodded. It was the perfect end to a perfect meal. I had enough material to dedicate a book of its own to Judy. There are times to complain on the spot and times to write a letter. You may feel that there were several opportunities to complain as the evening developed and you would be right and, I suppose, I did make my feelings clear. But there was a mesmeric quality to it all that stopped me performing to my peak ability. I had no intention of visiting again and assuming they weren't going to charge, this was just one for the scrapbook, one where I should just walk away. Then they gave me the bill (or check, another example of how they've managed to bastardise our mother tongue).

"What's this?" I asked.

"The check," he said.

"Are you having a laugh?" I asked.

He didn't know the phrase.

"Are you kidding me?" That he understood. "I'm not paying."

"But your friend has eaten his meal."

"But I haven't. And you've charged me for it. I'll pay for the other meal but quite frankly I don't think you should charge at all."

"I'll call Judy," he said. He did.

"Judy wants to talk to you." I weighed my options. Was another conversation with Judy worth the cost of the meal? It wasn't but it seemed churlish to refuse the call. Judy was sweetness itself. She comp'd the meal, she asked me back, she apologised. I felt really bad, but then maybe my complaints had taught her something. Maybe she would try and improve. Maybe she would grow and flourish and have a thriving business. Maybe the young waiter would become a superstar. As I now know she didn't. She closed her doors for the final time. The waiter, I've little doubt, is still dreaming of fame. I wish him and Judy all the best.

But for those of you who still have a little faith in restaurants, whether they be here or in Tallahassee here's your complaint check-list:

1. Were you able to make a reservation without being made to feel as if they were doing you a favour?
2. When you arrived at the restaurant was your table ready?
3. Was the position of the table acceptable and if it wasn't did they move you when you asked?
4. Were you told you had to vacate the table by a certain time (don't you just hate that)?
5. Was your waiter or waitress friendly? (or do they call females waiters as well nowadays like actors?). Thank goodness we've not yet adopted the word "servers" that they use in the States. "Hello, my name's Jim. I'm your server for the evening." What, are we playing tennis or eating a meal? And then he reels off all the specials and by the time he gets to the end you've forgotten what he offered at the beginning so you have to ask him to start all over again. Well, actually I tend to do that just for fun.
6. Were you offered a drink promptly and did it arrive in reasonable time?
7. Was your order taken in good time and without the waiter, or server, being sniffy about what you wanted?
8. Did your starter come within a reasonable time span and did all the starters come together? Nothing's worse than getting your meal in fits and starts.
9. Was the quality of the starters acceptable? Don't be polite. If a meal starts off badly it only tends to get worse and not better.
10. Was there a reasonable breathing space before the main course? And did they all come together too? And were they cooked as you had ordered them, or cooked at all?
11. Was the meal hot … or cold if it was intended to be?
12. Was the food fresh? And that includes the vegetables.
13. Were the staff knowledgeable about the ingredients of the dishes?
14. Did the waiters up-sell the drinks too strongly? As a customer I just hate it when a bottle of water or wine disappears because the waiter or sommelier gets too enthusiastic with the pouring?
15. Did the staff wait until everybody finished before clearing the

plates ... and did they scrape the plates at the table? For me that's a capital offence and I've seen my friend Robby, who has an even weaker stomach than me, threaten a waiter physically when he persisted having been warned not to.

16. Again was there a suitable pause before dessert? And again before coffee?

17. Was the whole evening leisurely and an enjoyable experience?

18. Were there any items on the menu which were outrageously priced? Everyone is entitled to a mark-up but, say, £15 for half a grapefruit is pushing the limits of the envelope.

19. Was the restaurant too crowded or too noisy?

20. Were you jostled by waiters as they served the food?

21. Did they leave the credit card open even though service charge was included?

22. Were you happy with the service and if not were you still obliged to pay the service charge?

23. Did any member of staff spill anything on you during the course of the evening?

24. Did the Maitre D' or the proprietor come over to you during the course of the evening to see if you were having a good time?

25. Were the staff as friendly as you left as they were when you arrived (assuming they were friendly then!)?

26. Did you feel overall that you had received good value for your money?

It doesn't matter whether you've been visiting McDonald's or The Ivy. You are still entitled to feel as if your visit was worthwhile. And if it wasn't then by now you know exactly what to do. Given that I've told you how to complain, again, if it was perfection, then make sure the restaurant manager or owner is told. The staff deserve that accolade. The only truly perfect eating experience I've ever had (not just once, but every time) is at the Grand Roche Hotel in Paarl, South Africa. In fact it's also the only perfect hotel in which I've stayed. That's why we return time after time and that's why we tell them why we return ... and that's why they, and

Horit Frehse, the General Manager, get a special mention and
thank you.

14

UNLUCKY FOR SOME

Actually, I was born on Friday 13th. Well, you'd probably guessed that already.

Judy's was a case for complaining on the spot, but Dougie's in New York (no anonymity there) was one for a letter. It had to be a letter because there was no-one there to whom I could complain. Nobody who served actually seemed to speak English ... or American for that matter. I visit New York City often. I like NYC. I like its buzz, its people, particularly for their rudeness, a trait with which I feel a certain amount of empathy, and its theatres, despite the tendency of audiences to clap, stamp and whoop, even at the end of a famous Shakespearian speech!

What I don't like is the service, and particularly the service in restaurants. I also don't like the taxi drivers who hardly speak a word of English either and who don't know the location of the Empire State Building. But you can't complain to a New York cabbie because he won't understand. There is a notice in the back of each cab giving you a phone number to call if you have a complaint and I've often been tempted, just to get some material for this book, but I've always resisted. What are they going to do? Increase the level of the licensing test so that the man has to know how to write and spell his own name or sing God Bless America? I don't think so. I give thanks every day I'm in the States for our own cabbies, and their knowledge. Astonishingly I've never had cause to complain about a London Taxi driver so I hope any one of them who may read this book, tell their mates and they all buy it.

To return to New York restaurants. I don't like the portions they give you either, but I don't think you can complain too much about being given too much food, even though I always feel as if I am at the foot of Mount Everest, about to ascend when I am handed my plate (which usually has to be carried to the table by at least three struggling and sweating waiters). That, of course, may well be how they make the soup. I bet none of you order soup in a New York restaurant ever again. So why bother to complain about the service? Or anything? All too often American complainees don't even bother to reply. That's probably because in their litigious society they think that if they apologise they may throw themselves wide open to a million dollar law suit arising from any admission of blame. The answer as to why you should complain is that if you are going to let people know that you are dissatisfied … and that after all is the mantra and creed of this book … then you can't be selective. You can't say, "I won't complain because it's a waste of time". It's NEVER a waste of time, and if you don't, or won't, believe that then reading this book is a waste of time. (Did I hear you say, "I'll drink to that?")

I genuinely believe we have to try to make the world a better place by raising standards. If service in a restaurant is appalling it's often because the management don't care. If they don't care then the staff don't care and if nobody cares then that flows all the way down to the customer. That wasn't the case with Judy. She did care, but she just didn't have the knowledge of how to run a restaurant and couldn't afford professional management.

So why do I pick on Dougie's for an onslaught. A friend in New York suggested we go there for dinner. They do great kosher ribs, she said. It's pretty casual but the food is to die for, she said. She got so excited at the prospect of returning to Dougie's on the Upper West Side, that she even downloaded a part of their website and sent it to me on my Blackberry. That's a plug for a piece of electronic gadgetry that I love, and which enables me to get my e-mails on the move on a wireless basis. Absolutely brilliant! I have no idea whatsoever as to how it works. It seems too small to contain the elves who deliver the elf-mails, but work it does. As I've been so enthusiastic about them, maybe they will stop charging me. Though probably not when they read the chapter later on that's partially dedicated to the back-up service on the machine.

Dougie's website is a great read. He is described as "legendary" and a "restaurateur extraordinaire" not to mention a "cultural personality." Now anybody who sets themselves up that high must be riding for a fall. He opened his first Dougie's in 1994 and was "determined to be truly new and unusual". He claims that his chain can "be confidently labelled a true success" and the "restaurant mogul has decided to expand his empire into other non-related businesses, including industrial grease and lubricants". Maybe he should let his customers decide whether or not they are related. He does say, bless his little cotton socks, that he "looked around and realised that these products are currently being produced in large quantities at my restaurants already. It's no big deal to bottle them up and ship them out". Excuse me?!

Just as a side-line this legendary personality who says he is "untouchable" as far as divine eternal judgements are concerned "started an Orthodox Jewish Escort service". It's amazing isn't it? Just when you think you've heard everything, someone like Dougie enters your life and makes it possible to start all over again. I've never met the bloke, and after writing this I doubt I ever will unless it's in court, but you have to admit that he does have chutzpah. Dougie's Angels, as his escorts were known, managed to gain a combined 158 pounds in weight in a single month, which rather blew the business out of the water ... or with that weight to carry sank it dead in the water. Nothing daunted Dougie who then started his own weight- loss programme (or program as he seems to spell it). It appears this consisted of "Poppers for breakfast, poppers for lunch and a sensible dinner". That too closed down with Dougie claiming that the hard truth was that "the only people who lose weight at my restaurants are the cooks." Hmm, now that gives one food for thought, doesn't it?

I have to say, after reading all that, my expectations were high for an unusual, provocative and I hoped gastronomically rewarding evening. I was going to have a "sensible dinner".

My friend, Hilary, had gone to the restaurant in the afternoon in the pouring rain, accompanied by her two dogs (yes, they are relevant to the story) and made us a reservation for two, at eight in the evening. I arrived some twenty minutes early. I'm always early, it's one of my more annoying traits, although the woman who has lived with me for thirty-three years may say it palls into insignificance alongside the innumerable others. I told the very bored looking receptionist that I had a reservation either in the name of Stein or Kramer to which she replied that they weren't taking reservations and that I could sit anywhere. I found myself a seat and waited for someone to come and offer to take my soaking wet coat. Fat chance! I hung it on the back of the chair and watched with some interest as a puddle began to form on the floor. After a few moments a young waiter came and tried to give me iced water. I hate plain water. It reminds me of school dinners.

I declined the waiter's offer of chilled water, and requested a Perrier, even making the request generic rather than specific by clearly stating my desire for sparkling water.

I sat there for ten minutes, read the menu, and regretted not bringing a book. No eye contact from anybody and certainly no verbal contact. Normally, my entry into an American restaurant does at least trigger off a little dialogue, something along these lines.

Oh, You're British. (Have the Yanks never heard of England? Always Brits, never the English?).

Yes.

I love your accent.

Thank you.

Where are you from?

London.

I've never been there. (Only something like 10% of all Americans have passports.)

Shame.

Is it always foggy and raining?

No.

Well, it always looks like it at the movies.

Yes, and in the movies, customers in restaurants always get served. It helps to move the plot along.

End of dialogue, unless they know someone who lives in England in which case the conversation continues along these lines.

Oh, you're British. I know someone who lives there.

Where does he live?

I'm not too sure. But his name's Andy. Big guy. Do you know him?

My sparkling water didn't come. I grabbed another passing waiter.

"Excuse me. I ordered a Perrier ten minutes ago?" I finished the

153

sentence by raising my voice to an inflection. The Americans understand that.

He nodded and disappeared behind the same door that had swallowed the first waiter some ten minutes before. They did not reappear. In desperation I collared a third waiter. Nothing wrong with the staff to customer ratio at Dougie's.

"I've asked two people now for a Perrier. Do you think I could have it now?"

Astonishingly, he too disappeared behind the same door. What were they doing in there? Planning world domination? Deciding whether or not to commence one of Judy's procedures?

Then all three reappeared. Without my drink. They began an earnest conversation in a language I didn't recognise. Hilary arrived. She was wet, but still enthusiastic.

"Well, what do you think of the place so far?"

I told her of my experiences. Her enthusiasm began to wane.

"We can leave you know," she offered.

"No, no," I replied, "you said the food was good and I trust you. Let's give it a whirl."

Another man appeared and offered Hilary some iced water. She's American so she accepted it.

"Do you think I could possibly have my sparkling water now," I asked. I'd been eating the crisps on the table and had a raging thirst.

"We don't sell sparkling water," the man said. I looked at the three to whom I'd given my order. They avoided my gaze and continued chatting. We probably should have called it a day then, but I was hungry, it was still raining and the menu did look appetising. Dougie talked a good game.

I ordered a diet coke. A waiter came with a can, a glass and a straw. He made no attempt to open it. We ordered our food. I chose some chicken soup in the belief that Jewish penicillin would calm me down. Hilary ordered chilli. For her main course she would have the buffet and I would have a steak and chips. For any readers still confused about all this when I make such a song and dance about vegetarian food the fact of the matter is that, let me make it clear once again, that I am a carnivore as long as it's kosher meat. What I have to be worried about is any non-kosher meat or fish products finding their way into the veggie stuff I order. Got that by way of revision? Good. You get a theological lesson as well for your money.

My soup came, as did Hilary's chilli. They came very fast. The soup had huge lumps of chicken floating in it. There was more chicken than soup. Hilary liked her chilli and asked me to transfer my chicken into her chilli. Now she had chicken chilli and I had chicken soup we were both happy. The operation had clearly caused chaos in the well-oiled machine that was Dougie's kitchen. They clearly allocated a specific time slot for a customer to consume his soup and I had exceeded it because, lo and behold, they brought my steak and chips.

"But I've not finished my soup yet," I pointed out without a question mark at the end of the sentence. This was very clearly a statement, not to mention a complaint.

The waiter (one of the trio who had failed to bring my non-existent sparkling water) put my main course on a side table as part of his time and motion process.

"No, no," I said, "take it back to the kitchen until I'm ready." He looked at me blankly and I gesticulated towards the door behind which he had hidden with his two compatriots when I'd been seeking my drink. All that seemed a lifetime ago. We had moved into a different universe. He seemed to understand and removed my food. I shuddered at the thought of what might be done to it.

I finished my soup eventually. It was not awe-inspiring. One rarely gets awe-inspiring chicken soup out in restaurants. I was going to use the word "memorable" then but just remembered in time that Winner has cornered the market in that phrase. For some reason chefs seem to think they have to tamper with the basics and stick all sorts of oddities into the mixer as ingredients. In my time I've seen raisins, apricots, nuts, croutons, even small slices of toast floating about in it. Hilary rose to get her buffet, leaving her chilli temporarily unfinished. She was feeling under pressure too, knowing my steak was coming back. I tried to grab a waiter's attention to request its recall, when, with my attention distracted, another waiter swooped and removed Hilary's chilli. If I had possessed false teeth I would have kept my mouth tightly closed, as clearly this was the sort of establishment where they were going to clear away anything that ceased to move. I couldn't be sure and I might have dreamt it, but I think I saw a customer who'd nodded off being carried through to the kitchen.

Hilary returned with her choice from the buffet, Dougie's famous ribs. I wondered, if he were on such intimate terms with the Almighty, that he might have suggested making a woman or two out of them. They could have been a regular assembly line for Dougie's Angels. She wanted to know where her chilli was. I was curious to learn of the whereabouts of my steak. Maybe they were meeting up in the kitchen. Upon request, the waiter returned her chilli. She now had the makings of a meal. My food had just been a ship that passed in the night. I asked again. Hilary munched her way through her meal. She was more than halfway done when mine was returned to me. It was OK, without being great. Dougie had rather overdone the expectations, not to mention my steak. I had asked for it to be really well-done, but I fancied they may have actually cooked it again when it went back to the kitchen. Or even stuck it in the famous microwave oven of which they are so fond.

We enquired about the desserts. We have black and white cookies, the waiter with the best (or at least minimum) command of the English language, said.

Now, to me, cookies, or biscuits, are not a dessert. They are something you might have with a cup of tea (if the Americans are capable of making a cup of tea) and dipping in it.

"What else do you have?" I asked

"Black and white cookies."

Well, I suppose he could have said, "white and black cookies "

"We'll try them"

"They're really good," Hilary said, trying to keep up her enthusiasm.

We did. They were huge and boring. I paid the bill, hesitating over the tip. Then thought what the hell. These guys are probably paid a pittance. It's not their fault they're not real waiters. They've followed the dream to America and all they get are people like me criticising them. So I added a gratuity, but at London rates. Hilary asked for the bones back from her ribs as they would be a treat for her dogs. A couple of young men were just finishing up their meal. The waiter whisked their plates away and added their debris of bones to the canine package. At last we had some real communication.

We then went in search of somebody to talk to about our "Dougie Experience" There was nobody around except the same bored receptionist (who didn't look like Dougie to me) the waiters and somebody serving at the buffet. I'll write I said. And I did. Here's the letter, though it may be a bit boring because you know how the story ends. So far it hasn't ended with a response from Dougie either. But then I suppose he's very busy being a cult hero, running restaurants, an axle grease business, escort agencies and diet clubs. I'll let you know what happens if we get to a second edition.

Dear Sir/Madam,

As a restaurateur in London, I always look forward to visiting New York and sampling the various kosher restaurants. Your establishment was recommended to me and I arranged to go there for dinner on the evening of Monday 8th March.

My dining companion went into the restaurant in the afternoon to make a reservation for 8 p.m. and booked a table for two.

I arrived at 7.40 and told the girl at reception that I had a reservation. She advised me that the restaurant did not take reservations and gestured generally in the direction of the interior of the restaurant. I took my seat and sat, waiting for someone to take my coat. No offers were forthcoming and I hung my coat on the back of my chair. After five minutes, somebody came over to offer me some cold water but I told them I didn't want that but wanted a Perrier or a sparkling water of any description. The waiter then disappeared into the kitchen, I presumed, to collect the drink.

Five minutes later, he had not reappeared and I caught the eye of another passing waiter and again asked for sparkling water. He too disappeared into the kitchen, behind the door.

My dining companion arrived and accepted the offer of cold water and, once again, I asked for sparkling water. The third waiter then disappeared behind the door.

Finally, someone came to offer us the menu and I asked where my Perrier was. To my astonishment, I was then told that you didn't serve sparkling water. I can only presume that the English of the three previous waiters was so poor that they simply didn't understand what I was saying.

I settled for a diet Coke and ordered chicken soup, a well-done steak and French fries. My companion ordered a chilli to start and then decided to take food from the buffet. Throughout this time there was no apparent presence of any management at the restaurant and certainly nobody came over to talk to us.

My soup and the chilli arrived and, when I was halfway through my soup, so did my steak and French fries! I told the waiter I wasn't ready, at which point he put them down on a side table. I told him to take them away and to serve me when I had finished my soup. My companion went to collect her food from the buffet, at which point the waiter swooped and took her half-finished chilli away. She returned with her buffet plate and asked for the return of her chilli. That came but my main course did not. She was well over halfway through her meal and I had asked for my meal to be returned twice before it finally reappeared. On several occasions whilst I was waiting at least three of your waiters were standing chatting to each other in their own language and the service was generally appalling.

I then asked for a dessert and was told that the only desserts you had available were "black and white cookies". We ordered one portion of these but to say they were dull and unappetising is an understatement.

We looked for some management on the way out so that we could express our dissatisfaction but, again, nobody was around, and we simply left.

As I say, as a restaurateur myself, the only way I feel we can improve our service is by feedback from our customers and I should be grateful if you would let me have some comments and explanation in due course.

Yours faithfully,

No reply, and as far as Dougie and I are concerned the love affair is definitely over. Even if he does want to introduce me to one of his overweight angels by way of compensation.

I'd really like to go back to Dougie's some time and meet him and ask him why he didn't answer my letter. Perhaps he never saw it personally. That sort of thing can happen and if there had been more at stake I would have sent it recorded delivery. There was nothing wrong with his food at all and maybe I just caught his staff on a bad day. However, I suspect this may be another establishment where I'm not particularly welcome. Which would be a shame because I just felt he ought to know what had gone wrong and I'm sure he would want to put it right.

15

NEVER DO IT YOURSELF

Beware of flat pack deliveries. Beware of anything that says it's being delivered flat pack. Beware of those two ominous words (or one if, in fact, it's hyphenated) "self-assembly". They should carry the same sort of government health warning as tobacco. You know, "DIY kills". I have been dragged unwillingly on several occasions to death traps with names like *Woodcare, Construction is Us* or *Mansworld*. I hate them all, particularly when Marilyn looks round at sweating figures carrying huge weights of timber, concrete and sand and tells me they are doing what real men do. I tell her that I prefer to write about what real men do, but she is always singularly unimpressed.

I have always found that when you buy anything that doesn't arrive on your doorstep in its completed, usable state, you may as well draft your complaint letter as soon as you leave the store or come offline. It's a racing certainty that the number of pieces to be assembled will bear no relation whatsoever to the instruction booklet, and the instruction booklet itself will be written in some kind of pidgin-tongue that bears no relationship to the English language. Who designs these instruction leaflets? Who draws the pictures? The fact of the matter is that, if you are seeking to follow the written directions for the assembly of any item, be it equipment, furniture or space rocketry, you might as well toss all the pieces in the air, dada-like, and hope they fall to earth in some vague approximation of the correct order.

In my particular case I'm not even sure I have the technical capacity to throw them in the air. We are, here, speaking of a man who can't change a plug and, indeed, struggles with light-bulbs. I'm always accused domestically (inter-alia, as I'm accused of many things) of not noticing if several light-bulbs have gone in a room at home. It's an unfair accusation, like most of those aimed at my innocent frame. I do notice. I just choose not to do anything about it in the sure knowledge that my wife will deal with it (whilst making the aforementioned accusations). The fact of the matter is that if I do put in a new light-bulb, the odds are that it'll fall out again well before its expiry date, so why bother?

Then, we are talking about the man who also never figured out how to change a nappy. This was back before the days of disposables. I don't say that in mitigation, as I doubt I would change a nappy today either. In fact everything in this paragraph so far is a lie. It wasn't that I didn't work out the mechanics of nappies, it was just that I didn't want to. And in fact, I never did. Indeed, I was never in the same room as a nappy being changed and rarely in the same house. Mind you I wasn't present at the birth of my sons either. I just felt that birth was a very personal moment between mother and child. I'm told by reliable sources (namely all the females I know who are under 35) that I wouldn't get away with that nowadays and I'd be standing there with my digital camera catching every bloody, noisy moment of the event, followed by sleepless nights and endless bonding with my boys as I gently swabbed their pink bums until they were shiny clean.

Now that I've provided all the credentials for my political incorrectness. I can return to my technical ineptitude, which is in fact, just another aspect of my male chauvinistic, political and social incorrectness. Flat-pack deliveries was the subject, just in case any of you have forgotten. As I recall it, my hate-affair with self-assembly started with a garden storage unit that I bought from a mail order catalogue nearly twenty years ago. It looked, from the picture, exactly what I wanted. But then they always do. That's the art of catalogue selling, I suppose. There it was, a nice green painted metal construction, discretely positioned in a rural setting with neatly mowed lawns, healthy fruit trees, hammocks, swings and cane furniture as a back-drop. The blurb said that it could hold a multitude of objects, deckchairs, garden tools, barbeques, small children, household pets, etc. The fact of the matter, as you've probably guessed, is that I'm not really a garden sort of person. When the kids were small I liked the lawn but only so that we could all play football and cricket and I tried at every opportunity to encroach into the flowerbeds which I generally regarded as superfluous hazards to our seriously competitive games. Our next-door neighbours had two teenage boys and if our matches had been played at professional level red cards would have been flying around in abundance. The real crunch is that I don't possess any gardening tools. Our builder, a rather debonair Jack-the-lad called John (who answers as if by instinct when I tell my wife we need to get a man in to deal with something major, such as changing a washer or a fuse) recently constructed a new garden shed for us and on demolishing and removing the old one he said, "I knew it belonged to Mel Stein. The only thing in it was a rusting rake." The rake was in fact the only surviving part of a garden tool set given to us as a wedding present by my cousin, who was unfortunately killed in a car crash and therefore had survived simply by virtue of its sentimental value.

Not only do I not possess any garden tools, I don't possess any tools whatsoever. No saws, no hammers, not even an itsy-bitsy-weenie screwdriver. Actually, that's not quite true. We bought a garden table and, for it to be fitted into my car, the salesman had to open a new set of spanners which I was then obliged to buy. I am thinking of offering them on e-bay. I have no idea of what to do with them. This technical hopelessness was endemic at my school and none of my contemporaries are what can even remotely be described as "handy". We had a woodwork teacher at school called Mr Stanford. He was a very nice man and in fact one of my friends in my year actually married his daughter. He had an area known as the "bleeding spot" where, if you cut yourself, you had to stand and drip. In the one year I did woodwork I suspect I gave enough blood to that spot to equate to a regular blood donorship. I never got beyond the first project, which was to make a boat. Nothing in my effort fitted and I ended up wodging it together with sawdust, which promptly sludged out when it was put in water. Neither handicraft nor science were my strong points, though I think my chemistry career was doomed when my team dropped and broke its chemical balance almost on our first day. We panicked and mended it with chewing gum which hardly made for precision in our results.

My wife has a tool-kit of which she is inordinately proud. I respect her property at all times and wouldn't dream of touching it. She got very upset (probably quite justifiably) some years ago when my late parents bought her a power-drill as a birthday present. Looking back, perhaps, it wasn't the most tactful of gifts, being not just a de facto recognition of my uselessness as a real man but a positive recognition and encouragement of it. Though my parents have passed on, the drill still survives and one day I'm sure my wife will find a good use for it by drilling a neat and tidy hole in my forehead as I lie sleeping and snoring annoyingly.

As far as the garden unit was concerned, I suppose I was a bit naïve in thinking it would arrive fully assembled, as I have no idea how they would have got it through my front door, manoeuvre it across the kitchen and finally lay it to rest on my patio. But, I swear I didn't see anything in the ad about self-assembly and if I had then I would never have bought it. Certainly what I didn't bargain for was it being delivered totally flat in what seemed like a hundred pieces and with instructions that assumed I had a tool-kit with the capacity to build a nuclear reactor. The delivery men took the tip, accepted the tea, and left. That taught me never to tip until you were satisfied you had got the best out of the delivery men.

I wrote to the manufacturers. They were unsympathetic and told me I should have realised it was self-assembly. I wrote to the mail order company. They said there was a very clear disclaimer as far as the goods were concerned but they would make it clear in future editions that it was self-assembly. That made me feel noble. I had done a great service to those who might follow behind, but it didn't help me. The flat-pack was fast becoming part of the furniture and I was wondering exactly what we could with it as it stood … or lay. These were before the days of the Tate Modern, otherwise I might have submitted it as an entry for the Turner Prize. "Unfulfilled Flat Packed Garden Unit" or some such resonant and symbolic title, in respect of which, I could have pontificated on chat shows for hours.

I changed my tack. I pointed out that there could not possibly be an implied term that I owned the tools necessary to assemble the unit. It needed a spirit level, for heaven's sake. So did I, after all this aggravation. I told both the manufacturer and the catalogue publishers that if I had to go out and buy the tools then I would send them the bill and wouldn't it better and cheaper for all concerned if they sent me a real man to assemble it. They did. The irony was that fifteen years later when my wife decided that the rusting abomination on our patio needed to be removed we had to pay another team of men to dismantle it and take it away.

We didn't seem to have a lot of success with our patio. We went to the Chelsea Flower Show (I know, it's not my natural habitat, but it was my wife's birthday and doubtless I was trying to make it up to her for some thought-crime I might have committed in my sleep). We saw some really nice furniture there and ordered it on the basis that, although it wouldn't come fully assembled it would be "child's play" to assemble it in a "matter of minutes". By the time we'd had a look at it on our own patio even my highly competent wife realised that a "matter of minutes" probably equated to about 1440 of them (I think that's twenty-four hours) and the only child who could have put it together in his playroom would have been a teenage Albert Einstein. Certainly not a middle-aged Mr and Mrs Stein.

Another letter. This time the response was that they could assemble it, that this was an option that was available to us when we bought it (not mentioned by the salesman who had told us how simple it all was) and it would cost a hundred pounds. You can well imagine my response. This was not a cheap set of furniture. The summer was moving along. We wanted to use it before Autumn. Words like "outrageous", "misrepresentation" and "county court" leapt to my lips. The company's resistance collapsed (that's why I haven't named them as they did the right thing) and they sent two very nice men who took a whole afternoon putting it together, whilst confiding in us between cups of tea and biscuits, that they had no idea how anybody without an engineering degree could have come anywhere near to completing the construction. I gave them both a generous tip and we enjoy our furniture on our metal-unit free patio to this day.

The exercise bike was another matter. We have a room at home which we always call the playroom. It leads off the kitchen and when the children were small it was a depository for all sorts of interesting junk. Oddly enough, I can't remember them ever playing there. It was a far more attractive proposition for them to lay waste to our lounge, TV room, dining room and bedrooms. They had one game that was basically a motor race involving every toy car they possessed. This race straggled its way upstairs and downstairs leaving death-traps in the shape of dinky cars at every twist, bend, landing and stair. It was all a bit of a waste of time, quite frankly, as they had one favourite car called Pete, as I recall, which won every single race. Hardly a betting proposition for the unwary visitor. However, it was slightly less expensive than a project called "Paul's Bank" founded by my younger son. Every depositor had to pay him at least a pound in return for which they got a cardboard badge that proudly bore the letters "PB" And that was that. No cheque book, no bank statements, no interest and certainly no access. He even got our unsuspecting au pairs to invest and any day now I expect some poor Spanish girl to knock at our door with her own children in tow seeking the return of her money and interest amounting to a four figure sum.

The playroom was called the playroom and thus it remains. A bit like the "au pair's room" which hasn't been occupied by an au pair for some dozen years or so and is unlikely to be so occupied ever again. Unless one returns and refuses to leave until Paul repays her money, as mentioned above. The "playroom" is now a mixture of gym and library. I say a library because every room in our house is filled with books. When I tell my kids that I prefer books to people and think I'm going to put a clause in my will to say they don't inherit unless they look after my books, the elder one, Nicky, says that he intends having a mass burning of my literary collection immediately following my funeral. I have to admit that I am pretty neurotic about books. I can't bear to read a book anybody else has already read. Well, a volume, I mean, otherwise reading for me would be a pretty lonely and elitist business if I couldn't read anything from the best-sellers. I have been known to hand total strangers on trains and planes a bookmark when they are about to break the spine of a paperback by folding it back to read or turn down a page to mark their place.

I now have a pretty good gym at home. A running machine, cross-trainer, steps, weights, a trampoline and an abdominiser. We have a TV and a video as well as a music system, membership if you want to join is a mere forty pounds a month, which you can pay by sending a cheque or a standing order to me care of my publishers. All that was missing was a bike and I calculated that if I had one I might even be able to charge fifty pounds a month for membership. By the way, when you run you get a very nice view of the garden with its newly erected shed and neatly assembled garden furniture, not to mention the plants on the patio where the unit once stood. You could open the conversation with other members by saying:

"I think the garden looks much better without that metal monstrosity. "

Or not, as the case may be.

So, we decided to get a bike. Son number two whilst still at home was the greatest user of the equipment (mainly because he always seemed to be recovering from some sports injury or another). When he was younger the X-Ray department at our local hospital knew him by name and on one occasion couldn't x-ray him because he'd be there so often that they were scared of the effects of the radiation.

Thus, he was designated to buy the bike. He did a reccie and I visited Lillywhites myself. For those of you who don't know, Lillywhites is the oldest and probably the largest specialist sports store in London, situated just off Piccadilly Circus. I found a really good bike in their sale, but by the time Paul visited that had been sold and he settled for another model (inevitably at a higher price). He paid with my credit card. Both my boys have the use of the card for emergencies and it's a standing joke in our family when they take my wife and I out for dinner that it is an "emergency" as they tend to "treat" us with my own card. Other such emergencies are petrol and clothes. They also have the use of my BT credit card and, whilst it's nice to hear from them when they are abroad, so does everybody else, as is proven by the bills.

Once again Paul was not told the bike would be delivered unassembled. Not only unassembled but unassembleable. We did have a go. Or at least the boys did, even summoning David (who is the most technical of all Paul's friends and is known within our family, of which he has become an intrinsic part over the years, as "Mr B").

David arrived with tool-kit in tow, eager to assemble the bike, mainly because he wanted to use it. A whole afternoon later he gave up. I went to visit Lillywhites. They did not seem very pleased to see me and I was told that I needed to speak to the manager and that he wasn't there.

"But somebody must be in charge" I reasoned.

Apparently not. He would call me. He didn't. I visited again. He still wasn't there. I made it quite clear that I expected his call that afternoon. He called. I told him I either needed him to deliver an assembled bike or to send someone over to assemble it. He took my point, albeit after a little persuasion and mention of Trade Description Acts. A young man arrived with some very interesting skin diseases. He managed to put the bike together, but hadn't been supplied with any batteries so couldn't see if it was working. I supplied the batteries and lo and behold my gym was complete. Or so I thought. After a week of fairly light use, the batteries wore out. We replaced them. When we went to use the bike a week or so later they were dead. I phoned Lillywhites. They suggested that I needed to remove the batteries after every use. I pointed out that this involved unscrewing the back of the battery holder. I didn't point out I didn't have a screwdriver. I don't think they would have believed me. We tried that over a period of time and squeezed a bit longer out of the batteries but not much. Eventually my patience wore out. I wrote to Lillywhites:

Dear Sir/Madam,

You may recall some earlier correspondence that passed between us in relation to an exercise bike that was purchased last year.

I have continued to experience problems with the bike. If batteries are left in for more than two weeks, this results in them having to be replaced. Consequently the batteries have to be taken out at the end of every single use, which as you are aware, because of the design of the bike, actually involves unscrewing the cover.

If this were not bad enough, the bike has now ceased to function altogether as various wires have come loose from the most modest use.

The bike is clearly not suitable for the purpose for which it was acquired and I should be grateful if you would confirm that you are prepared to exchange this with a suitable replacement.

I look forward to hearing from you at your earliest convenience.

Yours faithfully,

They didn't answer. Instead a young man called Mark called from the supplier company, was very helpful, referred me to various websites and said they would upgrade me. I looked on the websites and couldn't find a mains operated bike which was what I wanted. I tried to phone him back on the 0870 number he had given me. Nobody ever answered. After a dozen or so attempts I wrote again to Lillywhite's as I had no idea who Mark was or where he was based.

Dear Sir/Madam,

I refer to my letter of the 18th February (a copy of which I enclose herewith for ease of reference). Although I have not had the courtesy of a reply to that letter, I did receive a telephone call from somebody called Mark who gave me two website addresses and suggested I select another bike from them so that my existing bike could be replaced.

I told him that I did not want another machine operated by batteries and was quite happy to pay for any upgrade, provided this was discounted to reflect the inconvenience to which I have been put and the fact that I have been unable to use the bike that I have had for some time.

He told me to call him after I had investigated the two websites and gave me a telephone number.

I did look at both websites but could not find a machine which seemed to run from the mains. I did try to telephone him on the following Monday (February 23rd) but the number just rang out. I have tried on a daily basis since and the number either continues to ring out or, alternatively, cuts out without going to any kind of answering service.

Helpful as Mark may or may not have been, my complaint is against Lillywhites who sold me the product in the first place.

Could I now please have this matter dealt with by return to avoid any further action?

Yours faithfully,

I heard nothing. I wrote again.

Dear Sir/Madam,

I enclose herewith copies of my letters of the 18th February and 2nd March to which I have still not received a written reply. May I please hear from you by return.

Yours faithfully,

I told you this complaining business needs patience.

The end result was that the supplying company started phoning my son Paul. He told them to phone me. They didn't. Our paper suppliers chopped down another stretch of rain forest and I wrote yet again.

Dear Sir/Madam,

Further to my earlier correspondence, to which I have still not received the courtesy of a reply, I understand from my son, who placed the initial order, that he is continuing to get phone calls from the suppliers of the exercise bike. On each occasion he refers them to me but that message seems to go no further as nobody has contacted me.

As I have said previously, I have a phone number for them and a name, which simply doesn't work.

Could somebody please telephone me at my office this week to avoid the necessity of my taking further action.

Yours faithfully

At long last I got a call from a company called Icon. They didn't do mains connected bikes, but they would upgrade me and they would deliver. Nothing from Lillywhites who were, of course, the people to whom I had paid my money. No call, no apology and certainly no written response to any of my letters. They had, quite simply, just passed the buck (and the bike). Icon (belying their name ... you need to pause after the first letter to get the pun) were efficiency itself. I would hear from a delivery company called Tawny. I did. They would deliver on a Tuesday in the morning. They did. Unfortunately what they delivered was a flat-packed unassembled bike in a badly damaged box. I was back where I had started.

At times like these in the course of a complaint you begin to doubt yourself and your own ability to bring a complaint to a successful conclusion. But you can't give up now, however tempting that may be. As I was writing this I was on a train travelling to Leeds. Inevitably we were late. The man opposite me told me it was always late.

"Do you complain?" I asked.

"You just give up," he said.

"You mustn't" I replied, trying to instil some inspiration into him.

I told him about the book.

"I'll buy a copy," he said.

"Can I mention you?" I asked. He agreed, and so I have.

I was faced with the damaged box and the bits of what might or might not eventually be an exercise bike within. There was now a Tate Modern. Did I simply ship it to them? "Motionless Bike Without a Rider", was the title that sprang to mind, given that I couldn't spring into the saddle. Instead, I wrote one last letter.

Icon Health & Fitness Limited
Unit 4
Revie Road Industrial Estate
Revie Road
Leeds LS11 8JG.

Dear Sirs,

Further to your letter of the 25th March, a copy of which I

enclose for ease of reference, together with copies of my earlier correspondence with Lillywhites.

On Tuesday the 30th March, a replacement bicycle was delivered by Tawny. The box was badly damaged and, once again, the cycle had been delivered in a flatpack form. This is exactly where I came in nearly a year ago when I purchased the bike from Lillywhites and was not told that this was self-assembly. We tried to assemble it and after nearly a whole day's efforts (and calling in various neighbours), found it impossible. Eventually, Lillywhites sent one of their employees to assemble the same and I do require someone either from Icon or Lillywhites to do the same again. At the moment I am faced with a situation where I have made a relatively expensive purchase and have simply not been able to use it for more than a few weeks during the course of the past 12 months.

I am home all day this coming Friday, i.e. the 2nd April, and it would be very convenient for me if somebody could come on that day.

Yours faithfully,

My PA said I was wasting my time. She often says that, but then it's really her time I'm wasting because she generally types the letters. It's educational and good for her soul. She is very polite and politically correct and believes her mission in life is to save my moral soul and conscience. I possess neither but even after some twenty plus years of working with me she refuses to believe that. She said I wasn't giving them enough time, when I wrote the letter on a Thursday and told them they had to deliver the bike, fully assembled, the following day. I pointed out that far from being unreasonable it was very convenient for me as I don't work on a Friday and would therefore be home for delivery. Actually, I do work on a Friday because I write but then I suppose you might not call that work, and it's certainly not what real men do to earn a living.

And there I was in the midst of typing all this up when the phone rang and a very helpful man from Icon told me they would be sending me a fully-assembled replacement. They would have done it that day but they didn't have my upgraded model in stock.

It would be with me the following week. I shall be writing to Icon to congratulate them on their efficiency and customer service standards, even if I wasn't really a customer. I was a customer of Lillywhites. I won't be again. To this day I do not have one piece of correspondence on their headed paper. But at least I got a result. As a character sort of used to say in The A Team, "I love it when a complaint comes all together".

So, if you are buying anything at all that doesn't come fully assembled these are issues you may want to raise when you have reached the point of suicide on your assembly programme.

1. Were you told in the shop or the brochure (or in the online information) that there would be any degree of self-assembly?
2. If so, were you told the degree of complexity?
3. Did it say any special tools would be needed?
4. Did it say how long it would take?
5. Did it take longer?
6. Were there any parts left over after assembly? That's always a good pointer to the fact that you've done something wrong!
7. Were the instructions clear and in good English?
8. When you had completed the assembly did the equipment work, or did the item look exactly the same as in the sales literature?
9. Did you have to expend any extra money on assembly. For example on buying tools or paying a real man to do the work?

In my view if you have answered in the affirmative to any one of those then you have the right to complain. And if you have the right, then use it.

16

WATCH THIS SPACE

It's quite amazing how contagious complaining can become, like a genuinely infectious disease. Once I start regaling people at dinner parties with tales of my adventures, (as I have mentioned before I'm a real wow to invite) then you can be quite sure I'll receive a chorus from around the table of stories of deepest, darkest complaints, or "You should meet my mother-in-law, she's the best complainer I know". I've begun to realise that what began as an educational text-book is fast turning out to be my autobiography so I thought that round about here would be a good time to introduce other examples of complaints that emanated from third parties.

My wife is the worst complainer in the world and I mean that kindly, not as an insult. What I mean, and I can feel myself digging a pit here, is that she gets very embarrassed when I complain and would rather suffer personal torture than complain herself. It's no coincidence that she only goes on holiday with either me (well, I hope that would be the case) or her friend Ann, who is never able to settle into a hotel unless she has complained about the quality of the first three rooms she has been offered. In fact, they might as well save themselves the time and show her the third room first.

So, enough about me. Let's talk about friends and family. I have had doubts about my younger son, Paul. No problem with the elder one, Nicky. I recall many years ago, during a family holiday in Cornwall, he went missing on the beach. We had just bought him his first fishing rod. He must have been all of five years old. There he was, paddling in the shallows, rod in hand and suddenly there he wasn't. The usual blind panic that affects parents of a lost child swept over us. Had he been kidnapped? I have to admit that would not have troubled us too much as he was pretty horrible and any kidnapper would have returned him fairly pronto and with some compensation to boot. I dashed up and down the beach calling his name. We had lost him before in an hotel in Newcastle

173

when he had cheerfully toddled into an open lift to be carried away all of several floors, his plaintive cries drifting up the lift shaft. But this was different. This was a vast beach filled with holiday makers. Just as suddenly as he had disappeared, he popped up again walking back to the sea with a rod still in his grimy hand.

We raced over to him and swept him up into parental arms.

"Where did you go to?"

"The rod broke. I took it back to the shop."

What had happened was the net had detached itself from the rod. Don't suppose we could really have expected longevity from something that had cost about 20p. My five year old had thought otherwise and, as we discovered when we went back to the shop, had stormed in with his rod in two pieces and demanded a replacement.

"I told him it had only cost a few pence," the sheepish shop-keeper said, "but he was quite insistent."

And so he has been for the rest of his life. Even when I sent him to New York on my Virgin air-miles he managed to conjure up a complaint letter (justifiably, I may add) which earned him a few more air-miles of his own, when Virgin dealt with it as promptly, politely and efficiently as ever.

But Number 2 son has never been like that. He does complain to me from time to time about the fact I chose a middle name for him in the shape of Aidan, that he truly hates. There was a Newcastle United footballer at the time called Aidan McCaffrey who I thought would go far (how wrong could I be?) I also felt it had a bit of a literary sound to it and would add a bit of class to the run of the mill nomenclatures of his class-mates of the future. Meanwhile he ended up supporting Everton and rarely opening a book. However, since he has been a fund raiser for a national charity he seems to have toughened up a bit. On one of my travels in the States I went into a department store in Tallahassee (yes of Judy's fame ... and yes, they do have department stores there) and bought him a Fossil watch. I was rather proud of my choice and even prouder of the strap I selected. However, I forgot that Paul is the fussiest person alive when it comes to his clothes and accessories.

Anyway, Paul loved the watch (one-up for his old man's taste) but hated the strap. A not unexpected equaliser to bring me firmly down to earth. In July 2003 he went into the Covent Garden branch of Fossil in London, had them scurrying around with catalogues and selected a new strap, which fairly inevitably was not in stock. He was told (none too politely) to leave his watch there and they would order the strap, fit it and he would have an acceptable and wearable new watch within a maximum of five weeks. He left reasonably happy, carrying an order form but no watch.

He waited patiently for eight weeks, then phoned the store to see if his watch had been reunited with its new strap. A singularly unhelpful member of staff told him that he'd have to look in the receipt book (Paul had been able to give him the order number) and would call back. Either he had no intention of doing so or simply forgot, but either way Paul received no call. So, a week later he went to visit Fossil in Covent Garden once again. His visit was a lengthy one. He gave them a copy of his order form (which was, by now, beginning to yellow with age) and after it (and my son) had aged a further half an hour he was told they couldn't find the order as the member of staff who had taken it in the first place had departed.

Paul was persistent. It runs in the family. He asked to see the manager. He wasn't there. The "acting" manager was produced. His performance of the role was not particularly convincing. He was totally disinterested in the history of the watch and its poignant separation from its strap and blamed the distributors who, according to him, had nothing to do with Fossil. Certainly he did not see fit to apologise and merely said he would send the strap on when (and if) it arrived and would magnanimously bear the cost of postage. The fact that my son had made two trips to Covent Garden from his office in Hammersmith did not seem to have any relevance.

Summer came and went and so did Autumn. One hoped that somebody at Fossil was showing enough love and care for the watch to ensure it went back on to British Winter Time. By November neither watch nor strap, nor indeed the manager had surfaced. My wife and I were despatched to Fossil's store in midtown Manhattan (well, not literally, as we were there for Thanksgiving) to see if we could find a suitable strap, though on reflection that wouldn't have been much use without the watch itself. Paul, meanwhile, was taking matters into his own hands and went back into town and this time made friends with a very nice lady called Priscilla. Isn't it odd that this book is filled with very nice ladies who come to the rescue of me and my family when all seems lost? Priscilla, bless her, at least said sorry and said she would call back the next day. Not only did she say she would call but she actually did so.

Unfortunately, her news was not good. The distributors had, in fact, misplaced the watch. Even more depressing was the little tit-bit of information that the strap that had been ordered back in the lazy, hazy days of July had not been available then and was certainly not available now, in the midst of the bleak mid-winter. Priscilla (who seemed to be related to Lissa with two ss's) was nonplussed and went in search of the strap elsewhere. But to no avail, at which point Paul decided to get his watch back and fit the new strap that his doting parents had bought for him in New York. He was told he'd be called when the watch was safely returned to Covent Garden.

Christmas came and went. So did New Year. It was now 2004. The watch was obviously having problems finding its way home. Doubtless, with all the stress and strain it was feeling a little wound up. By mid January, Paul had had enough and resorted to his father's favourite instant remedy. The complaint letter which I reproduce here. Now, I have to say (and I say this quite proudly) this was all his own work.

Dear Ms X

I am writing to complain about the appalling level of service that I received from your store in Covent Garden over the past few months.

I first went into the branch in July last year to order a brown strap for my new Fossil watch that had been given to me as a present. I was told to leave the watch at the store and was informed that I would be phoned when the watch, complete with new strap, arrived back from the warehouse. In addition, I was assured that this would take no longer than five weeks (see enclosed photocopy of order form).

After eight weeks of waiting to hear about the watch I phoned up the store to enquire as to its whereabouts. The member of staff that I spoke to was particularly unhelpful and told me that he would have to look in the receipt book and would give me a call back. Unfortunately, I was offered no such courtesy and was left without any idea as to when, or indeed if, my order was to arrive in the store.

I therefore went to visit the branch the following week, which was the middle of September, over two months after my initial request for a strap. The staff once again shocked me by their incompetence and kept me waiting for half an hour whilst they looked in vain for details of my order (despite the fact I had brought one with my carbon copy). I was informed that the confusion was caused by the departure of the member of staff who took the order, but was offered no direct apology for the amount of time that I had been kept waiting.

I requested to see the manager, but in his absence was attended to by the 'acting' manager. I told him that I was most disappointed by the delay in receiving my strap and by the poor level of customer service that I had encountered. He seemed most disinterested about the fact that a member of his staff had failed to phone me back and took no responsibility for the failure of the store to produce my order in the allotted time. He stated that the distributors had caused the delay and that Fossil was therefore not accountable. Despite my protestations that your company had a duty to meet its stated deadlines, whatever the circumstances, he still refused to offer me any apology or suitable compensation. After much discussion he eventually only agreed to send the strap when it did arrive in store and to cover the cost of the postage.

Unfortunately, by the start of November (18 weeks after my initial order was placed) I had still not received the watch or strap, nor been contacted to explain the reasons for the extensive delay. I therefore once again travelled back into town to enquire as to the whereabouts of the items. This time I was dealt with in a more appropriate manner by a member of your staff named Priscilla. She apologised for the poor level of service I had received in the past and assured me that she would call back the next day to let me know the reasons for the delay.

Thankfully, Priscilla did ring me back, but informed me that your distributors had in fact "misplaced" my watch. They did manage to locate it the following day, but I was then told that the reason for the hold up was that the strap I had ordered had in fact not been available during this whole period of time. Quite why this had not been made apparent to me months earlier is quite incomprehensible. Priscilla kindly tried to locate a strap elsewhere, but to no avail. I therefore decided to cut my losses and requested the return of the watch. I was informed that I would be phoned when it arrived back in the store.

It is now approaching the middle of January, over six months after I made the mistake of ordering a simple strap from your branch in Covent Garden. I am still waiting for that phone call and have no idea as to the location of my watch, which I have not yet had a chance to wear.

I do hope that you will agree that for a company of your size and reputation this is an unacceptable level of customer service. I have wasted a great deal of time chasing up your staff who, for the most part, I found to be rude and unco-operative. I therefore trust that you will address all the issues brought up in this letter. Furthermore, I expect to receive suitable compensation to make up for my efforts in this farcical saga and for the absence of a present that was given to me over six months ago.

Yours sincerely

Paul Stein

Hopefully you can see some paternal influence on his style. The letter worked a treat. Telephoned by the Customer Services Manager he was told to go to Covent Garden and select a watch to the value of £75 (double the price I'd paid in Tallahassee). Doubtless both life and the cost of living is cheap there. On top of that, he was told he could have 25% off any future purchases up to £200. What was even better, from his point of view, was that upon returning to Covent Garden he was greeted (quite literally) by the acting manager who had, at least, to pretend to be pleased to see such a VIP customer. Of the watch I bought for him there has been no further sighting. Perhaps, it was so distressed by the continuing absence of its strap that it blew a spring (if modern watches do have springs). Perhaps, it has become a Time Lord. Perhaps it decorates the wrist of St Peter at the Gates to Heaven. For further news, just watch this space.

However, I did make the mistake of buying my wife a Fossil watch in Manhattan. It broke the second time she wore it. Nicky works in Covent Garden and tried to get it replaced but all she got was the address of their repairers. Whilst I felt another cmplaint coming on this time, a month after I sent it off, it returned, fully repaired.

I suppose this is a kind of revision of how to complain in store so don't forget:

1. Always ask for the manager.
2. Be polite, but firm.
3. Take the names of the people you have dealt with.
4. Take the receipt with you, but don't part with it.
5. Give them a reasonable period of time to deal with it before returning. Then repeat process as above.
6. Write a letter to the branch.
7. If you get no response assume it's been destroyed and write a letter to head office with a copy and a summary.

As to what you can achieve, my son has set the bench-mark and you must see if you can improve upon it.

17

IS IT ME?

I have just read a very disturbing article in *The Times*, headed "For some, things are just NOT fair." Beneath that are the words "Psychiatrist studying the Victor Meldrew syndrome say that certain people are simply beyond help".

Am I turning into Victor Meldrew? Am I perpetually railing at the slings and arrows of outrageous fortune and saying that I don't believe it? According to this article "For Victor Meldrew and his ilk, complaining is more than a hobby; it is a way of life." So that is what I have become, an "ilk" of that great TV character Mr Meldrew. I was almost too scared to read on. But I did. I had to know. If there were psychiatrists studying me then why didn't I know about it? I was about to learn.

It appears that the Meldrews of this world (and presumably their "ilk" as well) suffer from a condition called "querulous paranoia". This is according to a group of Australian psychiatrists, which explains quite a lot. We, of our ilk, "become so obsessed with a perceived injustice that nothing can be done to satisfy them". Whew! I mopped my brow with a relieved and quivering hand. None of my injustices are perceived and I am fairly easily satisfied by somebody doing something about them when I complain.

Fascinated, though, I read on. What if I weren't off the hook? According to this bunch of Aussie shrinks, these sufferers from querulous paranoia strike a mixture of fear and loathing into the hearts and minds of complaints officers, journalists, and ombudsmen. I'm not sure I've ever struck any kind of chord with journalists, though they've struck plenty with me. However, on reflection, I realised that I have written to newspapers on many occasions complaining about articles they've written about my clients, and me too, for that matter. In that respect I must take the opportunity to mention the Press Complaints Commission. There,

180

I've mentioned them. They're useless. They should be re-named the Journalists' Protection Society.

Anyway, these Antipodeans were writing in the British Journal of Psychiatry and it appears that people who complain are more often men than women (OK, I'll give them that) use coloured ink (what do they think I am, mad?) "issue threats" (right, at five feet four and weighing a mere one hundred and forty seven pounds … give or take a few) use wild language (well, perhaps) and "insist that their complaints raise issues of principle demanding a hearing in the court".

So that last one definitively gets me off the hook. As you know, I always say that courts are the last resort and if you have to resort to them then you have really lost. The art of complaining is to get where you want to be by reason and language, not by litigation. Yet, fascinated, still I read on. It appears that these people are never satisfied, no matter what painstaking or lengthy procedure they follow. The statistics spoke for themselves, as less than a quarter of the complaints were resolved when the files were closed. Goodness only knows how they researched these issues. (In fact, by gathering material from six ombudsmen's offices in Oz.) What was of historical interest, was that the psychiatric definition of queru-lous litigant fell into decay at the end of the nineteenth century, just as complaints procedures were being established. So, perhaps I was born in the wrong time. I could have been a trendsetter, though I have to say I wasn't aware of complaints tumbling in apace one hundred years ago. How many people, I wonder, wrote to the White Star Company complaining about the quality of the life-boats on board the Titanic.

Just to satisfy myself that I'm not querulous let me return to other peoples' complaints. The Chairman of the group of compa-nies to which I gave for seven years, before my retirement at the end of 2004, what was laughingly known as legal advice in-house, is an experienced world traveller. As his family lawyer I was forever writing letters about mishaps, both major and minor, but the best to date involved our old friends British Airways. He was flying to Beirut in early spring 2004 with his fiancée and her mother to choose a wedding dress. For her, I hasten to add, and not for him. They checked in six pieces of luggage at Heathrow onto a flight that would leave on a Tuesday night and arrive at 4.00 am on the Wednesday morning. When they got to Beirut there was a man with his name on a card. Oh good, he thought, BA are recognising a loyal and regular flyer and are going to fast-track my party through. Think again, my friend. The man was just there to tell him that it was possible, just possible, that a piece of his baggage hadn't made it on to the plane. Now how BA wouldn't know that for certain, I'm not sure. It's either on or it's off and if it's off then that's the reason why you have a man with a card waiting at Beirut airport at 4.00 am. It was off. But it would be on the next plane. The next plane was on Wednesday night arriving at 4 o'clock on Thursday morning, which is how his fiancée came to see her couturier wedding dressmaker wearing jeans, a t-shirt and tennis shoes.

At ten on Thursday he phoned BA. They had bad news for him. The case hadn't quite made it on to the Wednesday flight. Perhaps it had met my son Paul's Fossil watch and stopped to pass the time. In any event it would definitely be there on Friday morning. BA guaranteed it. (I've heard that one before.) He duly called again on Friday morning. It appeared that none of the "delayed" bags had made it onto the flight (the mind boggles as to why this might be) but it would be delivered to the hotel on Saturday morning and by the way would the young lady like to buy some clothes at BA's expense. What did they think she's been doing? Wearing the same jeans and t-shirt since Tuesday night?

He told them not to bother. He was returning to London on Sunday and would collect the bag at Heathrow. Would they please have it ready for him. (He's a lot politer than I am.) Yes, they would. He duly arrived back at Heathrow from Beirut on Sunday.

He went to the BA luggage office. He had the tag number of the missing bag which put him at some advantage over the BA staff. They checked and checked and eventually told him that he had three missing bags and that they had all been despatched to Beirut on three consecutive days. Still polite, he pointed out to them that this was not the case. They checked. They found the locator. The bag was in some storeroom at Heathrow along with thousands of other missing bags. They couldn't lay their hands on it right away but they would dig it out and deliver it to his home. They took his address. The bag did not arrive on Sunday night, nor indeed on Monday morning. I began to draft a complaint letter for him when he took the law into his own hands and phoned the BA Gold Card hotline. They had good news for him. The bag had been found. It had gone to Beirut on the Sunday night flight, departing well after he had arrived at Heathrow and sought to claim it. They would find it, bring it home and deliver it. The letter below went winging its way to BA's Chief Executive. He must have been pleased to hear from me after such a long time as I'd given up flying his airline since my last spat with them.

Dear Mr. Eddington,

I am the in-house legal advisor to the group of companies headed up by an executive gold card-holder with yourselves. His card number is …

On the night of Tuesday 30th March, Mr X, together with his fiancée, Ms Y (also the holder of a British Airways Executive gold card) and Ms Y's mother, flew to Beirut. This flight no longer has a First Class section but they flew Club Class. The purpose of their visit was for Ms Y to choose and be fitted for a wedding dress and this was a very important and emotional journey for them.

They landed at 4 a.m. on Wednesday morning and a representative of British Airways was there to greet them with a card with Mr X's name on it. Mr X thought that, as he was a gold card-holder and, in the absence of first class seating on the plane, special arrangements had been made for them to be escorted through immigration and taken to their hotel.

However, this was very far from the case. He was told that one of his bags had been checked in and "might not have made it onto the plane". Between the three of them, they had six pieces of luggage and indeed only five pieces arrived. Mr X was told that the piece of luggage would be on the next day's plane and, as that left on Wednesday evening, this would mean it would arrive very early on Thursday morning. Mr X gave your representative the name of his hotel and telephoned when he woke

up to ensure that his bag would be on the flight. To his astonishment, he was told that it would not be on the next day's flight.

This particular case contained all of Ms Y's clothes but there
was no indication that she should acquire clothes at BA's
expense. All she had were the clothes in which she had travelled, namely a pair of jeans, a t-shirt and a pair of tennis shoes,
hardly the appropriate clothes in which to visit a couturier
wedding dress designer. As you are also probably aware, Beirut
is hardly the place to buy quality ladies' clothing.

Mr X duly called on Thursday and again was told that the bag
had not made the flight but that it would be on that night's
flight, i.e. arriving on Friday, and that he should call at 10.00 a.m.
When he did call, he was told that the bag "didn't make it" and
it would be there for Saturday. Having telephoned again, he was
told that "no bags had made it on to the Friday flight" but it
would definitely make it that day.

As Mr X was returning to London on Sunday, he told your
representatives not to bother but to retain the bag for him in
London and he would collect it at the airport. He was then
asked for his home address "in case the bag got to Beirut". Mr X
advised them that they must ensure that it didn't get to Beirut.

Mr X arrived back in London on Sunday and went to collect
his bag. He was told that the baggage department at Heathrow
had received messages saying the bag had been sent on the 31st
March, the 1st April and the 2nd April. Mr X advised them that
this was not the case. He was then told that the bag was not lost
and that it had been "tracked".

Mr X received no call at his home on Sunday and, at the time
of dictating this on Monday 5th April, the bag has still not
surfaced, nor indeed has Mr X received any telephone call by
way of explanation or apology from British Airways.

This is not the sort of treatment one would expect for any
passenger, let alone a gold card-holder and I require an explanation, apology and offer of compensation by return.

Yours sincerely,

British Airways wrote back. Surprise, surprise, it was nothing to do with them. This was a deja-vu of my Johannesburg Com-Air incident. The route was operated on their behalf by British Mediterranean Airways Ltd. They wrote back. No explanation, though they did apologise. They would regard the bag as "lost" ... by then, it wasn't as it had finally found its way home ... But in those circumstances all they could do was compensate per kilo of bag-weight which meant an offer of under £500. It seemed to me that they were getting off more lightly by deeming the bag to be lost. We seemed to be entering a Kafkaesque world where things that were lost were found. It wasn't acceptable, and I told them so.

Dear Ms ...

Thank you for your letter of the 27th April.

Neither Mr X nor I was aware that British Airways franchised out the Beirut route.

The fact of the matter is that this is not really our concern. Ms Y's (now Mrs) baggage was not put on the plane at Heathrow and their tickets were booked with British Airways. As you are aware, Mr X is a British Airways Platinum Cardholder.

An offer of £416.40 by way of compensation is, to say the least, derisory. There is no doubt that Ms Y would have spent considerably more than that had she gone out and replaced the clothes in Beirut, something that was on offer to her from British Airways. I am copying this letter in to British Airways as it is simply unacceptable for them to "pass the buck" to yourselves and I await hearing from you or them with a suitable offer of financial compensation, together with an additional offer of Air Miles.

I await hearing from you.

Yours sincerely,

We finally got a result. Not only would they pay the compensation but would also give her 40,000 air miles, sufficient for a return flight to Beirut. Honour was satisfied. The case and all its contents had finally turned up and she had received a fair and equitable compensation for the distress. And that's all one wants, all one can hope for. That is the art of complaining reaching fruition in its purest form. Trust me I'm really not Victor Meldrew!

18

TIME SHARED IS TIME EARNED

Is there anyone out there, who at some time or other in his or her life, has not been offered a free or cut-price offer of a weekend in the sun at a glamorous resort? If you're young, pretty and female then you probably get those sort of offers all the time, but in the unlikely event of anyone from that category reading this book then this chapter doesn't apply to you. The rest of you now read on. It all sounds great. It's a personal invitation, so exclusive that if you don't take up your offer within a set time limit it will be be withdrawn before you can say, "hard sell". Did I say "hard sell"? I meant, of course, to say "time-share".

For the odd reader who may have been frozen in ice since the Neolithic Age (or for those young, pretty, female readers who persisted in reading on despite my warning) let me explain. A time-share is a system of shared ownership of a holiday home where you buy a week (or two, if the sell is really hard) in a villa, a house, a lodge or an apartment, which nestles romantically amongst five hundred identical units and where you can be sure that at any given time another five hundred are being built. It's so much your very own that the one-off payment you have made to buy your seven day eternal dream holiday home is supplemented by an equally eternal, albeit ever-increasing, service charge which probably pays for the ongoing construction of the other five hundred homes which will probably further increase the service charge. Hopefully, now, you will have got the picture.

There are people I know who have taken up the offer just to get their free weekend away without any intention whatsoever of buying. They have gone armed with resolve, garlic, crosses and ear-plugs, the latter to keep out the high-pitched whining of the commission driven salesman. Yet, still they have returned the proud owners of an annual week's holiday in Marbella, but with no recollection of ever having signed for it, or indeed handed over any money.

All you can get them to say, as they dazedly stagger off the plane and home to their much-depleted bank accounts is:

"I just wanted the sales-pitch to stop."

Time-shares. What mug would actually buy one when he's not been exposed to the sales-technique equivalent of the characters in "Glengarry, Glen Ross" That's a play by David Mamet, which, if you've not seen, then you have to. It's a movie too, and a very good one at that. How's that for a high-pressure sales-pitch? As for the mug, well, the answer is simple. Me.

Some years ago my wife and I actually accepted such an offer from a highly reputable company called Interval International. To be fair to them they did exactly what they said they would do. We had a great weekend up at Cameron House on the banks of Loch Lomond in Scotland, were exposed to the promised one-hour talk and tour of the property and then left to make up our own minds. It worked brilliantly. We were so impressed by their profession-alism and the stunning scenery, the view from "our" lodge over the lake and the quality of the furnishings and amenities that we bought the last week in June forever.

I'd like to say that was the start of a life-long romance with the concept of time-share, but if I could say that then there would be no *raison d'etre* for this chapter. As you may have gathered from my somewhat waspish introduction to this part of the book, there were problems. Not, I hasten to add, of the nature set out there, but certainly enough to give cause to complain. The first year we went everything was fine … except the weather. The following year again, no problem apart from the fact that my mother was taken ill and I had to drive back through the night to her hospital bedside. If you want to meet some really weird people then stop at service stations on the M1 at 3 o'clock on a Sunday morning. Can you believe that folk actually draw off the motorway to play video games involving car crashes? The next year, we exchanged it for a great unit in Williamsburg, Virginia. If you've never been to Colonial Williamsburg then you have to go. It's a re-creation of the town immediately before the American War of Independence (or the American Revolution as we prefer to call it on this side of the

Atlantic). History, is, after all, merely a matter of perception, or, as the brilliant playwright Alan Bennett says in his recent play *The History Boys*, "History, it's one fxxxing thing after another".

Williamsburg also has re-enactments of seminal moments leading to the Declaration. There are characters wandering around dressed in period costume making inflammatory anti-British speeches (no change there, then) and generally beating the drum to start the revolution. The guy dressed as Mr Washington and I had a ding dong verbal battle when I accused him of being a traitor. The exchange became rather heated and I quite forgot that the real Mr W had been dead for some two hundred years and eventually had to be led away by my wife to avoid futher confrontation with a howling pack of outraged American tourists who were showing every sign of turning into a lynch mob.

After a couple of years, we returned to Cameron House convinced we had bought a winner. In our absence the Lodge had changed, not for the better (you'll see what I mean when you read the letter below) and when we used the washing machine and tumble dryer, my wife pointed out that there was an odd smell.

"That might be because of the smoke," I opined. Black clouds of it were belching out of the tumble dryer, accompanied by a noise that might well have preceded an explosion. We called down to the main office. The lodge was largely made from timber, we pointed out. They seemed to know that as they had built them and promised to send someone. Nobody came. We called again and evacuated the lodge, me taking with me only my lap-top and the book on which I was working at the time. A man came, put out what was by now a minor fire, and thanked my wife for her prompt action. I told him proudly she had been a girl guide and a Tawny Owl with a Brownie pack. It didn't quite have the same resonance as claiming she'd fought on the beaches of Normandy or been with the French Resistance, but I did think he might have shown more interest in her paramilitary career than he actually did. What was of interest to me though, was the fact that all my T-shirts that had been in the machine had shrunk. I wrote a letter.

Dear Sirs,

Re: Cameron House, Lodge XX week XX, 2002

I recently stayed in our Lodge No. XX at Cameron House for the week commencing 29th June through to the 6th July.

For various reasons, we have not visited the Lodge for some four years (having acquired it some six years ago) and certain matters gave us grave cause for concern.

When we acquired the Lodge, it was furnished and fitted to a very high standard. This included a waste disposal unit and an answerphone system. My mobile does not always work in the area and I had left many people (including my wife's elderly mother) the direct dial number of our lodge and informed them there was an answerphone. To our astonishment, we were told that the answerphone was no longer a feature but that the hotel would take messages for us. In fact, I know for certain that at least two people called me during the course of the week and endeavoured to leave messages, but without success, on the Lodge direct line and they were at no time referred to the main hotel switchboard.

The whole atmosphere of the Lodge was one that had undergone substantial use and been refurbished to a much lower standard. I think the carpet had been replaced with a cheaper carpet and neither my wife nor I can recollect there being a glass table there. We thought there was a good quality wooden table and the glass table looked cheap, smeared and grimy. The seat covers on the exterior deck were torn and dirty and the towel rail in the bathroom simply fell off as soon as a towel was put on it. Similarly, in the course of the first shower I took, a tap in the shower came off in my hand.

I reported these various faults and, when maintenance came, instead of mending the towel rail, they simply turned on the heated towel rail !

Matters went from bad to worse. When my wife tried to have a spa bath, she found out that the spa was not working. Again, maintenance came and said that the system had shorted and they had to fix this.

Finally (and probably worst of all) when we put on the washing machine and spun to tumble-dry, this caught fire. I telephoned maintenance and got no response and eventually telephoned Lodge Services, telling them there was a fire, as smoke was belching out. My wife had the presence of mind to turn the machine off at the mains and closed the relevant doors whilst getting us outside, but it must have taken at least 10 minutes for maintenance to come. The gentleman told us that the machine was ruined and a replacement was sent. On this occasion, when the replacement was installed, a door was closed on it, breaking the glass at the front, so this could not be used either.

The items of clothing which had been in the tumble drier when the machine caught fire have all shrunk. This included some half a dozen t-shirts and assorted underwear and I assume you have some kind of insurance against which I can claim.

I trust you will agree that this is not the sort of holiday to which we were entitled and I look forward to hearing from you with your comments and some suitable offer of compensation in due course.

Yours faithfully,

Cameron House is a De Vere Hotel. I've never quite figured out the relationship between Interval International and the De Vere Hotel Group but be that as it may they behaved perfectly properly and speedily wrote back, not only agreeing to pay the cost of replacement of my t-shirts, but also giving us a long weekend at Belton Woods, near Lincoln, another De Vere unit.

So far, so good. A problem, a complaint, a satisfactory resolution, though we all have favourite shirts which are irreplaceable and my particular favourite was now of Lilliputian proportions. But now to turn back the clock to the previous Autumn. The way Interval International operates is to classify their units, so that if you own a share in a Gold Resort, such as Cameron House, you can exchange with a Gold Resort elsewhere which should be of the same high standard. As I said, Cameron House, is top of the range and we chose a unit with a Gold emblem alongside it within driving distance of San Diego.

191

We probably made a mistake by staying in the luxurious surroundings of the Beverley Hills Hotel for a few days before we began our trek south. We met up with some American friends (astonishingly I do have some) who lived locally and mentioned the name of the place we were staying, Ramona. They raised their eyebrows.

"Not a lot there but chickens," they said. We should have listened.

We drove and we drove through increasingly barren landscape, the roads getting narrower and steeper, realising these were roads we would have to navigate at night if we wanted to get to San Diego, which seemed much further away than the brochure had indicated, at least in time, if not distance. We came to the nearest town and went into the local store. It was like something out of a movie that fell into the Western/ Horror genre. A one-storey, dark and echoing building, filled with long shelves that led to one counter at the end, manned by an old guy in a Stetson, actually chewing tobacco. The shelves were filled with tin after tin, mainly baked beans, and I wondered if maybe this was where they had filmed *Blazing Saddles*. If we had hoped to fill up with supplies for our stay here then we were sadly mistaken.

After a long and exhausting drive we finally got to the resort. It was called Riviera Oaks Resort and it didn't look good. The fact that we were expected to haul our own cases up a winding staircase to a first floor apartment did not fill me with good cheer and nor did the cobwebs on the window when we actually located it. We made a policy decision, to leave the bags in the car until we had made a reccie and once we'd had a good look around we made a unanimous policy decision to leave. As soon as I could I dictated a letter to my long-suffering PA, Lucinda, from the States.

Dear Sirs,

Re: Cameron House – Riviera Oaks Resort

I am dictating this letter from the United States having visited Riviera Oaks Resort in Ramona, pursuant to an exchange with our resort at Cameron House, Loch Lomond.

Both resorts are deemed gold resorts in your brochure and we have always been told that an exchange would be to a resort of comparable standard.

It is not my intention in this letter to go into the shortcomings of Riviera Oaks in detail; save to say that it was the equivalent of a very moderate motel.

We have therefore booked ourselves into a hotel at a commensurate rate to that charged by Cameron House and will be looking to you for the costs of the same and, meanwhile, we also reserve all rights as to damages caused by the interruption and inconvenience to our holiday.

I will write to you further when I return to the United Kingdom.

Yours faithfully,

Having abandoned hope, the resort and Ramona I phoned ahead to the Hyatt in San Diego and, whatever complaints I may have had about Hyatts in the rest of this book, I've never been so glad in my life to see one of their portals.

I think, on this occasion, the best way to tell you about Riviera Oaks it is to print my complaint letter in its entirety.

Dear Sirs,

Re: Cameron House – Riviera Oaks Resort

Thank you for your acknowledgement of the 10th October. I now enclose herewith copies of my bills at the Hyatt San Diego and the Grande Colonial at La Jolla. In addition, had we been able to utilise the time-share at Ramona, we would have purchased food from supermarkets and cooked for ourselves whereas, as we were staying in hotels, we had to acquire food in restaurants. I estimate the additional costs at – say – £40 per day for the week.

With regard to the situation at Ramona, obviously I was not able to go into great detail when I dictated the letter to my personal assistant from California. However, the fact is that when we acquired our time-share at Cameron House, we were advised that any exchange would be to a property of a similar status and quality, provided the property concerned had a gold circle within your brochure.

In 2000, we had a very successful exchange to a property in Williamsburg where the apartment in which we stayed was certainly of the same quality as Cameron House, if not better. We were therefore entitled to assume that the property at Riviera Oaks would be the same.

When I made my selection, Riviera Oaks was only one of the choices and, indeed, my preferred choice was to be the Four Seasons Resort Club (FSA). However, when I was telephoned and advised that Riviera Oaks was available, I was told that I had to make a speedy decision and there was no guarantee that the Four Seasons would be available. I did confirm on the telephone at the time that this was of a similar status to Cameron House and was told that it was, as it was gold-circled within the brochure.

In fact, Riviera Oaks is totally remote and accessible only through a series of steep winding roads. It was described as "two hours" from Los Angeles, whereas the drive took us nearer three hours (and that was in daylight).

It was also described as being "in close proximity to many Southern Californian attractions but, in fact, nearly all of the attractions would have been over an hour's drive away. Similarly, whilst it might be an hour's drive from San Diego in the daylight, given the nature of the roads, I believe it would be considerably more at night, although we did not attempt this.

The check-in was decidedly uninspiring. We arrived late afternoon and were told that there was nowhere to get any supplies on-site, not even basic items such as fruit-juice and milk. If we wanted these, we were told, we would have to drive back the way we had come to a very basic grocery store. We were then told that we needed to drive to our apartment and, to our astonishment, we discovered that it was impossible to park outside the apartment. This was on the first floor, up a very rickety staircase and the lights, windows etc. on the exterior were covered in dust.

The main bedroom was dark and poky (not to mention dusty) and the furniture was basic, to say the least.

The cupboards had no backs to them and quite how the property could have been described as a two-bedroom apartment is beyond me. A pull-down bed in the lounge would have filled the room and the furniture in the lounge was hard, old and uncomfortable. The minute balcony overlooked a main road and it would have been quite impossible to sit outside with any degree of comfort.

The only swimming pool we saw was minute and certainly a description of "two large swimming pools" was nonsensical. Again, there was a very small Jacuzzi (which we assume is the "spa" referred to in the description) and this was filled with four people sitting in it. As already stated, there were no facilities whatsoever on site to buy even the most basic provisions and the communal room for "members" looked like the back room of an English public house, filled with cheap plastic furniture.

As we checked in, the receptionist was advising another party that the charge was $49 per night and that just about summed up the establishment, which was little better than a motel.

As you are no doubt aware, our apartment at Cameron House has modern, comfortable furniture, expensive electrical and kitchen equipment, a huge balcony overlooking Loch Lomond, shops, restaurants, excellent health and fitness facilities, daily newspapers and on-site parking. There was absolutely no comparison whatsoever.

I therefore immediately sought alternative hotel accommodation in San Diego itself at a rate commensurate with the rate charged by Cameron House for their hotel rooms. Utilising my Hyatt membership card I was able to obtain a reasonable rate at the Grand Hyatt for the week but we were unable to stay there for the weekend and moved on to La Jolla on the coast where, again, I was able to obtain a commensurate rate at the Grande Colonial Hotel.

Obviously, I require you to reimburse me for the cost of the hotels and the additional food costs, but I also believe we should be credited with the exchange week to compensate us for the inconvenience and annoyance caused and the loss of a whole day of our limited holiday.

I must say that there seems to be little confidence as to further exchanges utilising Interval International as I am not sure how much credence can be given to your gold circle within the brochure and we do still have the week in the bank for this year. I should therefore be grateful if you would also confirm that we will be priorities in relation to any exchanges and obtain our first choice in future.

I fail to see why I should have to wait 28 days for a response to this letter and I therefore look forward to hearing from you within the next seven days to avoid the necessity of my issuing proceedings.

Yours faithfully,

Letter of complaint followed letter of complaint. If I reproduce one of my letters here I think you will get the general gist of the correspondence.

Dear Mr. X,

Re: Cameron House – Riviera Oaks Resort

Thank you for your letter of the 25th November the contents of which I note.

I simply cannot accept that an inspection by yourself of Riviera Oaks Resort would regard it as being on a par with Cameron House. You have completely ignored the point I have made, namely that we were induced to enter into our contract to acquire Cameron House by the representation made to us that all Five Star status resorts would be of an equal quality.

Turning to the more detailed comments you make, I did not claim that there would be "shops" at the resort. I think it was not unreasonable to expect that any Five Star resort would at least have a facility to buy the basics such as milk, butter, eggs etc.

Your description of the resort is wrong; there is no "escape from the urban crowds" when the only view you have from your unit window is of a dual carriageway bearing a heavy flow of traffic.

You do not seem to address any of the other complaints that I made and I await your comments on these as soon as possible as I assume that, upon receipt of my letter, you have instigated another inspection of the property.

With regard to the question of a refund and your suggestion that I should have contacted you, let me make the situation absolutely clear. We arrived there at about 4.30 on a Sunday afternoon when it was growing dark. There was absolutely no way we were prepared to stay there even for one night and waste our holiday. There was nobody I could have telephoned at that time but what I did do was leave a message for my PA on her answerphone to send you a letter immediately the next day, which she did. You could have contacted us upon receipt of that letter but you failed to do so or, indeed, show any interest whatsoever.

Unless, therefore, you are prepared to meet my claim, we will have to deal with the matter formally.

Yours sincerely

Interval International had no inclination to pay for my week at the Hyatt. They said I should have contacted them before checking out of their resort. I pointed out again that this was hardly realistic on a Californian evening. And anyway what would they have done? Flown a magic wand in from Disneyland and transformed the resort into somewhere habitable?

Eventually my persistence paid off. We were compensated with a free week at one of the flagship resorts in the United Kingdom, Slaley Hall; we went there and it was excellent. Next year I think we'll go back to Cameron House. They do keep building units there but as long as my view of the Loch remains unimpeded and the tumble dryer doesn't catch fire I'm not complaining. I never do!

Now, by way of revision these are the sort of things you have to bear in mind as potential sources of complaint in relation to time-shares and the acquisition and use thereof:

1. If you go looking for a time-share, ensure that the sales-pitch accords with the inducement letter.
2. Find out how long the operating company has been in existence and make sure they are based somewhere that you can easily sue them, if it comes to that.
3. No hidden charges.
4. No silly management fees.
5. Facilities and furniture remain to the same high standard as viewed.
6. Construction on site is not excessive and view remains unimpaired.
7. Unit clean and ready for use and all repairs and replacements are carried out.
8. Ability to get the exchanges you want. If you put in three choices for three different weeks you should be able to get at least one of them and not be fobbed off with something inferior they can't otherwise let or exchange.
9. Exchange units accord with the brochure description and are of the same standard as your unit.
10. Accessibility and distances from towns is as described.
11. Ensure time-share management enforces the rules of the resort. If you have a pleasant lawn outside your house you don't want hordes of neighbouring kids using it for an ad-hoc international football match (yes, that happened to us at Cameron House as well).
12. That you have an adequate say in the running of the resort and are kept fully informed of any material changes.
13. Check them off and if you get more than a couple of positives then complain. You can hardly return the following year and complain about things you did nothing about when you had the chance.

19

COMMUNICATION CHORDS

Telephones are the curse of the 21st Century: Discuss. If that sounds like an exam question then let me give you the very simple answer. Yes. I'm as guilty as any of using them, but now they say they affect your virility. Lucky I got my two kids in early then. No chance for either of my sons to produce grandchildren though at their rate of usage.

The problem is the mobile itself and its network operators. Either it doesn't work or if it does then you get charged outrageous sums of money for calls you haven't made. I am tempted to advise you to complain as a knee-jerk reaction every time you get a bill. And that doesn't only apply to mobiles but to landlines as well. I've yet to meet anybody who doesn't have a telephone bill story to tell. Or indeed a story about the unavailability of their phone whilst the company cut through their connection whilst laying cable or digging for gold in Neasden, or whatever other excuse they can feed you whilst you desperately try to get the phone re-connected so that you can ensure that your 97 year-old great grandmother is alive and hasn't merely absent-mindedly left the phone off the hook whilst she's frying fish and setting fire to her kitchen.

The fact of the matter is that we are all so terribly dependent on the phone now and the phone companies know it. You land in New York and switch on your mobile. The phone immediately searches for a network and you have no idea whether or not it's the cheapest. It is what you are given presumably from your own home network. Like me, you probably have no idea how these things work though I'm sure there are ways to shop around and get the best bargain. I know people who do just that. The question is why won't your own network do it for you? I think you know the answer to that one.

If you do travel and do feel that you are being charged too much then, as ever, it costs nothing but a postage stamp to complain. There are all sorts of telecom watchdogs nowadays and, whether or not the big boys have any fear of them, one can but hope that a letter threatening to report them may have some effect, as the great majority of mobile phone users simply pay up. It's just another price to pay for doing business around the world in this techno-age.

What is really frustrating is making a call, being cut off because reception is poor and having to make another call at your own expense. I used to dial the operator when that happened, report it and ask them to put me through, just like the good old days of red call boxes and buttons A and B. I'm old enough to remember always hitting the B button whenever I went to make a call just in case a previous user hadn't bothered to get their money back if they'd not got connected. If three pence actually came out then you felt you had hit the jackpot. Now words like "user" and "connection" have their own meanings and so do "hits" in phoneboxes, I suspect. But to get through to the operator every time one is disconnected is just not practical, particularly if you are on the road. It's illegal in Britain now to use a mobile whilst you're driving but unfortunately nobody seems to have told the driving population of our great isle. Whether you are hands-free or sitting with the phone crooked under your neck you just can't be talking to an operator, even assuming you've been able to dial and explain that you lost your signal driving across Hampstead Heath and will they put you through at no charge. When you check your bill you'll find that you have been charged for the first call, the second call and some premium rate for just daring to call the operator.

So, what do you do?

Well, one thing is to make a note at the end of each journey of calls that have had to be redialled ... And in that respect train journeys are infamous. The phone company may say, with some justification, that they can't be responsible for tunnels on the rail lines, but what the hell. Morally, with what they charge, they are responsible for everything, even the outbreak of World War II. Once you have your list then write to the phone company and tell them for which calls you don't intend paying. When you get your bill knock off a suitable amount and send them your complaint letters with the balance of the bill. They may threaten to cut you off, they may even threaten to sue you, but the odds are that they'll just accept what you've sent them. The trick to that is to use this little magic phrase:

"This cheque is tendered in full and final settlement of all sums due to you of whatsoever nature and is to be held strictly to my order pending your acceptance of the same on that basis. If you can't accept it on those terms then you are to return it to me forthwith. I enclose a stamped, addressed, envelope for that purpose." OK, so it costs you a first class stamp but at least they have no excuses.

The same sort of principle applies to your domestic bills. Always ask for itemised bills anyway and then have a trawl through for numbers you simply don't recognise. Now it may be that the odd calls that stand out may have been made by your au pair, cleaner, plumber, gardener or burglar. More than likely, that if they are 09-something numbers they've been made by your teenage son. But it is quite possible that there are genuine errors in relation to calls that you simply didn't make and, indeed, were not made at all from your phone number. If that's the case then don't shrug and say to yourself that there aren't enough of them to bother. It's the thin end of the wedge and if you get complacent then who's to say that a three-hour call to Outer Mongolia won't slip through on some future account.

Part of the annoyance factor is trying to get through to make a complaint, which is why I suggest you restrict yourself to the written word. Have you ever tried to call the likes of Vodafone? I did. I have a Blackberry. No, I've not gone in for fruit growing and if I had then I wouldn't get very far with a crop of just one. Well, I suppose I might if it was exceedingly big and newsworthy or of such a funny shape as to attract the attention of the likes of Esther Rantzen or whoever is doing her type of programme nowadays. A Blackberry, and mine's called Bernie by the way, is a kind of mobile phone that enables you to pick up your e-mails anywhere in the world without any obvious dial-up connection. Bernie has a sticker on the back with a picture of a teddy bear telling me I kept still for my X-ray. I always insist on such a sticker when I go to the doctors. Now that they seem to have dispensed with biscuits and cups of tea you have to take what you can get. Bernie is a great business tool and saves you unpacking your lap-top for those somewhat over-zealous guys at U.S security and Immigration. I wouldn't mind complaining about the blokes at US Customs. Whatever the level of baggage I carry and whatever the purpose of the trip I always get hauled aside, asked to open my bags and then get quizzed as to whether or not I have $10,000 in cash on me. In case any of them ever read this book could you please pass the message on to your buddies that when that happy day arrives you will be the first to know about it.

Back to Bernie the Blackberry. From time to time he breaks down, probably because he's of a nervous disposition. I guess reading all my mail might have that effect on a sensitive soul, even if it belongs to a machine. There are all sorts of reasons for Bernie to go out of commission and by now I'm familiar with most of them. The problem is that if even one is able to self-diagnose, the fault can sometimes only be rectified back at the ranch, or in this case at the Vodafone HQ or Call Centre, in whichever country that may be from time to time. They gave me a phone number to dial when I first got the gizmo: it's 191. Unfortunately that takes you through to one of those multiple choice button pushing games that are so much an irritation of modern living. You know what I'm talking about. Press hash, press the pound sign, press one for the robot department, press two if you want to speak to a blue-eyed, blonde bimbo who has no concept of the technology under discussion but insists on giving you her name as if she is screaming out to be asked for a date, press four for entry to a competition to win a free mobile and run up a bill equal to the cost of the mobile while the rules are being explained to you and press five for an operator so that you can listen to ghastly muzak while you wait, and wait, and wait. I may have exaggerated a tad but you get the picture.

On this occasion I dialled 191 and hit the number that seemed closest to my enquiry. I was told I was on hold as all their operators were busy and the music began. I waited for some five minutes. I was then told to hit another number for GPRS services (these would seem to include Blackberries) I was also told to key in my mobile number. A lady called Sara answered and asked me to insert my mobile number. I told her that I'd already done just that but she was polite and persistent so I did it again. She asked how she could help me. I told her that the battery on my Blackberry had gone flat and since I'd recharged it I couldn't seem to retrieve any messages. She suggested I remove the battery. I told her the back of the machine was retained by screws and though it was remiss of me, I didn't have a screwdriver on my person. This seemed to exhaust Sara's technical knowledge. Presumably she tells everybody to remove their batteries. She then said she'd put me through to the technical department. She obviously knew her limitations. I was again put on hold as all advisors were busy and I was told to have my phone number ready. As I'd just supplied it twice I couldn't have been readier. I held on and held on, all the while fiddling around with the controls on my Blackberry. Eventually by trial and error I fiddled with Bernie (nothing sinister there as he is androgynous) and he sprang to life. I ended the call with Sara and her cohorts and then realised I would, presumably, be charged for a half an hour plus call to Vodafone. So I wrote to them.

Dear Sirs,

I am the owner of a Blackberry, telephone number *

On the 22nd June, my battery had gone flat and I needed advice as to how to re-boot the system.

I telephoned 191 and accepted one of the options by pressing the respective button. I was then put on hold for 10 minutes and, when I was finally connected to an operator, I was told that the extension was not suitable for Blackberry advice and he would transfer me back to the switchboard. I then waited another 10 minutes before I was given another menu of choices. I selected what I thought was the right option and waited a further 10 minutes before being connected to an operator. In the meantime, one of your advisors told me that I ought to remove the battery from my Blackberry and when I pointed out to her that the battery was screwed in and needed a screwdriver to release it, she then told me she would go and seek technical assistance and I waited a further 10 minutes for a connection.

All in all, as you will see, I spent well over 40 minutes on the telephone and eventually, simply through trial and error, while I was waiting, I was able to re-boot the machine myself.

I am sure you will agree that this sort of service is woefully inadequate. The telephone call was made on my mobile phone,* and I should be grateful if you would confirm that I will not be charged for the call.

Yours faithfully,

* you didn't really think I was going to give *you* my number, did you?

This is their reply

Dear Mr Stein

Re Mobile Number-XXX
    Case Number-XXX

Thank you for your letter dated 23 June 2004, which has been passed to me for review and reply.

I am sorry to read of the problems you have experienced regarding the telephone calls made to our Customer Service department on 22 June 2004 and can confirm that there is no charge for dialling 191 from a mobile phone. Please accept my apologies for any inconvenience this may have caused.

If you need any further information please do not hesitate to call our Customer Service department on 08700191191 or you can call 191 free of charge from your mobile phone.

Yours sincerely

It took them a while even to come up with that "in-depth" apology. Maybe I should have texted. But that's what trendy, young people do. I was trying to send my texts by selecting letter after letter with a gap between each one making my messages totally incomprehensible and, indeed, unreadable, at the other end. Then Nicky told me about word recognition and the world of texting became an easier place to inhabit. Until my text recognition switched to German. Nobody, least of all Vodafone, have been able to tell me how to get it back to English; this is a complaint that is only just beginning.

I am quite sure that many of my readers empathise with the Great Telephone Struggle of the 21st Century. Unfortunately we cannot turn the clock back to those merry days of yore when the Industrial Revolution was flourishing in Britain and reactionaries were rampaging the countryside smashing up anything that looked like a machine. But what we can do is to try and buck the system and do our best to ensure that if we are to be ripped off then we go down fighting, so here are my suggestions:

1. When you sign up for a mobile phone or, indeed, a land-line get them to confirm you are getting the best price and are on the cheapest system. Once they've told you that then write to confirm the conversation. If that proves to be untrue then write and complain.

2. Check all your bills and insist on itemised bills. Raise queries and complaints about anything that puzzles you. It may be that you've just forgotten you made the call in question but no harm in asking.

3. Complain about poor reception and cut-off calls.

4. If you can't make your complaint speedily, economically and efficiently then complain about that too.

5. If you're a high user of a mobile phone and they want to charge you for a new phone or an upgrade refuse to pay and threaten to change your company. Generally, it's a very competitive market and they'll give you what you want soon enough.

6. If your phone service is interrupted at home don't forget to take advantage of the credits on your bill that are on offer. They should be made automatically with a certain amount of compensation for each day you are without a phone, but be sure to check and if they've not been made then threaten to charge for your time in doing their job for them.

7. Ensure when you are abroad that you have the most economic server. If you don't, then complain.

8. Look out for hidden charges, such as connection charges, increased rentals etc.

9. If you've been persuaded to abandon BT for a cable company ensure that it really is cheaper and that the service is no less all encompassing. Believe me, I have no axe to grind for BT but they have been around a long time. If you do change and the new supplier fails in comparison with your old supplier then start a paper trail of complaints, just in case they want to start charging you penalties for early disconnection. If you can, before you do change, in whichever direction, see if you can get the new company to agree to a trial period during which you can cancel for nothing.

10. Examine the cost of long-distance calls, collect calls and charge card calls carefully. They can be a major source of complaints.

11. If you call one of these new-fangled directory inquiry numbers, goodness knows what was wrong with 192, don't get enticed into accepting their offer to put you through. They'll charge you. But they don't tell you that they charge you and if by chance you do get inveigled into agreeing and find the charge on your bill, then complain.

As far as phone companies are concerned, take no prisoners. They have no mercy on you. Oh, and always complain when people use their mobiles in restaurants and by the side of swimming pools. Tell the owner or the manager. If enough people complain they might just ban them and think of the dent that will make in the phone company profits.

20

DECKS OF CHAIRS

I've just realised that very little of what has been related in this book has gone on within the Stein household. I wouldn't like to give you the impression that this is a complaint-free zone. Far from it. There was a time when my house was not merely furnished with items that had arrived as a result of complaints, but was positively overflowing with such items to the point that I might have had to move out for lack of space.

To paint the necessary background I have to go back a few years to our first dining room table and chairs. I never cease to tell my children that when I got married our furniture consisted of two deckchairs, one card table and a 26" colour TV. No doubting my sense of priorities or romance there then. It was a big occasion when we had saved up enough money to go out and buy ourselves some proper furniture. Yes, in those days, I actually had to have the money before I bought. Now I find myself having to write books like this just to pay the interest on my credit cards, but don't get me started on credit card companies. I could give them a book of their own.

If my memory serves me correctly, it was Heals in Tottenham Court Rd, who were the lucky recipients of our money when we bought a glass table, with chrome legs and chrome chairs with white leather seats. We are talking about the 1970s, in case you had thought I had totally lost my stylistic mind. We had them for about six weeks when we noticed that, after they had been sat upon for a while, dark lines appeared through the leather. So, I wrote one of my first complaint letters (unfortunately long since consigned to the complaint heap in the sky) and we were invited down to meet a very pleasant gentleman, who was in fact the manager of the store. He saw the chairs, agreed we had been hard done by and exchanged them. This is easy, I thought, I must try this again.

It was John Lewis who gave me the opportunity. Now I have to say I have a lot of respect and, indeed, liking for John Lewis as a store. You have to give a lot of credit to a company who, for so many years, refused to open on a Sunday despite peer pressure, just because they didn't think it was right to open on a Sunday. To go with my new upmarket table and chairs from Heals we decided to order some dining room units. You must know the sort of thing. They are free-standing, with glass upper parts and cupboards at the bottom, within which you store all those items you never use but can't bring yourself to throw away because they were wedding or engagement presents. In our case every time you open one, the debris of our marriage falls out. Leather covered decanters (don't tell me you weren't gifted some of those) tarnished silver cande-labra, vases of various shapes and sizes and, in our case, all my single records and a life-time collection of alcohol.

We once had a burglary in my old house. The bloke broke into the kitchen and stole, as I recall, a fiver and some postage stamps. He left behind a perfect trainer imprint on the window-ledge which was scrubbed away by Nicky, who was then about five and who has never done anything else domestic to this day, because he said, it looked untidy. The purpose of the story (apart from embar-rassing the aforementioned son) was that the police asked if any alcohol had been stolen.

"Oh, no," my wife said hastily, "we hardly drink", at which point the officer opened one of the cupboards to reveal enough bottles of alcohol to stock an average off-licence. The fact of the matter is that so many people who visit bring us bottles that if we consumed them at the same rate as they arrive we would both be fully paid up members of Alcoholics Anonymous. I did start to redistribute them by taking them in to other peoples' dinner parties but gave up on that when I managed to give somebody back a bottle they'd bought us with their note still attached.

Back to John Lewis. At the time we ordered the units we still had the white furniture, although this had been exchanged for a considerably more expensive set, which no longer marked when someone placed a posterior on it for more than thirty seconds. We were the only people in North London whose dinner parties ended before nine o'clock. Mind you, even with the more comfortable furniture that relative affluence has brought (well, really thanks to the much-used credit cards, actually) I still find a temptation to go up and change for bed at ten pm.

Because of the white furniture we ordered units with a white front. They came ... or at least two of them did. The other one came with a black front. In fact the black front looked better. I thought that the black and white effect was good and made the point that the house supported Newcastle United. My wife did not agree. But she did think the black looked better. We contacted John Lewis. They readily agreed to exchange them. Three black units coming up. I told you they were a good company. The three units that we had filled an entire wall in our house. The new units duly came. Unfortunately we were not in so when we arrived home we had six units now filling almost the whole room. Four black, two white. I phoned John Lewis. They were apologetic. They came and removed three units. We now had three black units. Then we noticed one of them had a broken panel at the back. We phoned John Lewis. They apologised. They would deliver a replacement. They did. It was white. We now had three black and one white units. We phoned John Lewis. They apologised. They came and removed the white unit and replaced it with a perfect black one. We now had three, matching, useable black units which looked very nice in contrast to our white table. We had them for many years. What wasn't very nice was the invoice I received from John Lewis for eight units! I wrote to them. We are going back over twenty-five years and even I, hoarder that I am, do not retain my old letters (even the classical complaint ones) that long. It must have been a good letter. They called me. They were apologetic. They raised a credit note for all eight units to compensate for the trouble we had been caused. Which is how we came to furnish the downstairs of our old house for virtually nothing. As I said I'm a real fan of John Lewis's. They are truly a great company.

Now, when it comes to furniture you will probably have saved for it for some considerable time and spent an equally considerable time choosing it. You will also have probably put your marriage at risk with a tumultuous domestic argument in the shop. The point I am making is that you are entitled, not only to get what you want, but to enjoy it to the full when it arrives. These

are some of the problems to watch out for and to complain about
if they happen:

1. Did you get what you ordered or did the shop change some
   specifications, design or even the colour?
2. Did the item appear in a sale within weeks of your purchase at
   full price? If so, write, and if the shop is half-decent they will
   return the difference.
3. Did the shop assistant measure it up properly and if they
   didn't does it still fit in your room?
4. Was the delivery time correct?
5. If you complained about delays in delivery did the shop react
   promptly?
6. When it arrived was it suitable for whatever its use was?
7. Did any problems arise once you started using it?
8. Did any part of it not work or break? Like hinges on doors or
   extensions on a table.
9. Did the shop deal with your complaint sympathetically and
   constructively?
10. If there were problems did they agree to the return of the item
    or offer suitable compensation?

Even if you don't get your house furnished for free hopefully, if
you follow my advice, you will at least end up with furniture rather
then deckchairs and card tables.

21

HI-HO FOR THE OPEN ROAD
(If you have a car, that is)

I think you will have gathered by now that most machinery is a mystery to me. Of all the machines nothing is more mysterious than a car. How do they make them move like that? The only thing I do know about cars is that every so often you have to fill them up with petrol and somewhat less often with oil. I am not one of these blokes who stands admiringly as some monster purrs by me in the road or who will lean over the garden fence to chat to his neighbour about his recently acquired chrome and silver dream car that he lovingly cleans and polishes every Sunday morning. I never clean my car. I rarely clean my car out. That way you can be sure that if you are stuck in traffic you can find something to eat (usually either in the glove compartment or the side pocket and long past its sell-by date). My wife is even worse. I know when she has driven my car by the state of decay of the apple cores she leaves behind or, even worse, the chewing gum, carefully wrapped in a piece of tissue paper.

Just to show my total ignorance of the motor vehicle I once owned a Lancia. It was bright yellow. Now why, you may well ask, does somebody who denies any interest in cars buy a canary yellow Lancia? The answer is that I have no idea. That was a different person in a different time…and possibly even a different country. I was driving home on Christmas Day from my mother-in-law's home. There was an odd scraping noise from beneath the car and steering became very difficult. I put it down to the treacherous icy roads and drove home at about ten miles per hour. My grown-up sons suggest that I always drive at about ten miles per hour. That's unfair and I have speeding points on my licence to prove it. (35 miles per hour in a 30 mile limit. Doesn't that show how reckless I am? Mr Toad, move out of the way. I'm coming through. Toot, toot!) When I woke up in the morning and had a look at my car I could see that the whole of the under chassis was hanging off and scraping along the ground. Hence the noise. It had simply rusted away. The garage guy who arrived after Christmas, looked at it in disbelief and then looked at me with even greater disbelief that I had driven home in it. As it happened I complained to Lancia and they replaced the car.

Since then I've had various misadventures, though astonishingly (and here I'm touching the wooden top of my desk with every part of my anatomy) no accidents. I've also generally been happy with my cars. I've had the lot. A Morris Minor to start that was somewhat surprisingly stolen by an army deserter. What sort of deserter stoops to steal a Morris Minor with signals that flip out of its sides? How embarrassing to be caught. It's a bit like the old Skoda joke, where owners would leave the keys in the ignition hoping the car might be stolen. As it was, the deserter was involved in a police chase through London in my poor old Morris before writing it off. That was when I lost my faith in the accuracy of newspaper reporters when a paper carried the story of a "70 mph police chase". Yeah, right! In my little car. More like a twenty mile per hour chase with the foot flat down to the boards. Only the headline isn't as readable. I didn't know about the Press Complaints Commission then, though even if I had I very much doubt that they would have done anything about it.

I've had famous Friday Rovers, Escorts, Cortinas, Mercedes and finally a love affair with Audis. Until now. Until I met Sean at Audi's Head Office. Now, him I don't like. Sorry, Sean, I did say I would get you into my book but obviously that only works with pretty girls because he told me he'd be talking to their in-house lawyers.

It all started with oil. Bit like most of the latter day Middle-Eastern wars I suppose. Marilyn once asked me to check the oil in her car. I did. What I didn't realise was that oil isn't like petrol. You don't fill it up to the brim. I had taken the boys to Bournemouth for the weekend and she was going to have to go to work and drive down to join us later. In fact as she was driving through Epping Forest, clouds of black smoke began to emanate from the car's exhaust (and her ears when the AA man explained to her what I had done). We spent the weekend apart and she has never asked me to do anything with any of her cars again. Until the other week when she asked me to check the pressure in her tyres and I laughed. In fact we did it together, or rather she did it herself whilst I watched, my sole contribution being to bend my aged knees to unscrew the caps or whatever their technical name is) on the tyres. I can honestly say it was that rare occasion when I got down and got my hands dirty.

So it was with no great confidence that I came to the conclusion that the most recent member of my Audi family was using too much oil. In the past I had never had to put any oil in any Audi I'd owned between services. Given my track record a) with finding the bonnet release, b) with finding the dip-stick, c) working out where the oil went and d), and probably most importantly, calculating the right amount and pouring it in without liberally spreading it over the engine, that was not a conclusion that was likely to bear much weight with the experts, or indeed, anybody who knows me. I always give my cars names. My previous Audi was called Arnie. He was black and powerful, and following in the footsteps of an Audi Turbo called Tommy he did himself proud. As I'm a creature of habit, when it was time to put Arnie out to grass I simply ordered the same again and called him AJ (i.e Arnie Junior) I was rather sad to see Arnie go. The man who delivered AJ put him on the back of his truck and I could swear I could see tears trickling down his headlights as he rounded the corner and out of sight for the final time. I wasn't too dry-eyed myself when I realised I'd left my CDs in the compartment in the boot.

I've never understood why people don't give their cars names. In fact I name every inanimate object I own, which has had psychiatrists and close family members puzzling over me for years.

Returning to AJ and his oil problem, he was slightly different from his predecessor as he had a Triptronic gearbox. (I think I've spelled that right.) I'm not sure what that did but it seemed you just needed to flick the gearstick across and it magically changed gears. Clutches, of course, do exactly the same but they don't seem to be part of any sales pitch nowadays. I can't say the gear changes did a lot for me as I was more concerned about the fact that I no longer had a tape deck in my car (so I couldn't listen to The Archers Omnibuses I religiously record). The result of which was that my wife and I were, at one stage, ten Omnibuses behind, and were reading about fires, adultery and gay kisses in the paper whilst they were still light years away on our listening schedule. Just to show you how sad we've become we tend to listen to the Archers in bed at night.

They'd also reduced the drink holders from two to one (do they think everybody drives alone) and dispensed entirely with map holders of any decent size to hold a standard road map. There's nowhere in the boot to put anything to stop it rolling around and making a sinister noise whilst you're driving, either. I did write to them about all these little matters and they told me they were design improvements. Excuse me? But then they told me lots of other things about my car and none of them were true either.

So, after I'd had the car about three months (please remember that time period, it's important to the story and my dislike of Sean) I found that I had to top the car up with oil after every 500 miles or so. But what was exasperating (apart from the technological challenge of getting the oil into the right place) was that nobody sold the oil that was recommended to be used except Audi. Eventually I told my friendly neighbourhood garage at the top of my road and my mate Dino ordered it for me. In fact he ordered it for me by the dozen, as AJ liked it so much that he kept drinking it. Dino told me it wasn't right and I believed him. He knew about cars. I wrote to Audi.

Audi UK
Yeomans Drive
Blakelands
Milton Keynes MK14 5AN.

Dear Sirs,

Re: Audi 2.4 A4 saloon, registration No. XXX

In February of this year I acquired a new Audi 2.4 A4 saloon having enjoyed three previous Audis that I have owned. However, I have to say that I am, to say the least, disappointed with the new car.

I find that the vehicle needs to be filled with oil almost every 500 miles. The actual oil itself is of a type which is not freely available in normal garages and, on each occasion, I am having to return to my local Audi dealer, Knightsbridge (formerly Scotts) Audi in Victoria, to obtain the same, which is less than convenient. Indeed, having yet again run out of oil (this time the light came on after 400 miles !), I tried to buy some in a specialist auto shop locally. The shop did not sell OW-30 and the shopkeeper could not even find the specifications on the side of the container to enable him to supply me with an alternative.

I also fail to understand why you have designed the vehicle so that a) it does not have a cassette tape deck and b) it only has one cup-holder and c) there is no netting in the rear of the front seats to hold large mapbooks.

Having invested a considerable amount of money in a vehicle of this nature, I do feel that these are items that should have been considered by yourselves and I look forward to hearing from you with your comments at your earliest convenience.

Yours faithfully,

They suggested some alternate oils. None of the garages I went to for petrol sold those either. Dino continued to be my saviour. Audi also told me that the oil problem would clear up once the car had received its first service. First services ain't what they used to be. Do you remember those days when you had to drive carefully for the first 500 miles whilst the engine bedded in (or in the case of my Lancia rusted away) and then you had a service and then another at 1000 miles and so on and so on? Not any more. You have to wait until a little man comes onto your dashboard display and tells you it's time. It's almost Messianic in its tension.

I got tired of waiting.

Re: Audi 2.4 A4 saloon, registration No. XXX

I refer to our correspondence last year.

Whilst I have still not had a first service on my vehicle, I am still experiencing excessive oil consumption.

I have taken the car to the main Audi dealers both in Victoria and at H.R. Owen in the Edgware Road. The latter garage told me that they had checked the vehicle and could not see that there was any leakage but would not know whether or not there was any problem until after the first service which they could not do until I had done 18,000 miles. At present, I have done some 14,000 miles, even though I have owned the car for some 16 months.

H.R. Owen told me that the warning light comes on when the oil is about one-third empty. They said that I was possibly over-filling by using an entire litre. I therefore merely used about half a litre when the oil light came on and after 60 miles it came on again. I really cannot believe this is right and it is costing me substantial sums in purchasing the oil directly from a local garage as I simply can't find it anywhere in any ordinary garage such as BP or Shell.

I really do feel that this needs a full diagnostic test by your main specialist garage and I should be grateful if you would let me have a referral.

Yours sincerely,

I wrote again on 28th April 2003, again on the 25th November, after which they agreed to carry out an oil test. I took the car in, it was duly tested and they told me there was nothing wrong with it. I didn't believe them. The quantity of oil I was chucking down AJ's throat was equivalent to Popeye's consumption of spinach. I wrote and told them I wasn't happy but I would wait until the first service. Eventually that came around. Part of the benefit was that AJ returned squeaky clean as my nice Audi main dealer H. R. Owen (and more about them later), always clean the car before they return it to you. Within 700 miles of the service I was topping AJ up again. I wrote to Audi once more. This time they told me that, because of the Triptronic system it would use more oil than usual and hadn't I read that in the handbook? I pointed out that when I ordered the car I hadn't had the benefit of the handbook as it came with the car. In fact it didn't come with the car and they had to send it on, as I recall. I have to admit that handbooks and instruction books are not my cup of tea anyway. The only time I ever opened the handbook was to see what some light or other meant when it flashed on and off on my dashboard (like if it means the car will explode in five minutes, abandon ship, I suppose you should be aware of the significance of the little man leaping up and down with a sign that flashes danger in red letters). Oh, and I did need recourse to it to work out how to open the bonnet, and then further recourse to work out how the oil went in. Apart from that I am blissfully unaware of what came with the car or how it works or indeed if it is working at all.

I persisted and eventually they agreed to test it again. I left the car whilst they drained the oil, refilled it and then took it back when I'd done another 620 miles (don't ask, that's what they told me to do and I did it). They apparently weighed the oil and said I'd be hearing from them, after they had sent the results of the tests to Audi. Audi, head office that is, and not the garage up north from which, and for reasons that I don't need to bore you with here, I had bought it. After a few days they phoned me. AJ had failed his big test. Would I bring him in as he needed a new engine. I pointed out he'd only done 25,000 miles. He was still a baby. This would be a major operation. They would need him for several days. He'd never been away from home for that length of time. They then told me they couldn't do the operation right away as they couldn't get the parts from Audi and therefore I booked him into hospital for some three weeks time.

It was then I started thinking. I'd been right all along. Maybe I do have the makings of a mechanic. Who was to say this would work and anyway did I really want to be driving a car that had needed an engine replacement after such a short period of time, and indeed had probably needed it from day one? I wrote to Audi and told them that they should replace the car (I didn't know what I'd call the new little fellow) and reimburse me for the hundreds (literally) of pounds I had spent on oil.

And that was when Sean came on the scene. He's the Customer Service Manager at Audi in Walsall. He phoned me and left a message. I called him back at 4.55 pm. I was told he left at 5.00 pm. I pointed out he had five minutes to go. I was then told he was on the phone. Needless to say he didn't call me back. Obviously he had things to do which were more pressing than my car that needed a new engine.

He did call back and I called him. He didn't call back. So I called him again. And a third time. I was told that my call might be recorded for quality control. I was pleased about that. Eventually Sean and I spoke. I told him I'd been trying to get hold of him. He told me he'd been very busy. That did not endear him to me any more than his opening gambit which was:

"We're not going to replace the car."

"Why not?" I asked.

"It's too old," Sean said.

"It wasn't too old when I first started complaining about it." (Back in August 2002, if you'll recall, was the first letter) and nor was I, I thought, though I was beginning to feel it.

Sean cocked a deaf'un to that.

"Well, we're not going to replace it and that's that. We may do something ex gratia on the oil cost."

"Ex bloody gratia. You're obliged to do something."

We exchanged mutual threats. I told him that I was a solicitor, always calculated to get the dander up of anybody who's not. He told me he'd spoken to their in-house legal bloke. And that was where you came in on the story. I reckon the in-house legal bloke (who I never actually dealt with, by the way) must be busy if the likes of Sean were forever running off to him to tell tales about nasty men who wanted their duff cars replaced. In fact why would you need an in-house legal bloke if your product was perfect ? Big bad Sean (who tried to be very scary) said my contract was with the original garage from which I bought AJ and I should write to them and they would then pass the complaint on to Audi Head Office and it would doubtless return to the desk of the charming Sean and his anonymous in-house legal adviser. I asked to speak to the Manager. Sean told me he was the Manager, though I had my doubts. I told him that it didn't seem right to me to be driving up and down motorways in a car whose engine had been condemned. He told me it wasn't dangerous. I asked him if he was sure of that and could I have his word. That stopped him in his tracks and he said he'd check it out. I heard no more on the subject. So presumably Sean would have been quite happy to see me disappear in a cloud of combustion. In fact I didn't, as this book testifies, but I suspect this was no thanks to Sean.

I tried to persuade Sean that Audi had made the car. He accepted it had an "inherent fault" but he could not be moved, saying that it was irrelevant. Sean couldn't be moved. He had his rules. That was the way they did it there. He was like Lissa with two esses but without the charm. It was then he said something that threw me off my trolley.

"If you are a lawyer then you should know that the contract's between you and the garage."

If? *If?* And even if it is he'd told me himself that the garage was going to refer it back to him. "OK," I said, "I'll be writing to you." "Don't write to me," he said, "write to the garage." I decided to have the final word.

"And I don't want a new engine. I want a new car. You'll be hearing from me."

It didn't have the same ring as "you'll be hearing from my solicitor," but then I was my solicitor.

I decided to write to the garage (I forgot to ask them if they had found the CDs I'd left in Arnie) and tell them all about Sean, and I wrote to him too.

Re: Audi 2.4 A4 saloon, registration No. XXX

Further to our telephone conversation, I enclose a copy letter that I have sent to Massingberd Audi. I have to tell you that I have written this on an entirely without prejudice basis as I still maintain that you at Audi are fully responsible for my vehicle.

I must say I took the strongest objection to your attitude and, for you to say that my vehicle was "too old" to replace when I had been complaining about it since it was some three months old, is nothing short of an insult to my intelligence.

Yours sincerely,

I got a very supportive letter back from the garage who had sold me the car but, before Audi bothered to answer, it was time for AJ to undergo his operation. I took him in on Monday morning and they gave me a much smaller car by way of a loan. He (or she) had no personality and was not even worthy of a name. I told the garage I was going away for the weekend and needed AJ back Friday morning. It would take a few days and they were aiming at Thursday, but Friday should not be a problem. As it transpired it was a problem. On Thursday morning I asked my PA to call the garage to enquire as to AJ's health. They had just put his engine back and they were not confident he would be ready until late Friday afternoon. I then called, spoiling for a fight. I told them the car had to be ready by 9.00 because I was going away and if it wasn't ready I was going to go and take AJ's younger brother (or sister) with me. They didn't seem to like that. They told me the loan car had to be back by Friday whatever time AJ was ready. I asked them how they intended enforcing that. I could just see me bombing along up the M40 in the loan car with a train of police cars in pursuit, having been advised by the garage that it had been stolen by a mad complainer.

They did. The work was finished. He had to have one final check, then be road-tested, and although this would take a while they were confident it would be ready by midday. As luck would have it (for them) my wife had to go to work in the morning so we wouldn't be leaving at nine. It was almost the first time I'd been grateful to the hospital where she worked. I wasn't grateful when her on-call phone went off at midnight on the Thursday, so I woke on Friday in not the best of moods. This did not improve when the garage phoned me. They had installed the new engine. I told them again that I considered this rather a waste of time as I was going to try to make Audi give me a new car. They were non-committal. I suspected they agreed with me if only to get me off their back. The news was even worse. The operation had not been a success. The new engine that Audi had sent had a faulty water system and AJ was now leaking. I would have hoped that by nearly two and a half he would have been toilet trained but not a bit of it. And here were Audi telling me he was too old to be replaced. How absurd!

I think you can guess what I did next. I had to go away for the weekend with the tiny loan car, two passengers, their luggage and food. It was not a comfortable journey. Nor was the further complaint letter that I wrote to everybody.

Re: Audi 2.4 A4 saloon, registration No. XXX

Further to my letter of the 21st April, to which I have not received the courtesy of a reply, I duly took my vehicle in to H.R. Owen for the engine to be replaced (entirely on a without prejudice basis pending your replacement of my vehicle with a new car).

I needed the car for the weekend, as I had arranged to go away with my family. I was therefore appalled to learn that, even though the engine had been re-fitted, H R Owen had been supplied by you with a defective water pump attached to the engine which meant that water continued to leak when the vehicle was road-tested and was therefore unsuitable to be returned to me.

I was therefore forced to retain the loan vehicle (an A3, not an A4) for the weekend. My 81-year-old mother-in-law had to travel in the rear of this vehicle, surrounded by luggage as the miniscule boot could not accommodate the items that we needed to take away with us. Entry in and out of the car was virtually impossible for her.

I was not able to conduct my business during the course of the drive (or, indeed, during the course of the whole week) as the vehicle was not fitted with a hands free telephone unit, nor indeed was I able to open the sunroof of the vehicle as it did not have one. I have now been told that the vehicle will not be ready until Wednesday of this week, at the earliest.

It is quite clear that there are going to be continuing problems with this vehicle and, once again, I must demand that you replace the vehicle with a new substitute car. It is totally unacceptable that I am paying the full leasing payment for a vehicle that has only done 25,000 miles but which has already had to have its engine replaced, apparently without any guarantee that the problems will not continue to arise.

I look forward to hearing from you within the next seven days to avoid further action.

Yours sincerely,

Eventually, after the Bank Holiday, I was phoned by H.R.Owen to be told my car was ready. I could collect it at my convenience. I couldn't wait. My mother-in-law had experienced so many problems in getting in and out of the loan car that there was every chance I would be returning it with her still stuck in the back seat. It was an emotional experience seeing AJ again. We'd been parted for so long that when I was asked for his registration number at H.R Owen I couldn't remember it. But finally there he was all shining and squeaky clean. I felt guilty that I still had the intention of complaining to Audi until they replaced him.

Off we drove to Stevenage and back. Or nearly back. I turned off the M25 on to the A111 (you see, you get geography lessons for the price of this book as well) and there, just by the West Lodge Park Hotel (famous for Cup Final teams staying there in the past) AJ broke down. I was incandescent with rage. I was trying to get home for the Newcastle v Marseille UEFA Cup Semi-Final and had no intention of listening to the game on my car radio as I stood by the roadside. I phoned H.R. Owen and spoke to the service manager, called James. I don't think he really wanted to be in this book. But then, I don't think Michael or Bevan, the other two service people I had spoken to wanted to be either. There you go. We don't always get what we want, as Mick Jagger sang so many years ago. Not that there was anything he wanted that HE didn't get.

James said he would phone the RAC. I told him that wasn't good enough. I wanted someone there within ten minutes or else I was leaving the car by the side of the road with a note to the police telling them that it had been abandoned by James of H.R. Owen in the Edgware Road. James didn't seem to fancy that idea either and told me that he would not be responsible if I left the vehicle. I told him not to threaten me. I was not in the mood for threats. He then tried to placate me. That was marginally worse. I then spoke to my son who told me we didn't kick-off until eight o'clock and that did placate me. It was 5.30 pm. I was only a couple of miles from home. All would be well. I may seem to have said something nasty about H.R. Owen and thus broken my promise but believe me they did redeem themselves ... and in spades. Michael and Bevan there, are heroes and they didn't even sell me the car in the first place!

At 5.45 I'd not heard from the RAC and so I rang them myself. They put me on hold and played music. "It's a Beautiful Day ..." It wasn't. Eventually I spoke to them and was told help was on its way and would take about 25 minutes. Meanwhile interesting things were happening with the traffic. The A111 or the Cockfosters Road is the main road that leads south from the motorway. It is single lane either way. I was blocking one lane. It was the rush-hour. I was also at the junction of a side-road. Nobody exiting from that road could see the oncoming traffic as I hid their view. Nothing could overtake me heading south unless there was a break in the traffic heading north towards the motorway. That doesn't happen too often in the London rush-hour. People began to recognise me. A taxi-driver friend offered me a lift home. I was tempted to accept the offer. A bloke I didn't know stopped and offered me a push. He went off to park his car, returned and then told me that, as AJ was automatic, he couldn't be pushed. You live and learn. Not only have I learned how to open the bonnet of the car, to put in oil (frequently) but I also now know that automatic vehicles can't be pushed. I must be nearly qualified to pass a course in car maintenance by now.

Some cars which had passed me on the way north, cheerily waved as they returned heading south. The line of traffic grew ever longer. I am told I was featured as an incident on the traffic reports on the radio. Drivers grew ever more irritable. I put on a pair of sunglasses, seeking anonymity. More friends still recognised me, stopped for a chat and added to the tailbacks. It was growing cold. James rang me regularly. I gave him a countdown to kick-off. He promised not to leave until I was on my way home (I told you H.R. Owen would come out of this well). That was encouraging. We could chat to each other as the game progressed.

My mobile rang. It was Dominic from the RAC. He was now only a few moments away. Could I tell him exactly where I was? Just drive till you get to the traffic chaos, I told him, that'll be me. My mobile rang again. It was another friend who'd just passed me by, my cricket captain, in fact. Was there anything he could do and would I be home by Sunday to enable me to play? My phone rang again. At least I wasn't getting bored. This time it was my bank manager, who actually lived locally and wondered if I'd like him to come and pick me up. Now that's what I call a banking service.

Dominic arrived and so did my wife. She tried to calm me down and didn't seem to think that Newcastle in Europe was the most important thing on the agenda. Dominic decided that the car was beyond roadside repair (actually I think he feared for his life as the drivers in the queue were getting beyond aggressive). He towed me back home, used his diagnostic computer and said that it showed nothing. That, in itself, was a problem. I called James to report that I was home. He didn't seem as excited as I was that I was going to see my match. He would not be in on Friday but he would leave a message saying that I was to have a replacement car delivered as early as possible. I told him that if it was going to be the A3 again, he needn't bother. Not even if he wanted to return my mother-in-law. He assured me that it would be the equivalent of my car, namely an A4, 2.4 with a sun-roof. I hate air-conditioning and always drive with the roof open.

By nine on Friday morning I had heard nothing. I called H.R. Owen and left a message for Bevan to call me at home. He called me on my mobile. They were sending out an Audi diagnostic man called Louie. Just in case they couldn't get my car working they were also sending another loan car. Within sixty seconds of him calling, the phone rang again. It was Audi Roadside Assistance just to tell me Louie was on his way and would be with me by 11.00 am Another minute passed and the phone rang again. This time it was Louie himself. He was in the Finchley Road. I gave him detailed directions to my house. It was obviously going to be a busy morning.

My front door bell rang. Louie, I thought. Not a bit of it. This was Pete. He was also an Audi diagnostic man. Louie was not far behind. Louie's coming was fast, turning into the arrival of the Messiah and when another Audi diagnostic van turned up and parked I expected to hear heraldic trumpets followed by Nessun Dorma singing me a heavenly chorus. To my astonishment a third car arrived. This was Steve from H.R. Owen with my loan car. Obviously, in James's absence, their understanding of an equivalent vehicle was not the same as mine. What they had supplied was an Audi Estate 1.8, without a sun roof, in a rather ghastly shade of blue.

Louie and Pete went to work on AJ. Steve sat in the blue monstrosity and listened to the radio. Between them they had so much technology that they could have been tuning in to a satellite spy station. Brian Hanrahan (who counted them all out and counted them all in so famously) lives opposite me and I was half expecting to hear him reporting from Baghdad. The technology was all to no avail. AJ had other faults that were revealed, such as a problem with the water coolant system (that would have been fun as I overheated, bombing along a motorway with Sean sticking pins into my effigy) and they needed to take him away. They proposed leaving me with Bluey. I declined. I spoke to Bevan. I got the impression he was on the brink of losing it with me. That would have been a shame. He was a Kiwi and I'd told him when we first met how nice I thought New Zealanders were. I told Bevan I wanted the same car. He said he didn't have one and that he'd given me the nearest he had. I said I would go and hire one then. He said I could. I told him that I would expect H.R. Owen to pay for it. He said they wouldn't. The conversation became a little heated and he got just that one step closer to forgetting I was the customer and as such was always right. I just love that expression, don't you? It goes straight to the heart of the basis of complaining.

Eventually he accepted that I was justified (at least, I think he did as it was hard to understand what with the Kiwi accent and the clenched teeth) and would see what he could do to get me an exact replacement by the end of the day. Steve drove AJ away more than a little nervously, particularly after I had told him the history of his problems. Louie and Pete went on their merry way having got very excited when I told them they were going to appear in this book. They asked if I wanted to take their photos. Again as part of the complaint process I decided I ought to reduce the series of incidents to paper. Oh, and by the way, Newcastle lost. The referee failed to give us a blatant penalty for handball. I thought about writing a complaint letter and decided against it. I was too busy concentrating on Audi.

At about five o'clock Steve reappeared. This time he was driving an Audi 2.5 Quattro. This was better. It still had no sun-roof, it still had nowhere to fix my mobile phone, but it was better. There was just one thing. He wanted me to sign a form saying that I had to

225

agree to a £250 insurance excess. Bevan had bullied Audi UK into providing the car and this was their standard practice. I pointed out that I had no excess on my insurance and that I was only having to drive another car because Audi couldn't make my car better so why should I have to pay any excess. Bevan was not happy. He had obviously been delighted by the outcome of his efforts and I didn't want to seem unappreciative of them either. So, I signed under protest and wrote again.

By Tuesday nothing had cropped up with AJ despite extensive tests. Bevan told me that Audi UK wanted the loan car back by Friday. I said they were only getting it if H. R. Owen were able to find the fault on my car and could rectify it. Then, on Thursday they had a break-through. The engine light had come on during testing and they thought it might be electrical. They would continue to work on it and I could keep the car.

Massingberd Audi wrote to me and said they weren't interested (despite selling me the car in the first place) as I'd never brought the car to them to be serviced. I wrote back pointing out that they were in Yorkshire whilst I was in London, some 250 miles away, so no surprise there then. However, they weren't my target. They were a sub-plot introduced by the main protagonists themselves, namely Audi UK. They themselves also wrote to me offering an extended 12-month warranty on the car. As you will see from my reply I was under-whelmed. I'd given up on Sean and was now focussing on a lady called Jessica.

Re: Audi 2.4 A4 saloon, registration No. XXX

Thank you for your letter of the 7th May. To say that the facts contained in your letter are selective is an understatement.

I did indeed only contact Audi UK Customer Service in August 2002, but I had previously been complaining to the garages where the car had been taken for services, namely Audi in Victoria and H.R. Owen.

I cannot accept the accuracy of the oil consumption test carried out in May 2003. If it were accurate, why did I need to have a new engine installed in April 2004 ?

I have virtually not seen my car for a month now. After I had

had it for one day after the new engine was installed, as you are aware from my previous letter, it had to be taken back to H.R. Owen. They have been road testing it and I was telephoned last Thursday to be told that the engine management light had come on and was telephoned again on Friday by the most helpful Michael at H.R. Owen who told me that there was a fault with the secondary FO system (whatever that may be) and that the engine management light continues to come on. So far they have not been able to ascertain the reason why I lost power on the first day I had the vehicle and, until they do ascertain that, I am not prepared to take the vehicle back and run the risk of breaking down on the motorway.

I was told early last week that Audi UK wanted the return of the loan car that I had and I made it quite clear that I am not prepared to return this vehicle until such time as I have a problem-free car back from Audi. I am now quite convinced that my vehicle will never be returned to me problem-free. I am continuing to pay all the leasing payments on it and the situation is totally unacceptable.

I cannot believe that you do not see fit to apologise for providing me with a loan vehicle that was totally unsuitable for my needs. Even the vehicle I currently have, an Audi 2.5 Quattro (like for like), does not have a sunroof and, further, and far more inconveniently, it does not have a hands-free telephone kit which I require for my business.

Returning to your offer of the 12-month extended warranty, as I say, I fail to see what good this does me when I lease the vehicle anyway and all repairs are paid for by the leasing company. What good would the warranty do me if I were to break down on a motorway (which seems to be highly likely given the problems which continue to arise with my vehicle)?

At present, I have no faith in the Audi brand. As I have told you before, this was the third consecutive Audi I have purchased and the only one with which I have had any problems. Why can you not see that there are inherent defects with this vehicle which mean that it should be replaced?

Let me assure you that I am not going to go away and nor am I to be fobbed off with hollow offers.

I am quite happy to have a meeting with yourselves if you want to discuss this matter further with a view to resolving the issue.

Yours sincerely,

On the following Thursday I finally got AJ back. I decided to write to my friends at Audi one more time, pointing out that at the very least they seemed to have forgotten their "ex-gratia" offer of reimbursing me for the cost of the excess oil I had used. But I was still determined to get a car that had not had an engine replacement before its third birthday. However, within days the light was back on my car, I was driving another loan car, had written two more letters to Jessica as new and interesting warning lights had erupted onto my dashboard and, oddly enough, there was not even a description of what they signified in the handbook.

I had gone beyond the boundaries of the handbook and also the boundaries of Jessica as our old friend Sean replied to my letters to her (after a suitable three week delay) to tell me "Jessica has moved to another department". I bet she had ... and with alacrity I wouldn't wonder. It was at that point I felt the need to introduce some new characters into the plot.

On the 1st June 2004 I wrote to Audi Finance from whom I leased the car and, even if I say so myself, that was an inspirational, seminal moment in the saga. After a minor skirmish I found myself dealing with an excellent gentleman called Alan. He seemed both sympathetic and receptive to my arguments and, whilst Massingberd Audi by now felt the need to instruct their lawyers to get rid of me, Alan was coolness itself. It did take two more visits of my car to H.R. Owen and two more loan cars (I do feel I now have a book in me about the Audi range of vehicles) but eventually Alan came good and we came to terms over the replacement of AJ with a brand new vehicle. I met another nice man called Paul, who was the manager at H.R. Owen and he agreed to try to source me the vehicle of my choice. Suddenly I was once again singing the praises of Audi. I felt like writing to Sean whatever and saying "yah, boo, sucks, I told you I'd get a new car," but triumphalism is just not my style. However, before I could celebrate there was to be another twist in the tail.

I went on a business trip to the States in mid-June, 2004. The light had come on in my car yet again. The long-suffering and ever patient Michael at H.R. Owen agreed to pick up AJ and have him made well and returned to me so he'd be waiting when I got back and he was true to his word.

I drove AJ on Thursday and Friday and then on Sunday the light came on again. I phoned Michael. I took the car in on Monday. I asked where my desk was as I was spending more time in their office than my own. I met Paul. The poor man seemed positively delighted to see me. I seemed to have acquired a bit of a reputation. I did point out to him that it was fortunate that Michael Winner preferred Rolls-Royces to Audis. Well, he would, wouldn't he?

Paul and his Finance Director, Tom (is there anyone in Audi's great all-encompassing family I've not yet met?) helped me fill in some forms, confirmed that there was one solitary model available of the car of my choice, that it was in Germany but would be with me in a week or so. While I was with him the technical team ran my car through the computer, found the fault was the same one as before, thought they had rectified it and I drove away happy in the knowledge that the nightmare was nearly over. Then on Wednesday morning I got stopped by the police. My reverse lights were on. I pointed out to the policeman that this was not possible as I was driving in a forward direction. He was insistent. He had seen what he had seen. He told me to get my car to a garage as soon as possible and couldn't understand my hysterical laughter that came as a response. I phoned H.R. Owen. Poor Michael had been carted off to hospital with a cyst, so the unfortunate Bevan had to deal with me. I told him I was coming to Edgware on Thursday and would drop it in. He expressed no surprise. However, fate once again intervened. On Wednesday night I went to a meeting and parked my car outside, I returned to AJ a couple of hours later and he refused to go into reverse. I finally persuaded him, revved up and we jolted backwards. I repeated the process for drive and then decided this was not a good idea and went off to phone the RAC. It was a wet and windy summer's night in London and as I was waiting in the dry and warm I did not seem to be a priority. I was told that it would take about an hour to get to me.

There was football on the telly and I decided after a while to try again. I got AJ started this time and thought I'd take a chance and try to drive him home. It was a sad journey as we both knew that this was the last time we would journey together. He would go to the Audi graveyard, I to a new glamorous vehicle. It was only when I got him home that the imminent parting became even sadder. Whilst I'd been parked the car had been keyed all along one side and had the word "shot" scratched several times on his paintwork … once misspelled by the way. I had wanted to shoot AJ myself at times but we are what we are made and AJ could not be held responsible for his own manufacture nor his sad end. However, to add insult to injury, Paul Greenberg did ask if I had claimed on my insurance. You can imagine my reaction. In fact, there's no need to imagine it because here's the letter I wrote.

Audi Finance
Brunswick Court
Yeomans Drive
Blakelands
Milton Keynes MK14 5LR.
Dear Mr. Duckett,

Re: Audi Saloon A4 registration No. XXX

Further to our innumerable conversations, you might be interested to learn that I was stopped by the police yesterday morning, when driving in, because it appears that the reverse lights are permanently on in my car! Fortunately, they did accept my explanation of the problems with the vehicle but they did warn me that I should not be driving with the car in that state.

Later in the afternoon, I drove to a meeting. Upon returning to the car, I found it would not go into gear. I left the car and called the RAC. They said they would be 1 hour. I waited. Eventually, I gave up and returned to the car and found it vandalised.

I finally managed to get the car into gear and drove home by fits and starts and then called the RAC again. Another hour's wait. Eventually, someone came and told me he could not fix it and he thought it was a gearbox problem.

Enough is enough! I have called H.R. Owen today and told them to collect the car once and for all. I have had to cancel my meetings out of town as I just can't get there without a car. I have had to phone my insurers to be told I have a £220 excess to repair a car I shouldn't even have been forced to drive.

H.R. Owen are trying to source me another car today but that will be too late for my purposes.

I think you will understand when I say that I have just about come to the end of my tether with this catastrophic vehicle.

In any event, I confirm that we have now agreed that you will be supplying me with a brand new vehicle to the specifications discussed on the telephone and that I will be charged my current leasing rate for the balance of my current leasing period and this will then increase by £18 per month.

I believe you have agreed in principle to the reimbursement to me of the cost of the excessive oil I have been using over the last two and a half years and I have dealt with that amount in earlier correspondence. I also enclose copies of the latest Congestion Charge payments I had to expend in addition to my normal payment on my current vehicle because I was using a loan car. We also need to discuss the insurance claim I now unfortunately need to make.

I am sure that you, like me, will breathe a sigh of relief when this saga is brought to a conclusion.

Yours faithfully,

The gallant Michael had returned to work from hospital and he arranged for AJ to be collected from my drive during the day on Friday. I left the key hidden outside and fully expected him to be gone by the time I got home. It would be less painful that way. But when I did make it to my front drive he was still sitting there, sad and accusing. Eventually, just as England ran out onto the pitch in Lisbon to face their fateful opposition in Euro 2004, in the shape of Portugal, some unfortunate guy came to drive AJ away and delivered to me yet another loan car. There were three more loan cars after that whilst I awaited AJ's replacement, I calculated that, including the cars I had refused, Audi must have supplied me with over ten cars during this period. Good call from Sean to take the stance he did at the start of the debate.

So that was it. Two and a half football seasons, one World Cup, one European Championship, innumerable letters, a host of characters from Audi (most, apart from Sean, rather likeable) and the RAC, not to mention two garages and the odd law firm, phone calls, threats, enough visits to H.R. Owen to justify the charge of some rent, eleven loan cars and finally I was getting what I should have had three months into my ownership of AJ ... a new car. Was it all worth it? I think so. Justice, in my view, was served. The good guy (that's me, by the way, if you've lost track of the plot) won. They reimbursed me for everything; oil, congestion charges, lease payments and insurance excess. And I got enough material for one of the longer chapters in this book.

So if you buy or lease a car these are some of the issues about which you can and should complain, sooner rather than later:

1. Does the car fit the specifications of the vehicle you ordered? If you wanted a multi-change CD player don't settle for a single action one.
2. Is the car using too much petrol or oil? If it is then don't be fobbed off with technical excuses. Put your concerns in writing at an early stage. The same old story of creating a paper trail.
3. If your car is persistently off the road then demand a replacement vehicle whether it's part of your deal or not.
4. If the fault seems to you to be unrectifiable then ask for the vehicle to be replaced.
5. If you make no progress with the garage from whom you bought the vehicle then go to the car manufacturer.
6. Never make a threat that you won't carry through. If you tell the garage you'll go to the manufacturing company then do so. If you tell the manufacturing company you'll go to the press then do so. You can only make a hollow threat once. If you're caught out in a bluff then you can't bluff again.
7. If you feel there are design faults on a car then tell the manufacturer. They may just be grateful and you never know what they might offer you.

8. If you have a problem with the first car you buy of a particular make then complain in the most effective way and don't buy another car of that brand. Don't forget in my Audi story AJ was the third Audi I'd had and I'd been really happy with the first two so felt it worthwhile giving them another chance with a fourth. I bet Michael and Bevan, the kool Kiwis at H.R. Owen are really delighted with the prospect of having me as a customer for the next three years at least. They are probably saving up right now for the return fares to New Zealand.

22

DOLPHINS ARE NEARLY HUMAN AND COMPUTERS POSITIVELY ARE

I promised my wife that I'd keep this book clean so let's talk about showers and bathrooms. Oh, and bathroom floors whilst we're about it. It was some five years ago that my wife decided that our bathroom needed a face-lift. I suppose I should have been grateful that she didn't decide that it was her who needed the face-lift. As I think you would already have realised it was unlikely that I would have noticed the state of the domestic washing arrangements. There could have been mould and mushrooms living side by side, but as long as the cold tap produced cold water and the hot tap complemented it nicely by producing hot water, I would never have commented. Men are like that. Well, at least most of the men I know.

Now, I am a simple soul. I read the colour supplements of the Sunday papers, see the glossy pictures of patios, kitchens and bedrooms and truly believe that, with the flick of a magic wand and with the flash of a cheque or credit card, they could be transported perfectly to my own humble household. Naïve me. I know now, and I'm sure you've discovered long ago, that it just doesn't work like that. For a start, you don't get the glamorous models and endless sunshine that seem to be a part of every such advertisement. And then, of course, your house is not the virgin territory where these glossy pictures are always shot. Your house has probably endured, and may well continue to endure, children.

I can't remember which came first, the desire for the bathroom or the attractive advertisement, which, as I recall it, was also linked with a special offer. I love "special offers". They lure you on to the rocks like the sirens of old. Three for two books at airports where you end up buying three books you'll never read instead of the one you might have thumbed your way through on the beach. In any event, from the moment my wife saw the pretty pictures of the bathroom to come our old bathroom was doomed.

The man duly came from Dolphin Showers, actually I think it was a woman. He/she looked at our existing bathroom, shook their heads in dismay, then nodded in acknowledgement of our decision to replace it. There was much talk of colour schemes, whirlpools, etc and eventually it appeared that they would gut my prehistoric facilities, install the new bath and sinks, design the room into which they would be transplanted, but it would be our responsibility to get in our own builder to decorate and tile the same. They would have to have access to the pipes beneath the floor but they would "make the floor good".

They came, they worked to their time-schedule. They installed a beautiful bath and spa and things could not have gone more smoothly. My wife was happy, I was delighted that she was happy and we were getting ready to recommend Dolphin to all our friends as the company who managed to make the dream pictures of beautiful rooms into reality. Well, almost, because all we had was me and the missus and not a trace of the half-dressed models in the adverts. But then, you can't have everything.

They left. And they left behind an uneven floor with floorboards that squeaked so much they over-rode the noise of the toilet flushing. Believe it or not, I complained. My wife made me. Well, at least that's my excuse. Unfortunately, she'd signed a certificate of completion. I say unfortunately, but in reality all she'd acknowledged was that the work had been completed. It had. It just hadn't been completed properly. I love it when I think like a lawyer. A whole world of semantic nit-picking just rolls out before your very eyes.

Dolphin came back like a shot. They seemed to do everything very quickly. They referred me to their terms of trading, which were, indeed, set out on the back of their contract. Within them it was stated that the "structure, condition and suitability of the property" was our responsibility. They wanted me to pay them the balance of their contract, all of £930. I declined. They gave me seven days. I had the feeling that at the end of that seven day period they didn't intend nominating me as "The Dolphin Customer of the Month". But I do so hate ultimatums. Unless I'm giving them, that is. In any event, I wasn't worried. Marilyn had signed the contract and it was her that they were threatening to sue, not me.

I re-read all the papers. They had sent a surveyor. I assumed the surveyor knew what he was doing and would not have allowed them to proceed without the property being suitable. In my view (and back to semantics again) it was only going to be suitable if they were going to be able to do a perfect job. Floorboards that played Beethoven's Ninth when you tread on them and a slope to the floor that required a ski-lift to ascend, did not equate to perfection in my book.

I wrote back to Dolphin.

I got my builder to inspect the work. He shook his head and tutted in very much the same way as the Dolphin man, or lady, had done when they had first visited us. I called in a surveyor and he wasn't impressed either.

Dolphin then threatened to sue me, or rather my wife. Their Operations Controller, was getting very hot under her collar. She needed to take a nice, cold shower to calm her down. The relationship seemed to be deteriorating rapidly and I threatened to sue them back. (The last resort reached at a very early stage – I told you Dolphin did everything quickly)

Re: Contract No. XXXX

I am in receipt of your letter of the 22nd February. Would you please cease communicating with my wife and have the courtesy to write to me? I appreciate that she may well have signed the contract but this was simply because she was at home and I was not.

Whether or not major building work is required to the floor in the bathroom is an irrelevance. You sent a surveyor to inspect the bathroom. I assume that he inspected the floor. At no time were we told that there was a problem with the floor and indeed, if you look at the Agreement, it specifically says that you will "make good the floor". This is quite unambiguous and anybody, even having a cursory inspection of the bathroom, would have realised that there was a problem with the floor. We did not think there were going to be major building works but we did think that you would be able to carry out works to ensure that there was no longer any movement in the floorboards.

If you look at your own Terms and Conditions, you specifically say in Clause 3 that "if it becomes apparent that the installation has been under-priced beyond the reasonable expectation of the agent ... the company will inform the customer within ten working days after the survey was undertaken and give written reasons".

Your workmen obviously were aware of the problems with the floor (as indeed must have been your surveyor) and nobody contacted us. Had they done so, we could have considered whether or not we would have agreed any revised price or indeed whether we wished to terminate the contract.

Given that you had a lengthy survey, it is clearly implied that the premises were suitable for the installation as to "structure and condition".

I must make it absolutely clear that we would not have considered spending such a substantial amount of money on the bathroom had we thought that it would not be finished to a reasonable standard and, with the floor as it is, this is not a reasonable standard.

I can only repeat that you have an obligation to "make good" the floor.

I have tried to contact you today by telephone with a view to endeavouring to resolve these matters. However, if you wish to issue proceedings in the Small Claims Court, so be it. I must make it quite clear that these will be strenuously defended and will be subject to a counter-claim within the limits of the Small Claims Court.

You are, of course, fully aware that you will not be able to recover costs and, as I am a solicitor myself, the question of costs does not concern me.

I do hope that you will have the courtesy to return my call so that we can endeavour to resolve this matter one last time amicably before things get too out of hand.

Yours sincerely,

Meanwhile, my builder thought he could rid us of the squeak and reduce the slope to acceptable levels. He would, not unpredictably, charge us for the privilege. Eventually Dolphin saw sense, but not before I had to write several more letters to the doubtless delightful Operations Controller, culminating in my letter of 24th May 2000.

Re: Contract No. XXXX

Thank you for your letter of the 17th May. Given that neither you nor your surveyor have inspected, I do not know what was "not included in the costing of the bathroom".

I am not asking you to make a contribution towards the cost of rectifying the floor. What I am asking you to do is to indemnify me for monies I have had to pay to my builder to carry out works that your builders should have done. Your builders put a flimsy hardwood over the floorboards. My builder has been able to remedy the situation by putting down a more substantial covering and thus levelling out the floor. He has taken photographs of the work "before" and "after" which he is happy to produce at a site meeting.

Whilst the payment I have made to him is more than £100, what I am prepared to do is to agree a reduction of £100, rather than the £50 you have suggested, and I am enclosing a cheque for £330 herewith which is tendered in full and final satisfaction of all claims of whatsoever nature that you may have either against myself (or my wife). The cheque is to be held strictly to my order pending your acceptance of the same upon those terms, and is also tendered conditionally upon your making the necessary arrangements for the re-fitting of the bathroom carpet to our satisfaction. I note you are taking the appropriate steps to avoid any repetition of this in the future.

Yours sincerely,

They agreed to give me a reduction. The amount covered the cost of the work of my builder. My wife had the bathroom of her dreams. Everybody was happy, with the possible exception of

Dolphin, and their Operations Controller in particular. They did send me their guarantee and I'm delighted to say that we've never had to claim on it. The bathroom is still green, the floor is solid and level, the spa bath works a treat and my wife still tells me off for not cleaning the bath properly.

Whilst we're on the subject of warranties and guarantees, how many of you have ever tried to claim on those warranties they give you when you buy an electrical product for your home or office. I've now got to the stage where I'm very rude to retail salesmen who try to sell me extended warranties. The $64,000 question to ask them is why are they trying to sell it? Have they no faith in the longevity of the product? Is your £1000 plus computer or stereo equipment going to break down the minute the manufacturer's warranty has expired? The answer is, probably not. And by the time it breaks down it will be cheaper to replace it than repair it. If you were to squirrel away the money you would have spent on the extended warranty insurance premiums you'll probably have enough money to buy a replacement.

I'm typing this book on a Dell lap-top computer. I like Dell, and they didn't pay me to say that either. But I liked my old Apple Mac as well. And when I say old, I mean OLD. I bought it in 1993 and it still works today. It has a funny face with rabbit's ears around its screen and is called Arthur. No, I've not taken leave of my senses. Someone bought me one of those animal screen surrounds that gives a computer a personality and Arthur certainly is not short of that. He may well be one of the oldest computers in the world by now but age has not wearied him. Well, maybe just a tad.

When I bought Arthur I did take out an annual service contract, not just for him but also for his friend, Peter the Printer. I did that because I had never used a computer before, let alone owned one, and I was terrified they would both go wrong and I would lose all the original work that was in the process of creation. Many of my more famous and erudite tomes were written on Arthur and printed by Peter. *Marked Man, White Lines, Red Card, Gazza, My Life In Pictures*, I'm sure you've read them all.

It was a big leap for me to move from pen and paper to computer screen, particularly as I made computer illiteracy an art form in itself. My friend, Gerry, to whom I'm eternally grateful, taught me the basics and to his amusement I wrote everything down. I do mean everything. Like "Press switch at back to turn computer on" I did say we were talking about basics. I followed my written instructions religiously, line by line, for many a long moon, panicking when the result was not exactly as Gerry had predicted during our lessons. In that event Gerry would get a phone call (often a daily occurrence) during the course of which I'd tell him I had "lost" everything. He would explain patiently that this was practically impossible and would then talk me down from the heights of my hysteria by explaining, step by step, how to retrieve my daily quota of words from cyber-space.

It took about eight years of usage of Arthur before anything went wrong. I do keep giving these companies plugs without any reward and must remember to get myself a decent commercial agent. (Nothing whatsoever wrong with my literary agents, David and Diana by the way ... another free plug for MBA.) However, when Arthur did go wrong, it seemed, at least to me, to go wrong in a big way. The screen froze. The mouse refused to move. I encouraged my extremely fat cat, Cleo, to come upstairs to give it some encouragement but all was to no avail. Nothing happened on screen. It was like watching an Ingmar Bergman movie. I phoned Gerry. I phoned everybody I knew who knew anything about computers. It may seem odd, after paying enough in premiums to buy the most sophisticated computer invented, that I didn't go straight to the company who provided the insurance cover, but I just thought it might be a simple problem that Gerry would make go away. When nobody else had the magic cure, I did phone them.

It took me a long time to get through and when I finally did I was given another number to call in relation to Macs. I tried to call it and was told I was in a queue. Eventually I gave up. I hate queuing. I began the whole process all over again. Eventually I was connected to a man. Yes, a real live human being. Mind you, I'm not too sure what kind of sad individual lives his life next to a phone diagnosing faults with Apple-Macs from long distance, or maybe even from outer space. I mean, are these people for real? Why don't they get a life and take on board some sensible obsession like supporting Newcastle United or complaining?

I asked the sad man when he could come and see me (and

Arthur, of course). Alternatively, if he were personally too busy answering the phone then when could he send someone else to see me? (Is that an even sadder career, being sent to see people by the man who answers the phone to deal with their problems regarding Macs?) It transpired that the sad man could neither see me nor send anybody else to see me either. But he could try and cure the fault over the phone. I suspected that was his area of expertise. He then began to ask me all sorts of questions that involved megabytes, hard drives and various keys and buttons I didn't even know I possessed. I explained to him that I was probably the least technical person in the world and he had to be both gentle and patient with me. In fact he was neither. He asked me what sort of computer I had. I tried to tell him.

"It's an Apple Mac. I wouldn't be speaking to you otherwise, would I?"

"Yes, but what sort of Apple Mac?"

"Well, it's got big furry ears ..."

He wasn't impressed. He asked me how old it was. I told him. He laughed cruelly.

"That's not a computer, it's an antique."

That was when I decided a state of war existed between me and sad apple-man. I told him in no uncertain terms that he and his company had been happy to accept my premiums for many years without suggesting I was paying for an "antique" and neither objected to receiving the money, nor insulted my computer, when it had been behaving properly. This was now pay-back time. He told me, (quite aggressively as I recall it) that I had not been paying his company, or, indeed, him personally. He was merely a sub-contractor. For some reason that fact neither surprised nor interested me. I told him I'd expect his company to visit me on a date and at a time convenient to me. He told me that if I wanted to arrange an appointment then I had to phone another number. At this point I was close to losing it. I had books to write. I suppose at this stage in the story you may feel he was doing the literary world a favour, but it didn't seem that way to me at the time. My whole career was stretching before me, leading on to my Nobel Prize. I did try to phone the number. I did, honestly. I tried several times. It was permanently engaged, doubtless with other folk who had been duped into believing that a service contract meant that service would be provided by a veritable army of eager-beaver technicians on twenty-four hour stand-by. At this point I resorted to the old tried and trusted technique. I wrote a letter of complaint. I told them that if they didn't want to do the work then I'd get somebody else in who would.

I think the threat of my actually paying somebody else to do the work got to them. It worked with Dolphin as well, of course, and is highly recommended to all apprentice complainers. They probably knew that the fee I'd pay would be on a par with emergency plumbing rates. I once acted for such a plumbing company. They were actually quite good but also knew how to charge. They also knew what to do with clients who didn't pay. They'd return to the scene of their work on some pretext or other and fill the recently unblocked drains with liquid cement. Beats a complaint letter every time and don't think I haven't thought of it in moments of frustration.

In any event sad man sent his even sadder man. He actually admired the handiwork of a machine built to last. He mended Arthur and I've never had to make another claim. As Arthur now approaches his 12th birthday (which is probably equivalent to 155 in computer years) I think it's time to put him out to grass. It will be a sad moment.

Bit of a mix, on reflection, in this chapter but here are your bullet complaint points to which you have grown accustomed:

1. If you are having work done read the contract carefully to see the extent of the work and the making good.
2. Make sure that the small print doesn't mean you surrender all your rights. If you don't like the contract and the company won't change it then find another contractor.
3. Don't pay all the money up front.
4. If you are in doubt about the quality of the work then get your own expert in to look at it.
5. Complain as soon as you think there is anything to complain about.
6. Don't be browbeaten by threats of litigation. Give back as good as you get.

7. At the end of the day if you are not happy get a surveyor in so that you can send his report in with your complaint letter.

    a. Try and negotiate on the phone but confirm every conversation in writing and always make contemporaneous notes;

    b. When it comes to guarantees for work done, or for things bought always read them to see what is covered;

    c. This may sound obvious but keep all your warranties and guarantees together in a safe place. Not so safe that you can't remember where it is, though;

    d. Any complaints that are not dealt with immediately put in writing;

    e. Don't take any back-chat either from the guarantee company or their workman. You've paid good money to have the work done and generally they just want you to buy new equipment;

    f. Don't worry if your equipment is old. As long as it works or can be repaired you shouldn't have to replace it;

    g. Don't accept any delays in getting the work done. You've not delayed in paying your premiums.

Don't forget. You are the customer. You are always right. You are the one who is guaranteed that your equipment will be repaired. So let them get on with it.

23

THE PLAY'S THE THING

The London theatre is not a cheap place to visit. Well, it is, unless you want to see a play. Nowadays you can expect to pay up to £50 for a ticket for a performance that, in some instances, can last less than ninety minutes without an interval. Actually, on a per minute basis Wimbledon is probably the best value for money you can get at any place of entertainment, that is if you call seeing our so-called tennis stars thrashed by an unseeded wild card entrant from Bosnia Herzegovina, entertainment. For about £30 you can get to Wimbledon at around eleven in the morning, watch the outside courts and on a good day, in an English summer, you can watch tennis till nine at night. But, as I say, in the theatre (and I have seen plays as short as an hour ... or less if they are written by Pinter) you could be paying a pound a minute. Well, in my book, at that sort of rate there should be no pregnant pauses, you want dialogue that fairly crackles along, just to get in as many words as possible to make you feel as if you have had some return on your investment.

Now, how on earth do you manage to complain about the theatre. It is what it is. Well, for starters I'd like to complain about the man or woman who invariably comes on stage before the curtain nowadays and asks you to turn off your mobile phones and digital watches. They then go on to say, "Enjoy the show". Show? *Show?* It's a bloody play, for heaven's sake. We're not in America, we're not in the old Finsbury Park Empire to which my parents took me every Thursday.

Some plays, not shows, are good and some are bad. That's fair enough. I do accept that it's a lottery when you pre-book. You can, of course, wait until the play is reviewed, but then if it's raved about by the critics you run the risk of not being able to get tickets. I usually adopt the policy of booking long in advance when I know the author ... not necessarily personally. Although I do know

David Hare, he says shamelessly name-dropping, as his sons went to the same school as my boys.

My wife reckoned that I had no idea how my sons' studies were doing but knew everything about David's latest work in progress. My finest hour was when he gave me a signed copy of one of his plays and I solemnly gave him in return a signed copy of *Gazza, My Life in Pictures*. Well, it was signed by both me and Gazza so I figure he got the better part of the bargain. And I got his sons free tickets for a Crystal Palace match so I do feel I have been somewhat influential in his career to date and a definite contributory to his knighthood.

I also tend to book at certain theatres where I am a member and get the forthcoming programmes on a priority basis. I'm almost as sad as Mr Computer Geek as I have to admit to getting a thrill when I receive the programme for the likes of the National Theatre on London's South Bank, the Royal Shakespeare Company in Stratford-upon-Avon (and can I use this page as a platform to complain about their abandonment of their London base at the Barbican ... What a load of pretentious rubbish they put on now that the RSC have moved on) the Donmar in Covent Garden, where I was for many years on the Board of Directors, the Hampstead Theatre (before they moved as now what they put on is not only not worth going to see but doesn't even justify a complaint as it's so bad) and best of all The Open Air Theatre in Regent's Park. The arrival of their early booking form means that summer's on its way and we can once again rejoice at sitting in the pouring rain watching *A Midsummer Night's Dream* for the zillionth time and wondering if the ending is still going to be the same. I do that with all my favourite plays (will *Hamlet* survive and marry Ophelia?) in films, will Gary Cooper fall to a stray bullet in *High Noon* and in books will Little Nell survive to grow up, marry, have kids and get divorced?

As I say, you can't really complain about the play. Someone, somewhere along the line must have thought it was good, even if it was only the writer's mother. Actually, I was once moved to write a complaint letter about an actual production itself as it was just so appalling that anybody involved in it should have realised that it was an affront to human intelligence to put it on in public and, to add insult to injury, to charge for the privilege. The play, and I use the word loosely, was *Time*. I have the feeling that Dave Clark (without his famous five) was involved somewhere along the line and they even had a holograph Laurence Olivier involved. Mind you, he was in Neil Diamond's *The Jazz Singer* as well with the most unlikely Jewish accent I ever heard, so his presence (or holographic presence) didn't mean a lot. I couldn't believe what I was seeing and hearing. It was supposed to be a musical and gave a whole new meaning to the phrase *Doing Time*. I left at the interval and wrote and complained. I received a letter of apology expressing regret that I'd not enjoyed an experience which according to the producers had been "well received" and they sent me six more complimentary tickets for the production! I gave them away to sworn enemies.

I think the best way to complain about a bad play is to talk with your feet and not return after the interval. I have found that things rarely get better and if it was bad in the first half it's likely to get distinctly worse in the second. Nothing tells a theatre so succinctly and graphically that it has a flop on its hands than whole patches of empty seats that were occupied when the performance started. But there are occasions where there is nothing wrong with the play or the performance, yet there are extraneous elements interfering with your enjoyment. And if that's the case then not only can you complain, but you must.

In every theatre (apart from those modern purpose built auditoriums like the RSC and the National) there are some seats from which you simply cannot see, either partially or in the entirety. If you forget your glasses and have a seat high up in the Upper Circle then you can hardly blame the theatre for your poor view of proceedings. Similarly, if a seat is sold at a reduced price because it has a restricted view you can't complain about that either. But if you pay full price and can only see half of the stage and have to guess as to what is going on in the other half then you have every right to complain and not only demand the return of your money, but also a ticket for another performance.

I went to see a very fine play at Her Majesty's Theatre in Haymarket called *Breath of Life*. It was a two hander about the conflict between a wife and a mistress, both with memories of the same man. I was accompanied by my wife and two friends. I could see from the start that there was going to be a problem but could do nothing about it as the house was full. I sat at the end of the row and had to settle for a view of one actress at a time, desperately trying to fill in the gaps in that part of the stage, which I simply couldn't see. I had people shushing me when I asked my wife what was happening and eventually I just gave up. I wrote to the theatre. Do I hear a sharp intake of breath in awe and surprise at my action?

Dear Sir/Madam,

I attended a performance of *Breath of Life* on the evening of Tuesday 26th November with my wife and the Chairman of the company for which I am the in-house Legal Advisor and his wife. I had bought them the tickets as a present.

We were seated in the Royal Circle in Row C, seats 25, 26, 27 and 28. The price of these seats was £40 a ticket and there was no indication given to me when I booked on the telephone that there would be any problem with regard to sight lines.

In fact, the seats clearly had a restricted view and for a good part of the play, I could see only one actress and was at times unable to see all of the stage or to see the actresses as they moved towards the wings.

Whilst this was a dazzling theatrical performance, it was marred by this difficulty and I should be grateful if you would let me know why we were not warned that these seats had a restricted view, why we were charged full price for them and what proposals you have to make for compensation.

Yours faithfully,

The theatre behaved impeccably and immediately wrote back giving me a credit for my ticket and indeed, for 50% of my wife's ticket as our mutual enjoyment had been impaired. Mind you after 33 years of marriage I'm not quite sure what mutual enjoyment there's left to impair. Serial killers get released earlier.

Some years earlier I had also had cause to write to the National

Theatre. We went to see one of my favourite plays *Oh, What a Lovely War*. Somebody had the bright idea of putting this on in a large tent right next to the river. Very atmospheric. All we needed was shrapnel flying past our ears, bodies rotting on the wire and rats scurrying by our feet and we could well have imagined ourselves on the Western Front. And then there were the planes actually flying overhead, and the noises from the river. Yes, we were bang in the middle of a flight-path and as jets roared by, towards Heathrow, or Gatwick, or City Airports, the actors might just as well have been miming. I fired off another letter (sticking with the military metaphor) and sure enough I received back my money and an apology.

Although I love the Almeida to bits they too felt the wrath of my pen.

Dear Sirs,

As a member of the Almeida and a regular attender at the main theatre, I decided to purchase two tickets for the performance of *Richard II* at the Gainsborough on the 1st August.

I have to say that it was not a happy experience. Whilst our seats were in the front row of the First level, there was not even room to place a small shopping bag between the seat and the end of the balcony and the seat allocations were so tightly spaced together that my wife (who is not a large woman) could hardly sit down. She endeavoured to use the Portkabin outside toilets before the performance but found herself at the end of a long queue and panicked when she heard one of your American employees shouting out, that "the <u>show</u> was about to start in three minutes".

Whilst it has always been my understanding that Shakespeare was performed and not shown, we hastened to our seats and then sat there for fully fifteen minutes waiting for the performance to start.

The first half, at an hour and half's length, was intolerable as the heat within the building made it impossible to concentrate and, indeed, difficult even to breathe. The performance was interrupted by the constant noise of people moving and, indeed, some people had to leave the performance because they felt faint.

In the interval, my wife began to queue again for the ladies' toilet on the first floor level and by the time the performance was about to start the queue still extended beyond the door. Unable to get back to our seats in time and feeling quite ill because of the lack of any air conditioning (or indeed any air circulation) within the building, both of us left.

Given that the tickets cost us £30 each and given that the actors had played their part in what appeared to be a magnificent performance, there seems to be no excuse for the Almeida seeking to cash in on what was obviously intended to be a once-in-a-lifetime opportunity given the impending development of the Gainsborough Studios.

I am well aware of the problems encountered by theatres like the Almeida as I am myself a Trustee/Director of the Donmar Theatre and mindful of the fundraising needs of theatres like ours. However, I really do not believe there can be any excuse for putting people through the misery of the Gainsborough on a hot night. Having spoken to several friends of mine who attended other performances, I gather that they too were very unhappy both with the heat and the toilet facilities and I look forward to hearing from you in due course.

Yours faithfully,

Again a positive response and the wait for their new theatre was well worth it.

So far, so good. I was beginning to feel confident that theatres were good people to whom to complain. They had an intellectual grasp of the concept. I was wrong. I went to see a play called *Dinner*. This was in a small theatre upstairs at the National. The stage set was merely one long dinner table and the whole play took place during the course of a meal. We were seated so close to the stage that I expected us to be served a glass of wine along with the rest of the cast. What I didn't expect was for most of the dinner guests to light up fags and smoke continually during the performance. Didn't anybody tell them it's rude to smoke when other people are eating (or watching a play)? I suffer from mild asthma. We were bang in the middle of the front row. There was no escape and so I coughed and wheezed my way through the evening. Naturally I wrote a letter of complaint.

Dear Sir,

As a regular theatre-goer and Friend of the National, I duly attended a performance of *Dinner* on the night of Tuesday 19th November.

Throughout the performance, one of the actresses chain-smoked. There was no warning regarding this and the play itself had no interval. My wife and I were at the end of a row furthest away from the door and there was no way we could leave. Therefore, as an asthmatic with an acute aversion to smoke, I was forced to endure some two hours of sitting in a small smoky room and suffered a very bad asthma attack on the way home.

I should be grateful for some explanation and, at the same time, could I please suggest that you do post some warnings on the publicity for this play and outside. I am sure I am not alone in my situation.

Yours faithfully,

The reply was not sympathetic. Obviously the bloke who wrote it was a smoker. The small print on the literature for the play said there were scenes that contained smoking. I should have read them. Maybe it did, but it didn't say it would be like a visit to an opium den. Whatever I felt, they weren't going to do anything about it. I thought the play was lousy anyway, but what do I know as it transferred successfully to the West End some little time later. I wonder whether it was one of the theatres that operate a non-smoking policy?

A problem I encountered at the RSC in Stratford was a little more delicate. We went to see a production of *The Taming of the Shrew* and with the curtain about to rise there were five vacant seats to my right. This was unusual, as well-reviewed productions such as this were normally sold out. However, as far as I was concerned this was a bonus. I could stretch out, toss my jacket and programme on a seat and relax. As is often the case at the RSC the cast were on the stage as the audience were drifting in. Just as the action started for real a family, obviously tourists, took up the seats next to me. A mother, father, elderly relative, two children of about nine or ten and, to my horror, another child so young it had to sit on its mother's lap. Now, unlike W.C Fields, I have nothing against children in the theatre. If they can understand the play then why not give them the chance at the earliest possible age to enjoy the magic of the spoken word. My Paul and his bosom buddy David saw *A Midsummer Night's Dream* when they were about six and were Shakespeare fans for life. Mind you, they did take theatre-going to extremes as for a while they insisted on taking the full text of each Shakespeare play they saw with them into the auditorium and following line by line. I did tell them they could have got jobs as prompters but they preferred to annoy me.

These kids next to me, however, were not devotees and they were never going to be, as far as I could tell. The elder one wriggled throughout and the younger one steadfastly refused to go to sleep, and had to be placated by the mother with a bag of sweets throughout. I'm not sure if the rest of the family got the point either as they chomped their way through the goodies as well, to the point, that not only could I not concentrate, but I wanted to scream. I hate people eating at either the cinema or the theatre and have actually cut down my movie visits for that reason. Mind you if you visit the Barbican cinema at least they don't allow food inside and the seats are to die for. I once went to the opera in Prague with my old mate Len and our respective wives. Neither Len nor I are known for our love of so-called classical music. To me, the classics are Bob Dylan, the Rolling Stones and Springsteen and anything that hit the charts between 1960 and 1967. However, Prague is a city of culture, Mozart did something there (not sure what, born, composed, played, died, decomposed) and Kafka certainly WAS born there. I like Kafka. I hate Mozart. Mind you I hate all classical music. To me it's the *King's New Clothes*. I can't believe anybody can actually prefer to sit through 12 hours of Wagner than listen to Roy Orbison singing *Only the Lonely*. Still, each to their own. Len summed it up when we went into the Opera House, looking around and saying, "It's a nice stadium".

He then proceeded to eat tic-tacs. Try eating them silently. He then finally and mercifully fell asleep. I did not. The noise emanating from the stage kept me awake. I told people after that I had been to The Opera. When they asked which one I asked if there was more than one. They all have the same plot and the same non-tunes. Fat bloke sings. Fat woman sings. Fat bloke and fat woman sing together. Fat bloke or fat woman fall in love with another person. Fat bloke or fat woman die. They die shouting at such a volume that it's hard to see how anybody writing out the death certificate could not have suspected foul play.

At the interval in Stratford, by now feeling great sympathy with the Prague audience who had to endure Len's tic-tacs and snoring, I discussed with my wife whether or not I should complain. I have to say that had the family been English I would have had no hesitation, but I didn't want to cause an unpleasant international scene. I just hoped that the noise levels would subside and that a few side-long looks from me that were linked to "Tutts" and "Shushes" might suffice. They didn't. The small child just got more and more irritable and so did I. To say the play was ruined was an understatement and I felt sure that if I wrote to the RSC I would receive a sympathetic reply. Not a bit of it.

Dear Sir/Madam,

Re: *The Taming of the Shrew*

As a full member, you will note from my booking record that my wife and I are regular attendees at the RSC and, indeed, have bought a house in Blockley mainly so that we can visit even more often.

I purchased three tickets for the performance on Monday night of *The Taming of the Shrew*. Some 60 seconds before the play commenced, the five seats to my right were empty but these were then taken by a family consisting of a mother, father, two children aged about ten and eight and a child of no more than 18 months, who was carried in his parent's arms. I had no time to comment on this before the play started, at which point the child began to cry. The parents then noisily fed him sweets and continually sought to silence him throughout the first half. The child was not to be silenced and, if he was not making a noise, he was tapping his fingers or kicking the seats around him. I did comment to the father in the interval that perhaps he should take the child out in the second half to allow those around him to enjoy the play, but he demurred.

The family were in full sight of your ushers and management, none of whom commented in any way. I did not feel I could complain directly to them as the family were Asian and I felt sure that this would be misconstrued as an act of racism. I therefore asked the parents once again to keep the child in order during the second half of the play but they were no more successful until the child finally fell asleep some five minutes before the end. I know I was not the only person whose enjoyment of the play was ruined, although I am not sure if anybody else actually complained.

I should be grateful if you would let me know whether or not there is any lower age limit for performances of adult theatre at the RSC because, if there is not, I really do feel this should be implemented forthwith. If there is, then I wonder why a child of that age was permitted to be in the theatre at all.

Yours faithfully,

They replied and told me that nobody else complained, but then nobody else was sitting next to them.

It is quite incredible that they don't exercise any policy as to the minimum age for attendees and just want to get in as much money as they can, even if that offends loyal patrons such as myself. As I've said before and will, doubtless say again … Whatever.

The lesson I learned from that is that if you are at, what is for you, a one-off event, such as play or a concert, then you must complain on the spot and complain quickly before you make yourself into a martyr. All too often, seats are not banked, which makes it impossible for somebody as short as me to see. There's no point in writing in about that. If I've paid £70-£100 for an evening in the theatre for the pair of us why should I let it be spoiled because the bloke in front of me is seven feet tall and the seats are all on the same level because the theatre thought they could pack that many more punters in by ignoring suitable banking?

So, in circumstances like that complain on the spot. There's a reasonable chance they may find you another seat and if they refuse at least you have something else to put into your complaint letter. Or you can always simply walk out and demand your money back from the box-office. You've paid to see a play and if the theatre can't deliver on that then in my view they're in breach of contract.

Sometimes it can be a long hard haul to get to see something, which, in the end, may not even be worth seeing. I was foolish enough to be inveigled into seeing a production called *The Black Rider* at London's Barbican. As I mentioned I have been disenchanted with the Barbican ever since they let the Royal Shakespeare Company leave. I'm not sure who was responsible but whoever it was, both parties should get together as soon as possible, as what has followed great theatre has generally been a load of pretentious twaddle. I suppose I should have realised that *The Black Rider* was likely to fall into this category. Poetry by William Borroughs, that well-know fan of certain forbidden substances, music by Tom Waits, he of the desolation of the soul and starring Marianne Faithful, who has not been adverse to forbidden substances herself in another life.

7.45 pm start, running time two hours, so I figured I would be back for any penalty shoot-out there might be in the First Division Play-Off between Sunderland and Crystal Palace that was being televised that night. So, when I got there at 7.00 pm and was told even at that stage that there would be a ten minute delay in starting, I was not best pleased. I was even less pleased when at 8.10 we had not even been allowed in to take our seats. Eventually, they did open the doors and we now sat inside the theatre and waited. A man came on stage.

"They're going to abandon the performance, just wait and see," I said to my companion, David Swede, a bit of a Tom Waits fan.

Not a bit of it. The show would go on, but in ten minutes. I looked at my watch. 8.15. 8.25 start, 10.25 finish. Bang went the football. Still, hope sprang eternal that this was going to be good. It wasn't, it was worse than terrible. Terrible didn't come close to describing it. And at 9.45 pm (the time it was due to finish) we were still in the first half. I wanted to go to the loo. I wanted to go home. I wanted to be anywhere but listening to and watching the extraordinary things that were happening on stage. I won't even begin to try to describe the plot, save to mention that it involved Ms Faithful as a military (male, I think) character called Peg-leg who may, or may not, have been doubling as the devil, and a pet duck which got shot and fell from the sky on to the stage ... oh and a scene straight from a nightmare Mary Poppins where the romantic (and I use the word loosely) leads, flew across the stage on less than invisible wires. The man who'd said that the play would start in ten minutes had also asked us to bear with any glitches as this was the first night of previews and there were some very adventurous sets and special effects. My view was that it would have been impossible to recognise any glitches. The whole thing was a glitch as far as I was concerned.

My companion suggested to me that they might have abandoned the interval because of the delay in starting. He was worried, because his wife was away and he had left his kids with a baby-sitter (who was costing him such an hourly fortune, if I had been him, I would have abandoned the girls and moved without leaving a forwarding address). Not a bit of it. At 9.50 pm precisely we broke for drinks. Or everybody else did. Me, I went home and saw Sunderland miss their penalties in a shoot-out (so at least I had got one prediction right) and exit the play-offs to Crystal Palace. I rang David the next day who told me the whole evening had finally wound up at 11.10 pm (only an hour and a half late, then) and he had finally got home at midnight.

The next day I was moved to write my letter of complaint.

Dear Sir,

I attended with a friend a performance of *The Black Rider* on the evening of Monday 17th May. Both our wives were away and he had to arrange for a baby-sitter for his young children.

We arrived in good time for the performance, only to be told that the curtain would be "ten minutes late" going up. This was mildly annoying but, as we had still not got into the theatre by 8 o'clock, clearly the estimate was inaccurate. We took our seats and waited. And waited. And waited. Somebody came on stage and said that the performance would start in ten minutes. It didn't. Eventually it began at twenty-five past eight.

I had telephoned through during the day to find out the finishing time because, as I say, my friend had to arrange for his baby-sitter to be taken home. I was told it would take two hours, including an interval, and therefore should have finished at 9.45. In fact, the interval did not commence until 9.50. At that stage I decided to leave but my friend, who had juggled around with his baby-sitter, did not reach home until midnight, as the performance finally finished at about ten past eleven, with a running time not far short of three hours, as compared to the two hours specified in what passed for a programme.

I must take the greatest exception to the fact that no programme was available although the leaflet said that programmes would be available from the 21st May.

As you will appreciate this was, to say the least, a less than enjoyable experience and I look forward to hearing from you in due course with your comments.

Yours faithfully,

Again I got a result. The Barbican were very apologetic and gave me two free tickets for any production I chose in the future. Maybe I'll wait until the return of the RSC. Or go to the Barbican Cinema which is so blissfully popcorn free.

So here are your public entertainment bullet points that are worth complaining about.

1. Broken or uncomfortable seats.
2. Restricted view.
3. Inability to hear.
4. Noisy neighbours.
5. Dirty theatre.
6. Warm interval drinks.
7. Poor access to the bar so you don't get your drink ... or it takes so long to get it that it gets warm! (We once went to see

Chicago and never even got to our pre-ordered drinks!)

8. Allowing latecomers to interrupt when you have dashed there because the ticket said latecomers would not be admitted.
9. An impossibly bad production.
10. Rip-off programme; £5 for a whole load of ads; a few photos and the cast-list.
11. Late running for no good reason and no information on the delay.
12. Insufficient toilets (particularly to ladies).
13. Insufficient banking of the seats.

That's your check-list. Oh, and enjoy the show.

24

MY LAWYER CAN BEAT UP YOUR LAWYER

"Let's kill all the lawyers," wrote Shakespeare in *Henry VI*, putting the words into the mouth of a character called Dick the Butcher. Even as a member of that dishonourable profession that seems good to me. Although I also have to say that I wouldn't mind having a tilt at the butchers as well, particularly the kosher ones given the size of our domestic meat bills. You may think that I might find it a bit compromising to tell you how to complain to and about legal advisors, but not a bit of it. You see, I know exactly what you should complain about. It's a bit like being a freemason, and I'll probably have my tongue cut out for disclosing trade secrets, but I'm prepared to take that risk. And while we are at it why not also learn the art of complaining about your accountant, or indeed any other professional adviser, surveyor, architect, estate agent. Whoops, let's draw the line right there in a chapter about professions and tuck them in somewhere else. Like how to complain to your mugger, for example. Bit harsh that, I suppose. Some of my best friends are estate agents. Well, actually, only one that I can actually name with any confidence ... and he's very good at what he does and very honest. Which is why I use him all the time and why I exempt him from the slur on his breed and even go on holiday with him. But as for the rest of them, whatever I say, whatever anybody might say, it's probably true. Shakespeare had probably never met an estate agent (realtor for our transatlantic reader) but if he had then he might have said he would kill the lawyers second.

I have a t-shirt given to me by a client which says "Trust me, I'm a lawyer". If my memory serves me correctly it was a gift from my pal Michael Brandon who has recently starred as Jerry Springer in *Jerry Springer, The Opera*. Great play if you missed it. Bloody sight better than *The Black Rider* that's for sure. Michael recently had some complaints of his own about the over-enthusiastic parking attendants outside the theatre. He did a very good complaint letter to Westminster Council and, received some compensation by way of a refunded clamping fee, if not his requested month's free parking.

Dear Mr. X,

RE: PCN No. XXX – Earlham Street

I am a professional actor at present appearing as the lead in the play *Jerry Springer – the Opera*.

On the 19th May, I parked my vehicle in Earlham Street on a Pay and Display meter where it clearly indicated that the maximum stay was two hours. I originally paid for 13 minutes and I enclose a copy of my receipt. I then extended my time at the meter (still within the 2 hour maximum stay) and enclose herewith a copy of a further receipt.

Notwithstanding this, my vehicle was clamped and I had to wait two hours to be unclamped. I had to pay £115 for the clamp release fee and also the parking fine on top of that.

I think this is yet another case of over-enthusiasm on the part of your parking attendants. I am, of course, appealing against the fine but that does not rewrite history or in any way ameliorate the inconvenience that I have suffered.

I should be grateful if you would look into this matter and I await hearing from you with some explanation. Meanwhile I suggest the very least that Camden could offer me, while I continue to appear in *Jerry Springer*, is a month's free parking within the Earlham Street environs.

I look forward to hearing from you.

Yours sincerely,

Mind you, Michael also gave me a t-shirt that said "My lawyer can beat up your lawyer," so given my puny stature, what does he know? The fact of the matter is that generally you can trust lawyers. Not every single lawyer, of course, as there are a fair sprinkling of them giving internal advice in Her Majesty's prisons, but as a breed you can be fairly sure they are not going to nick your hard-earned money. What you can't be so sure of is that they are going to represent you in an efficient manner. If you've ever bought a house and found a pedestrian right of way meandering straight through your living room then you will know what I am getting at.

The fact is that most of us only use solicitors when we are buying or selling houses, making a will or dealing with the estate of a deceased loved one (particularly adored if they left you in their will) getting divorced or buying or selling a business. There are loads of other things solicitors do. As a sports lawyer myself I negotiate footballers' contracts *inter alia*. I threw the latin in there just to prove that I know what I'm doing. That's what a lot of legal advisors do, by the way, try to hide behind the legal jargon, so if your solicitor or barrister come out with something technical that you simply don't understand, bully them until they put it into plain English so that you do. Then there are corporate lawyers, music and entertainment lawyers, insurance lawyers, tax lawyers, shipping lawyers, media lawyers (never been too sure that justifies an area of specialisation, but merely the ability to watch so much television that eventually you become a Class Z personality and thus part of the media circus) and, of course, our old mates and part of the media scene, the criminal lawyers. You know them. They are always the plump, balding ones who get into camera shot as their serial killer client enters into court protesting his innocence. It's the criminal lawyer who has to give the interviews when his client has gone down for a twenty-year stretch, a fact which has never much commended their services to me, given their lack of success in keeping their client on the right side of a twenty-foot high wall topped by barbed wire.

Now I would suggest that all of these lawyers have one thing in common, namely that at some stage in their legal careers they have perpetrated some act worthy of a client complaint. I was taught at a very early stage by principal, during my articles (that's what they called them back in the dark ages) that solicitors never apologise, they "regret", that they never lie, but they do "obfuscate". So what I have to do is teach you to recognise causes for "regret and obfuscation", so that you in turn, can learn when to complain about them.

When we are talking about complaints to solicitors and the like we do have in place a professional disciplinary body in the shape of The Law Society, which is there to regulate solicitors and to protect the public against any malpractice. By their rules and regulations solicitors have to maintain sufficient professional indemnity insurance to cover themselves against the sort of levels of matters with which they are dealing. The medical profession around the world has similar controls, but I'll deal with doctors and dentists a bit later. Actually, I'd rather not deal with them at all as they both scare the living daylights out of me, but I feel I have some kind of duty to my readers to push the envelope as far as I can where they are concerned, notwithstanding my own squeamishness.

I do not intend going as far as explaining how to bring proceedings against your legal advisor. I want to keep my practicing certificate. I've held it since 1968 and I'd quite like to take it to the grave with me, thank you very much. The fact of the matter, as you've probably gathered by now, is that this book is about complaining rather than suing. If you get to that stage then you failed as a complainant. In fact I was a bit disappointed when the English courts changed the nomenclature on writs from "Plaintiffs" to "Complainants".

The obvious place to start is with fees and charging rates. When you instruct a solicitor he is duty bound to send you a retainer letter setting out what he, and anybody else in his firm who deals with your matter, will charge, on an hourly basis. You may take a sharp inward breath when you see that he charges more in an hour than you spend on the household in a week, but by way of some kind of explanation, I would urge you to understand that he doesn't see all of that. There are little matters like rent, wages, business rates, telephone charges, technical support, insurance, etc, that come off the top before he receives his miserable pittance. However, it is very important that you know what you are being charged and that you make a note of every communication with your lawyer. That way you will know, when you receive a bill for an hour's telephone call, that the conversation only took fifteen minutes and ten of those were spent chatting about your respective golf handicaps and the weather. If you are going to complain about charges either during, or at the end of a transaction, then you must have the ammunition with which to fight. Just relying on your memory is not enough and will cut no ice if a dispute comes before the Law Society over charges. When you get your bills analyse them. It's not enough for him to charge you £2000 for ten hours work at £200 per hour. What was done, who did it and was the time taken to do it reasonable?

That brings me nicely to one of the most common causes of complaints to the legal profession and that is delay. Delay is not in itself negligent, though it can prove to be, but it is annoying, particularly when you are in a hurry to complete a transaction like a house purchase. Failure to return calls, either on the same day, or at all, is just downright rude as far as I am concerned. In the days when I was in private practice and before the days of mobile phones allowed you to transfer your office to your car, I would not leave my workplace until I had at least tried to return the calls of everybody who had tried to reach me that day. That left my wife complaining but, hopefully, not my clients. There, don't you wish you had known me back then? Mind you, those were the days when most solicitors were Jacks of All Trades. If somebody came to see you then whatever they wanted, you would try and deal with it yourself, or if it became too complicated, you would instruct counsel to advise. None of this calling in seventeen departments for a transaction as so often happens with the larger City firms. I'm not suggesting that they are not excellent at what they do (and if I did they would probably bring a class action against me ... they're a bit like that when they feel their reputation is being impugned) nor that they don't have expertise that out-experts the lads who put rocket ships on the moon and specialisation that means they conjure up somebody to advise on magnesium mining contracts in Outer Mongolia, but you do pay for the privilege and it's a bit hard to identify exactly who is YOUR solicitor. None of my clients were ever in doubt as to who was representing them. Even if I didn't actually do their divorces myself (I just couldn't take the lip-stick on the collar when weepy wives threw themselves at you for comfort ... Bit hard to explain to the wife when she is trying to scrub aforementioned lip-stick out as well) but I did know exactly what was going on. If a client couldn't get hold of the minion or partner who was dealing with the matter on a day-to-day basis then they would get hold of me and I would actually know where they were at in the matter. Just try that with a five hundred partner City or Wall Street firm nowadays.

But back to delays. Again harping back to my youth, one did have breathing space in a transaction. A typical phone call would be:

CLIENT	"Have you dealt with my letter yet?"
SOLICITOR	"I haven't had it yet."
CLIENT	"But I posted it first class yesterday."
SOLICITOR	"Well, you know what the post is like. As soon as I get it I promise you it will have top priority."

Now, he may well have been obfuscating when he said he didn't have it. Maybe it was still in his firm's post-room, perhaps his secretary (in the days when there were mere secretaries and before every typist became a Personal Assistant), had not passed it on yet. The solicitor in the above, largely fictional, call had bought himself another day to deal with the transaction and enable him to deal with the letter he said he'd not got the day before. Then came Telex, the facsimile machine and then the mobile phone, the car phone, e-mails and finally the ubiquitous blackberry. There is, consequently, no longer any hiding place. Nor any reason for delay. If something has been sent to your solicitor he is lying (whoop, sorry, obfuscating) through his teeth if he says he hasn't got it. And if he doesn't deal with it promptly then that is a ground for complaint. What is even more annoying and totally unacceptable, is if you get charged for the time the lawyer takes in dealing with your complaints about delay. In a world of time-recording gone mad he will log every phone-call and if you have spent twenty minutes justifiably ranting and raving at him over his prevarications there is every chance that twenty minutes will go on the computer as chargeable time and will have cost you another sixty odd quid to add insult to injury.

In a property market which is over-heating, your solicitor's failure to respond speedily may well cost you the property you desire. Complaining about earlier delays may well mean that he reacts more swiftly as the transaction proceeds. If he doesn't respond, whether it be to a letter (if you still send them) a phone-call, a fax or an e-mail then you need to let him know very early on in the transaction that you are not happy. Make sure you create a paper-trail. You do not want to get to the stage where it is your word against that of your lawyer. Remember my t-shirt. "Trust me, I'm a lawyer". Far more convincing than "Trust me, I'm a client". Delays can be even more fatal when dealing with wills. Again, at a very early stage in my career, I was asked to visit a client in hospital to make a new will for him. Unfortunately, nobody bothered to tell me that the bloke was at death's door and by the time I got there the following day he'd actually stepped over the threshold. So, no new will. As luck would have it he'd scribbled out what he wanted on a piece of paper, a couple of the nurses had witnessed it already, and that was good enough to get probate. But it could have turned out all so differently. After that, I was seeing clients at breakfast when they'd so much as sneezed in the night, to ensure their affairs were in order.

If you are not dealing with a partner in a firm then never hesitate to complain to the partner in charge. This is not an instance where you should worry about getting somebody into trouble. If you do not complain then there is every possibility that you will be the one in trouble. I suspect that trainees today do know a bit more than I did when I was articled. I treasure the memory (and so will she if she reads this) of going to a property completion with a female articled clerk on the other side acting for the mortgage company. As luck would have it neither of us had attended a completion before. We were both completion virgins, though back in 1967 you might have hesitated before using the "V" word to a strange female in public. Ah, those innocent bygone days. Anyway, we were faced with a mass of documents that included the Land Certificate, the proof of title issued by Her Majesty's Land Registry. It's quite an impressive document, all tied up with pink tape and having various official-looking seals affixed. They are official looking, I suppose, because they are official. Neither of us could decide who should take custody of the Land Certificate which, once the mortgage company had had their wicked way with it, would have become a Charge Certificate. Looking back, it's as clear as daylight that she should have taken it as security for the money she was giving my client to buy the damn thing, but at the time it seemed more logical for us to divide this document in two and for each of us to take away half and, here we thought we were being particularly clever, to give cross-undertakings to ensure that whoever was entitled ended up with the whole. It was only later that I saw the message on the front cover that said it was a criminal offence to tamper with the document.

If you do not understand what is being said to you in letters you receive, or if you feel you are being fobbed off, or matters are being glossed over, then complain. Don't worry if you feel you are making a nuisance of yourself. Trust me, you will not be the client from hell. I had most of them in my time.

It is a little hard to get a time scale for a property transaction as your solicitor is, to a certain extent, dependent on his opposite number. However, it's not unreasonable to ask for a schedule of what is going to happen in the transaction (particularly if you are a first-time buyer) before you kick off and at least you can follow progress (or lack of it) as you go along. It's a little easier in a piece of litigation, where there are strict time limits now and your solicitor should be able to set out the various stages right at the very start. Ditto for your divorce. Your ex-partner may find all sorts of ways to get his or her revenge, though maybe you are the vengeful one, by delaying the matter, but if you know what should be happening and when, then at least you are in a position to question the delays and, if necessary, to complain.

Complaining about your lawyer is very much a gut-feeling process. If you get prompt responses, clear advice and the transaction seems to be proceeding without glitches then it is very likely that he is doing a good job. He may, of course, get you into your house on time and only afterwards do you find he was negligent in not discovering the right of way, but that's a matter for a negligence claim on his insurance, not for a complaint.

There is a confidence issue. You may have been delighted with your solicitor up to the point of getting to court, but then you find that the barrister who has been handling the case isn't available on the day and you are lumbered with counsel who has only seen the papers the night before, or, worse still, on the actual day of the hearing. Now, that really is a cause for complaint, even before you discover the outcome of the case. Maybe it was your solicitor's fault that the barrister was under-instructed and maybe not. But if he knew the barrister of your choice wasn't going to be there and either didn't bother to tell you, didn't brief the substitute properly or promptly and didn't seek an adjournment if appropriate then all or any of them may have affected the outcome of the case and given grounds for complaint.

I talked about fear of the medical profession. The fact is that the lay public used to hold the legal profession in awe as well. Give a bloke with a law degree a big office, a pair of half-moon glasses over which to peer and he has the upper hand. How can you possibly complain when he so obviously knows more about the matter than you do? That's where you would be wrong. It's your piece of litigation, your divorce, your purchase of a house or company. If you want to put in your two pennyworth, then do so. If he ignores you and it all goes wrong, then put your complaint in writing.

Obviously, I can't tell you everything that can go wrong in a whole myriad of transactions, but I can give you some bullet points as to the sort of things you should be looking for to complain about:

1. Delays.
2. Failure to return calls.
3. Refusal to have meetings with you or delay in setting a date.
4. Over-charging.
5. Failing to follow your specific instructions.
6. Agreeing something with the other side without your authority.
7. Breach of confidence.
8. Rudeness on the phone, which can include cutting calls short because he's too busy.
9. Failing to keep you informed of developments in a timely manner and not copying you in on all the correspondence.
10. Conflicts in the matter that he didn't disclose.
11. Downright incompetent advice that you know is patently wrong.
12. Failure to know the subject on which he's supposed to be advising.

13. Fobbing you off on a junior or even someone unqualified.
14. Going on holiday without bothering to tell you.
15. Telling you he's going on holiday and not bothering to pass the file over to a colleague with a full explanatory note.
16. Sarcasm, failure to take you seriously, lack of sympathy, condescension, patronising you.
17. Failure to supervise either his own staff or your barrister.
18. Letters coming to you unchecked with loads of typing and spelling errors (spell-checks have improved that situation) but you'd be amazed about what that tells you regarding the level of care that's being given to a transaction.
19. Telling you something is being done that day when it isn't and general failure to meet deadlines and targets.
20. Failure to explain things to you patiently when you ask politely.

Now, reading those you may think I've set extraordinarily high standards for the profession. In fact, you can apply almost all of those criteria to accountants as well, or surveyors and architects, in fact all those professions I mentioned before; except estate agents. But then that's why they are called professions. They are meant to be professional. You have to ensure that you get what you pay for. You will certainly be paying enough. I know. Trust me. I'm a lawyer.

25

PHYSICIAN, HEAL THYSELF

If we have a natural inbred fear of lawyers, they even make me nervous and I am one, then we tend to be in awe of doctors. Dentists less so. They are, after all, just guys with strong arms and wrists who couldn't go the course in medicine. (That's my dental fan base gone and it's also probably the last time I get an injection before a filling.) My dentist, is, of course, an exception. He always wanted to be a dentist. It was his life's dream when he got his own spittoon and he could have been the finest surgeon in the land if he hadn't followed his chosen career. Dentistry's gain is surgery's loss. So that's me and him sorted out and now I can say what I really think about the medical and dental service in this country and why there are not enough pages in the Encyclopaedia Britannica to contain all the complaints that could be made about them.

I do seriously except our own GP practice from criticism. Their prompt action in the past has saved my younger son's life when he had a very bad asthma attack and one can always get to see them the same day in case of an emergency. However, they are the exception rather than the rule. The problem is, when one looks at the steaming, yet crumbling, ruins of what was once the envy of the world, namely our National Health system, where do you start your complaints and to whom do you make them?

The fact of the matter is that the buck should start and stop with Government. I'm going to deal with complaints to government bodies and institutions later in this book, but I do think that the National Health Service and, I suppose, to a slightly lesser degree but not that much lesser, the private sector, deserves its own chapter at least. The fact that I've spent more words telling you how to complain to Audi about a duff car than I have in pointing your way through the minefield of medical malpractice complaints, is not to suggest that I regard it as any less serious issue

268

than the fact that my car is more off the road than on. Nor is this intended to be a political tirade. I don't like Mr Blair, if for no other reason than he purports to be a life-long Newcastle United supporter when he palpably isn't. Actually, I don't like him because of everything he stands for, but then, I suspect I'm not alone there. So, if I can make life just a teensy-weensy bit more difficult for him by having him inundated by complaint letters that are so professionally constructed that he has to reply, then I feel somewhat satisfied. The fact of the matter is that Tony Blair is a bit like the Chairman of British Airways, or the General Manager of Loew's Hotel in Miami Beach, insofar as he isn't going to be arsed to reply himself, and all you'll get back is a standard letter from one of his minions. But when it comes to the issue of health you have to persist. Keep writing to him; involve your MP. Everybody who has lived all their lives in this country has their own nightmare story to tell about the health treatment here and it's about time those stories got shared with those in charge, those who make the decision to spend millions of pounds on invading foreign countries but are quite happy to cut back on A & E Departments in those hospitals they have condescendingly left standing.

I've just re-read the last paragraph and I sound like a 1970s' socialist. I suppose I was. I have to confess to actually voting for Harold Wilson. Now I'd rather gnaw my toes down to the bone than vote Labour. But enough of this polemic, let's get down to the nitty-gritty of what to complain about, how and to whom. As I mentioned, if you've been absolutely satisfied with the treatment you have had from doctors etc, in the United Kingdom you are either the healthiest person alive, a patient at our local surgery or The Queen, because otherwise I don't believe you.

Where to start, oh where to start? The agony of choice. When we spoke about lawyers we talked about cost and delay amongst other things. Now the NHS is supposed to be free. But, of course, it's not. Every worker in this country pays for it whether they use it or not, because of the contributions deducted from your pay-slip or included in your tax if you are self-employed. I suppose if you have been unemployed for some thirty years you could proudly claim to have obtained free medical treatment, but think of all the forms you have to fill in to obtain it. It's not free either when you go to collect your prescription from the pharmacist. I nearly fainted the other day when I had three items to pay for. "What do you do if you can't afford it?" I asked. "You get exemption," my friendly neighbourhood pharmacist said. I suspected that entailed the completion of the sort of forms you might have to fill in if you were applying for a job with MI5 but I hope I never have to find out. I'll talk about such forms and the elderly a bit later. This is now the serious bit of the book that should encourage chat show hosts to invite me on for some in-depth discussion of these controversial issues. (And if I can promote the book at the same time then I'd be really rather grateful.) It is, certainly, outrageous that the prescription charge for an item can be greater than the cost of the item, assuming you can buy it over the counter. That can't be right. Surely the cost of a prescription should be the lower of the two. Agree with me? Then write and complain. And while you're at it, write and complain about the delay you will have to suffer if you want an operation in this country. What is it, three years for a hip replacement? If a dodgy hip is as painful as an arthritic hand, and I've got one of those and I suspect it's a lot more painful, then to expect some poor old dear to hobble around in agony for three years or more, depending upon where you live, is just not acceptable. We Brits are a stoic race. Stiff upper-lip and all that. Pip, pip, chin, chin, don't you know! And, as I said almost at the start of this book, we are not a race of natural complainers. Moaners, maybe. Just travel on the top of a bus one day, or stand behind a line of pensioners at the Post Office (soon, you won't be able to do that) and you'll see what I mean. Grumblers, rather than moaners, on reflection. Yet, generally we accept our lot. But we shouldn't. If you are told you have to wait for an operation or even an inordinate length of time to see a doctor, then complain. Complain to the Minister for Health. Complain to the Prime Minister. Complain to your Member of Parliament and complain to the relevant hospital's director or the Practice Manager of your local surgery.

Actually, the last of those complaints is the most dangerous of all. Good doctors' practices are so hard to find that most of them aren't even taking on new patients and if they have a patient who is troublesome they may well try to rid themselves of the "turbulent priest". But should that be a reason not to complain? The point I am coming to is that there are times when even if you think you have every reason to complain, when you are absolutely on the side of the angels, that you have to think through the consequences very carefully. I know it's not right and it's not fair, but are you really going to start taking your local GP to court because he says he won't treat you any more because you wrote him a complaint letter (and also sent copies to various other parties up to the Prime Minister!) We have reached here an interesting dilemma. My view is always to do what you think is right, and if you feel that you have been treated badly (and this after much thought and discussion with loved ones ... and partners) then go for it. But be prepared for a fight.

Hospitals are easier targets. If you get barred from a local hospital how would you tell? The places are so hard to get into anyway. I mentioned earlier the instance of my wife dropping off her mother and looking for somewhere to park. Just try looking for a bed in a hospital. My wife's elderly aunt spent a night on a trolley in an Essex hospital. Actually I nearly did as well but made such a fuss that they gave me my own cubicle in A & E. They still wouldn't admit me even though I had blinding pains in my head and kept being sick. They did suggest I had a brain scan which I dealt with privately but, again, ill as I was, if I hadn't been such a pain (being in such pain actually made me reach new heights of obnoxiousness, my wife said) I wouldn't have even achieved that height of luxury.

Not that you want to get admitted to one of our National Health Hospital wards. My late mother did and promptly caught some kind of bug or infection which killed her. Of course I complained. But somehow "I want my mummy back" coming from a fifty plus year old man with a grey beard and little hair doesn't carry the same emotive ring about it. I'm quite sure that she's haunting the ward anyway. Can't see my mother letting somebody get away with them bumping her off.

The quality of doctors can be a bit of a lottery as well. Some years ago I made the mistake of having a wisdom tooth removed at University College Hospital. What I didn't sign on for however was that it would be done by a student in front of a class of other students. Needless to say he buggered it up, broke the tooth (and for all I know the drill as well) and I left the hospital bleeding profusely. This was just before I got married so we are going back some thirty-four years and I hope the student has not only qualified, learned to remove a wisdom tooth in one piece, but like every other dentist I know has made enough money to buy himself a property abroad and retire there. On returning home the bleeding continued apace. My parents didn't drive so I rang Marilyn, my then fiancée, who got her dad to take me back to UCH where I sat in Casualty, or A & E, as they now seem to be called, still bleeding. Now when it comes to vital juices I'm not very good. I don't like the sight of blood, particularly my own. I could either spit or swallow, sorry for the graphic description. It seemed I was swallowing because by the time I was seen by a very young registrar I was choking on my own blood and managed to do a very good impression of the girl in The Exorcist and promptly drenched the doctor's tie in red gore.

I was admitted, put on a drip, and told I'd come in to hospital just in time as I would have probably choked to death in the night. And then this book wouldn't have been written and what a loss to the world of literature that would have been. And how grateful British Airways, Audi and Loew's Hotel would have been. But I didn't choke to death. I lived to tell the tale. Mind you, I couldn't shave for nearly a month and that's how I got my beard which I vowed to keep until Newcastle won the cup, so that's with me for life then. I must have made threatening noises to the hospital at the time, but I didn't have a lifetime's experience of complaining behind me so here's how I would have dealt with that now:

Dear Sirs

Last week I underwent some dental treatment at your hospital. I was seen by a young and inexperienced practitioner who, without my consent, sought to remove a wisdom tooth in the presence of a group of students.

Due to his inexperience the tooth broke and I was subjected to considerable pain and discomfort. The tooth was finally removed and I was sent home by public transport even though I was still bleeding and clearly in considerable distress.

The bleeding continued unabated and all a telephone call to yourselves produced was the advice to lie on my side and to return if it persisted. It did persist and upon being brought back to the hospital I was admitted on an emergency basis and told that had I not returned then my life might well have been in jeopardy.

I was detained in hospital for some 48 hours and put on a drip and have been advised that I will not be able to return to work for at least a fortnight.

I require some explanation, an apology and a suitable offer of compensation and look forward to hearing from you within the next seven days.

Shame I didn't do that as I could be a wealthy man today if I'd invested my ill-gotten gains as a result.

Actually, my son Paul has also had grounds to complain recently. He went to see his National Health dentist, who actually works from a surgery where all the other dentists only do private treatment. Paul was in pain and the dentist told him he had a gum infection. A week or so later he was in agony. He called the emergency line of the surgery on a Saturday morning and was referred to another local dentist (still on the National Health). She saw him, took X-rays and told him he had a huge hole in his tooth which the other dentist had completely missed. She gave him antibiotics and then said he needed root canal treatment to complete the filling. I made a point of speaking to the senior partner at the practice.

"Well," he said, "it's the National Health. What do you expect?"

I said I expected my son to be diagnosed properly and treated accordingly. The dentist shrugged.

"The whole system is falling apart."

"But he was seen in your practice," I continued.

"Well, he should have gone privately."

"But he can't afford it."

"Then he should go to one of the teaching hospitals ..."

Which is where I came in.

And that attitude in the private sector is certainly worth a complaint. Have you ever been seen by a specialist who treated you as if you weren't there? Who muttered to himself his diagnosis as if there was no chance you could possibly understand it? Now, believe me, if you, or your private health insurer, is paying through the nose for private medical treatment then you are entitled to be treated like an intelligent human being and if you are not then you should certainly complain. To the specialist, to the General Medical Council if his conduct borders on the unprofessional, and even to the private health insurer. No medical practitioner wants to be removed from their approved lists, it's too remunerative.

As I said, I don't want to get into the realms of medical malpractice as that involves letters before action, insurance companies and possibly courts and who knows, maybe even lawyers (the final word to be spoken in hushed reverential tones). There is a distinction, even when it comes to the medical profession, of what justifies a complaint (and no, I won't repeat the Spike Milligan pun even though I really, really want to) and what needs to be taken that extra mile. Only you can decide that but, again, here's your check-list to keep by your side when you visit the doctor, dentist or hospital:

1. Delay in getting an appointment or delay in being seen. It's just not acceptable in 21st Century Britain to wait six hours in Casualty.
2. Delay in having a necessary operation.
3. Lack of courtesy when finally seen. However busy or tired the doctor may be there is no excuse for that. You have gone to see him because you have something wrong with you, unless you're a hypochondriac ... in which case you still have something wrong with you and you do deserve some sympathy, compassion and understanding even if you are not paying £200 an hour for the privilege.
4. Failure to explain to you properly what is wrong or treating you like an idiot.
5. Having students present at an examination without your consent.
6. Over-charging. Yes, it can happen with doctors too.
7. Misdiagnosing where it doesn't turn out to be too serious but does impair or delay recovery. Obviously, if it is serious then you need to consult a solicitor.

8. Fobbing you off with another practitioner when you've made a specific appointment to see a specific person.
9. Rude and unhelpful receptionists.
10. Dirty surgeries, hospitals, wards, etc.
11. Lack of privacy, and, whilst I'm on the subject, mixed hospital wards. Do you really want your grandpa to be in the next bed to your neighbour's granny? Who knows? If they get better they may end up in the same bed.
12. Poor food in the hospital.
13. Inconsiderate, careless or non-caring nursing. If you have an elderly, sick relation who may be incurable, they still deserve the same time and respect as anybody else. As my mother used to say: "I paid my taxes."

Again, as I've listed those I realise just how lucky my family has been with our GPs. None of those comments apply, but I suspect we are in the minority. The art of complaining about your medical practitioners is to survive long enough to do it. Oh, and still manage to keep on somebody's panel.

25

POWER TO THE PEOPLE!

Authority. With a Capital "A". We all rebel against authority at some time in our lives, but generally that's when we are young and disobeying our parents or teachers and that can hardly be deemed to fall into the category of complaining. But by Authority, I mean Local and Central Government and the Police, or anybody in uniform for that matter, including any "Jobsworth" of whom you may fall foul.

It's not difficult to find things to complain about when it comes to Government and to achieve a successful complaint you don't need to burn the Union Jack in Trafalgar Square, or anywhere, for that matter. Though have you noticed that the tossers who burn the flag in public are the same people who fight to the last appeal for their right to remain here? Bit odd that. If it is such a lousy country you'd think they'd want to rid themselves of its sand between their toes. Perhaps, after reading this they may realise that it's more constructive to complain than burn flags and I suspect that this book is cheaper than the cost of a full-size British flag anyway.

It has always seemed easier to me to complain about local rather than national issues. If your road is a death-trap because cars use it as a rat-run to avoid the main arterials then you can get a petition together, present it to your local councillor and there's a good chance he'll get some kind of traffic calming system installed. However, if you want to complain about Government policy on health spending, any letter addressed to the Prime Minister or Minister for Health is likely to produce a stereotypical response from some assistant secretary who can't even be bothered to sign his or her own name and if they do it's more than likely to be illegible and have you branded in officialdom as a crank. So it is better to plant your little acorns locally and hope eventually they turn into giant national oaks.

So, what is there to complain about locally. Well, why don't we try, road-safety, environment, schools, hospitals, playing fields or lack thereof, noise, traffic, development and dogs not kept on leads in public places for starters? Let's begin with the most important. Yes, that's the wild dogs. I have to say I don't like dogs. Or rather, to be more accurate, dogs don't like me. Whichever way you want to put it the feeling's totally mutual. So that's yet another readership fan base I've alienated, which is why I left this revelation until towards the end of the book and yes, you'll be relieved to know that the end is in sight. My pet hate (not meant to be a pun, that, but suppose it's not a bad one) are owners of salivating Hounds of the Baskervilles telling me that their creature of the night wouldn't hurt a fly and there's no need for me to be trembling and quivering in a corner at the sight of his saliva-flecked jaws and blood-shot, blood-lusting eyes. My theory (and response) is generally that if the animal were to tell me that himself then I might believe him, but why should I take the word of his owner who doesn't even speak the canine language? The famous line, when I hesitate at the portal of a dog-owner's door, is that I should come in because "Fido never barks" I enter and am greeted with the sort of aggressive baying usually reserved for Spurs when they run onto the pitch at Highbury.

"That's funny, he's never done that before," the owners say as they try to persuade me down from the top of a bookcase.

I may hate dogs, but I do like running, and I particularly like running around the park. What I don't like is having to run a zig-zag as I try to avoid dogs that are running wild without their leads. If you try to approach an owner to tell them that parks are for the use of people they will tell you that you are quite incorrect and that these have been designed and nurtured solely and exclusively for the use of four-legged friends with all the attendant joys they bring with them. So, I complained.

And the result was a sign referring to by-laws and an injunction to keep dogs on leads. The fact of the matter is that a fair number of pooch-lovers ignore it and I find myself in the role of a one-man vigilante group as I seek to enforce the law. However, if you ask a leash-less dog walker for his, or even worse her, name or address you are just as likely to get a torrent of abuse or a black eye as the information. Or worse still they will set their animals on you. But I did get the sign put up, so 1-0 to me in my fight against authority.

Joking aside, and turning to more serious issues, this Government came to power dedicated to saving playing fields and making life ever more difficult for developers who want to build on them. One of the more attractive features of our house when we bought it some years ago (under a Tory Government) was that it backed on to open school playing fields. I cost the local authority a few million quid by seeing off a plan to develop the field into houses, only to see the scheme raise its head again some years later (under a Labour Government) and this time the bastards won. I complained and complained and what I did achieve was the preservation of a copse that contained a family of foxes, even though they had bitten the head off our pet rabbit Garfield some years before. The rabbit had just undergone some rather expensive surgery so I was particularly peeved. I also managed to get a small buffer zone of trees between the development and my rear wall, and neither of these would have been achieved without a constant barrage of complaints. It did always strike me as rather odd though, that the one listed part of the school that was to be redeveloped got burned down in a fire that was not extinguished for some time, even though the fire station backs on to the school as well. Still, I'm writing a book about complaints, not mysteries.

I complained about the noise and disturbance when they laid cable in our street as well. I didn't see why we should have to put up with this (even to the point of my not being able to get my car onto my own drive) when it was purely for the profit of a private company (always a good point to make in a complaint letter). They still put it in and I then suggested that I should be connected for nothing. They declined. I argued. I failed. This was over ten years ago and I suspect I might be more persistent today. If you do have disturbance, either from someone like a cable provider, or a developer, or even a noisy neighbour, then you are entitled to complain. The first point of call should be the actual noise producer and after that you should be going both to your local council as a whole and to your councillor in particular. You know, I've just decided to devote an extra chapter to noise. Aren't you pleased about that?

Certainly, in terms of local issues it's worth getting to know your councillor. He will usually be your near neighbour as well, unlike your Member of Parliament who probably only visits the constituency for a monthly surgery or to scrounge for votes before an election. Actually, I've been blessed with two really good local MPs. Michael Portillo was always there for a cause. He certainly tried to help me save my playing fields and his successor, Stephen Twigg, who does live locally, does react immediately to any complaints or inquiries. But if you aren't so lucky and your local complaints fall on deaf ears, whether those belong to your councillor or MP don't hesitate to complain. A good way to complain about your representatives is to complain to the local press. Local people read the local press and local people vote. Politicians are always very wary of losing votes.

If you are a parent and can't get your child into the school of your choice, or if you have got them there and the teaching is not up to standard, then again you have to complain. Your child's education is not something with which to take chances. Many moons ago my younger son was being taught stuff he, and the rest of the class, had learned the previous year. We complained to the headmaster who was actually grateful that we had brought the matter to his attention and the teacher was removed. She'll probably read this, realise what happened and I'll be found face down in a gutter with a steel ruler impaled through my heart. If that does happen there may be a couple of suspects because we also complained about a teacher who had lost control of the class which meant my son was learning nothing and she too was moved on. Complaints about education are far better dealt with by a visit to the school than a letter. At least, if the head teacher is sensible, you can gauge the reaction and know immediately if anything is going to be done about the problem. Particularly in GCSE and A Level years, time is of the essence, and a couple of months of poor teaching or anarchy in the classroom can make all the difference to your child's educational prospects.

Central government is a trickier problem. Nowadays, Big Brother is watching us and not just on television. He comes in the shape of databases, computerised information and endless form-filling to achieve anything. I was chatting to my friend, Jeff Caire, the other day, who told me his 92-year-old mother had just received a huge form to complete in respect of her pension. It appears that very soon it is no longer going to be possible just to amble or limp or shuffle as the case may be, down to your local Post Office to collect your pension. Those pension-day morning queues will vanish, yet another piece of our fast disappearing heritage. They were part of my childhood, all those old men and women lining up a good half an hour before the Post Office opened just in case they ran out of money. The women with their shopping baskets, purses tightly gripped in their hands, hair neatly and newly permed, the men with a fag in their mouths, or a pipe in more sophisticated cases, and a tabloid opened to the racing page all ready for the day's investments once they had received their pension cash. What is now planned is that all these pensioners will have to have either a bank account or a Post Office account and their pension will automatically be paid in, thus removing a fairly important element of their social lives, namely the conversation outside and inside the Post Office itself. Quite frankly, so many local branch post offices are going anyway that some pensioners would have had to travel about 100 miles to get to one that had survived. They wanted to close down our local branch, but we set up a petition, in conjunction with a couple of the more active local councillors, complained vociferously, and it was saved.

So, this 92-year-old has the form to complete. By the time her son, my pal, had arrived from his home in Ireland she had mislaid it. The conversation went something along these lines, I am told:

"Jeffrey, I've had a letter. If I don't send it back they're going to put me in prison."

"Well, give it to me and I'll fill it in for you."

"I don't know where I've put it."

"Why don't you give the letters you get to the warden?" (the old lady is in sheltered accommodation, not prison, I may add).

"What, so that she should know my business?"

Now Jeff is about to complain to the relevant Government Department. How on earth do they expect elderly citizens who may be vague, blind, confused or totally alone to cope with forms like this? It's quite incomprehensible that this plan has sneaked under the door and the procedure itself is beyond belief. There has been no Government explanation, no home visits and once this arrangement is in place who can be sure that pensioners will actually receive their proper due. Now if Jeff is complaining then so should any of you who are either pensioners yourselves or have an elderly relative who will be affected by this change of tradition. As I may have mentioned before, pensioners on pension day can be quite brutal and ruthless about collecting their monies, but even if the loss to the pensioner is the gain to the casualty department it is simply not acceptable, and is a fine example of something that can only be changed by mass complaints.

Then we come to the police. Mind you, if the pensioners rise as a man and lay siege to the post offices then the police might come to them. My money would be on the oldies. Now generally speaking the police do a good job. However, they are sometimes the subject of complaints and there is, ultimately, a Police Ombudsman to ensure that the service our boys in blue give to the public is fair and even-handed whatever may be the colour, race or creed of the citizen. Blimey! I sound like the American Declaration of Independence don't I? Mind you that document seemed to have a fair number of exceptions, like if you were a Red Indian in the 19th Century, a black in the Deep South in the 20th Century or a "suspected" terrorist or "captured" fighter in the 21st Century. Not a lot of suffering of the poor and needy to come to the old Mother Country as far as any of that lot were concerned. Yet, there are times when we do need to complain about our cops without even going as far as requesting a formal Ombudsman investigation.

For example, how many times have you been stopped in your car by a couple of policeman who are having a quiet night. Generally, one is older than the other or one is male and one female and in either case you get the feeling that the elder or the bloke is showing off to his partner as to exactly how powerful he can be. It's quite some time since I got called "Sonny" by a policeman (though they do seem to be getting younger all the time, don't they?). I've not been called "Gramps" by one as yet though I'm sure that pleasure has yet to come. The fact of the matter is that whether we are stopped for nothing, or because of a genuine suspicion or, indeed, a genuine offence like speeding, we are entitled to basic courtesy. And, you may be interested to learn, that if we are not, then the policeman in question is in breach of the Police Discipline Code. (Jeff told me about this as well, so if any policeman out there are peeved by this chapter then it's him you should be harassing officer, not me.) If that happens to you, then, having made a note of the policeman's number, go to your local police station, ask to see the senior officer on duty and lodge a complaint under the Code. They have to investigate it and they have to be polite to you when they log it. If you hear nothing after you've made such a complaint then that is the time to put it in writing, setting out the incident that triggered it off, the time you visited the station, and the name of the officer you saw. Just by the by I've still not been asked to complete a crime report form in respect of the keying of AJ which was nearly six months ago.

The nub of the matter is that you mustn't be scared just because the entity to which you are complaining is bigger than you, (most entities are bigger than me anyway) and has more resources than you and will, almost certainly have a deeper pocket. If you just shrug your shoulders, on the basis that it's too much hassle, then the one racing certainty upon which you can put all your pension money, in the unlikely event of it ever being received at the right destination again, is that it will re-occur.

The Tax Office is another potential source of complaints. They are very quick to complain to you if you don't pay them on time so why shouldn't you be inundating them with complaints when they either over-charge you, or fail to send you back your rebate that may be due in a timely manner. You may well have an accountant who deals with all that and if he's not somebody who falls into any of the categories of my professional adviser complaints then you can probably safely leave things to him. But many people either cannot afford accountants or, in these days of self assessment, think they can do it themselves. It's an unequal fight. Or at least it would appear to be so. But if you think a mistake has been made, then make the effort and write the letter. They can only say no.

So here, in the space I have, are some Authoritarian issues about which you should complain if they have happened to you.

1. Vehicles being able to drive too quickly down your road.
2. Uncut hedges making it dangerous to get out of your drive – because you can't see what's coming.
3. Persistently noisy neighbours.
4. Inefficient rubbish collection.
5. Uncontrolled developments.
6. Dirty streets.
7. Deprivation of leisure facilities.
8. Closing of hospitals and post offices and other social services.
9. Uncooperative social services.
10. Poor gas, water or telephone services.
11. Bullying police.
12. Pension payment and collection problems.
13. Unreasonable Council Tax demands, an appeal is a sort of complaint.
14. Flight-paths disturbing you at night.
15. Poor public transport in your area.
16. Ruthless parking wardens waiting to swoop even as you go off to get change for the meter.
17. Failure to get the school of your choice for your children.
18. Sub-standard education for your children, whether you have got the school of your choice or not.
19. Local councils failing to live up to, or implement, election promises
20. Poor library service.
21. Absence or delays in providing emergency services.

Oh, and allowing packs of wild dogs to roam uncontrolled through your local parks.

27

I WOULDN'T HAVE DONE IT LIKE THAT

Builders complain about each other, so how can they not expect us to complain about them? It's in the blood as far as they are concerned, a knee-jerk reaction whenever they see a competitor's handiwork, that sharp intake of breath, those pursed lips and then the shake of the head and the deathly silence that you know signifies the mental arithmetic that is going on in their head to correct the awful mess before their eyes.

But how to complain to a builder? Here we have a trade that very often doesn't even have an office from which to operate and whose idea of correspondence and a filing system are some jottings on the back of a cigarette packet. Obviously that doesn't apply to the big boys, but how many of us use the big boys to decorate our front rooms or lay a new patio?

To avoid repetition let me make it quite clear that when I talk about builders I'm including plumbers, electricians, carpenters, plasterers, painters, joiners and even gardeners. These are all people who ply trades of which I, and I suspect the greater proportion of the Great British Public know very little and therefore it is all too easy to be taken for a ride. That is assuming you haven't bought your car from Audi and have one that works, or is at least in your possession for a reasonable number of days a year.

Now I'm sure I don't need to tell you that, even before you start learning about how to complain to and about builders, you need to take every precaution to avoid the necessity for complaints. Basically try not to use a builder you don't know or who hasn't been recommended to you. I know that's a bit unfair to all the young builders out there graduating from building school (or wherever it is they graduate from) and that everybody has to start somewhere, but it's a bit like dentists. Let them learn their trade somewhere else before they are let loose on you and your property.

Almost everybody I know has a builder story so, I have to admit,

I've been fairly lucky. Apart from some jobbing bloke who managed to hang the wallpaper in our front room upside down (and I think I should have been wary of him by virtue of the fact that he'd been sent to us originally as a contract cleaner, who then turned into a baby-sitter, and I'm sure if I'd asked him to perform brain surgery on one of my kids he would have claimed to have been competent to do that as well) I can't think of any major problem I've had with the people who've worked for us over the years.

Now when I say major problems that doesn't mean I've not had cause to complain. My regular builder, John, who dresses in designer clothes and never seems to get his own hands dirty did a very impressive job on our kitchen and then left a sink in the front garden. I made the major mistake of paying him all I owed him and the sink stayed where it was. In fact it was becoming a veritable feature and I contemplated filling it with plants and leaving it there, but however I might have disguised or decorated it, a sink it would have been. I phoned John and phoned John. It was time for threats as this was clearly a language he understood. If the sink were not collected within 24 hours I would personally deliver it to his house so that he too could have a sink-feature in his front garden. The sink duly vanished to the great sink heaven in the sky. I have to say that for a while I actually missed the damn thing.

The problem is that builders always like to be ahead of the game, at least as far as money is concerned. When it comes to schedules, however, they are always miles behind the game, even assuming you can work out the rules of the particular game that builders play. A friend, who bought a house in France, went through three building firms before she worked out that the game they play over there (apart from taking the diametrically opposite stance to anything we Brits believe in) is first to deliver all the building materials to the property. Next come the tools and if one is lucky some workmen accompany them, but they don't stay for more than a day and the materials only arrive because they've been paid for in advance. As time passes no men appear but strangely the materials slowly disappear and so, eventually, do the tools. This is presumably because the process is being repeated on site after site all over the country. The only way to get work done in France, it appears, is to supervise it oneself on a daily basis.

Now, annoying as that is, the situation is made far worse by the fact that money has been taken on account by Bob (or Robert in the French case) the Builder allegedly to buy the materials. Some payment for works is also generally required on account. And thus it is that the builder becomes so far ahead of the game that he is virtually lapping himself. The fact of the matter is that most builders won't start work until they have some dosh on account. There is a strong argument for writing out a cheque, tearing it in half, and handing across one portion to Bob, retaining the other in your top pocket until Bob has done the work to your satisfaction. However, builders don't seem to recognise cheques as a method of trading and work only in that rather grubby commodity known as cash.

I know this is meant to be a book about how to complain but I can't write a chapter about builders without mentioning Les, who does all the building work for us in our house in the Cotswolds. When we first met Les we asked him how much he wanted on account and he looked at us as if we had insulted him.

"When I finish the work and you're happy with it that's when you pay me," he said.

I'm not going to give Les's surname as he's mine, all mine and nobody else can have him.

Les, unfortunately, is the exception that doesn't prove the rule. He is unique and I have to tell you how to complain about the other 99.999% of the building trade. I would like to say that, as with most areas of complaint, you need to create a paper trail, but the problem is, as I have already mentioned, that paper is not really a commodity in which builders deal. Maybe that's why they have their aversion to cheques as well. However, if you are going to be in a position to complain effectively, you need to have something to complain about. If he does shoddy work then that will speak for itself, but if he takes too long or charges too much how are you going to prove either of those.

So, what you need is to ask for, not only a written estimate, but also an estimated time for completion of the works. If he won't give it to you, or fobs you off by saying he'll let you have it once he's on site, then find another builder, because the likelihood is that you'll never get them. If he asks for money on account (which he will unless his name is Les and he supports Birmingham City ... that's another clue to his identity) then for heaven's sake get a receipt, even if it is just a tacky scrap of paper because of his avowed paper allergy (a well-known affliction amongst the merry men of the building trade). If the money is for him to buy materials then ask him for the receipts. He may just buy wholesale and charge you retail. I know that may be another scurrilous slur on a noble profession, but there you go. I'll take my chances that I won't get a whole army of blokes with tattoos, ear-rings and buttock cleavage milling outside my house the day after this book is published. If the work involves any kind of substantial construction get the builder to enter into a formal contract. There are standard forms you can obtain from H.M Stationers which relate to "small works" (they may be small to the builder but they are mammoth for you) or more major works. Again, if the builder doesn't want to sign, then find one who will.

It is ever so easy to be lured into spending and spending once the job starts. Problems which were concealed from the naked eye, suddenly add hundreds of pounds to your bill as they come to light. And then you feel you are so far in that you have no choice but to continue to spend. Builders are a bit like lawyers in that respect. It's also not difficult to give them a day or two longer than they anticipated to finish the job. Materials haven't arrived; the weather's been bad; Bob's grandma has died; the District Surveyor didn't keep his appointment or there's been a crisis on another job. Did I not tell you that no builder worth his salt had less than three other jobs going contemporaneously with yours and materials, tools and manpower seem to switch, by magic, between all four projects? They are like magicians, or, in fact, more like cardsharps, demonstrating the three or four card trick. Now you see it, now you don't. Now you see workmen, whoops you looked away, so now you don't.

The fact of the matter is that it's a sign of weakness, a potential disaster, to cut them any slack at all. If they say they will finish on Thursday and by Wednesday it's obvious that they won't, then complain. If they are getting very near to the budget and you can see there are several thousand pounds' worth of work to be done, then complain. If any part of the work is unsatisfactory as it goes along, don't accept an assurance that it'll be dealt with at the end. Complain and ensure it gets rectified at once. Of course, there will be times when you know that it's either your fault or something totally outside of Bob's control that is to blame. If there's external work to be done and we are having a typical English summer with pouring rain, hurricanes and blizzards on and off then he'll have a good excuse not to have brought the job in on time. If you have changed your mind and decided to have a patio laid instead of decking then he might just have the teeniest reason not to bring the job in on time. But if your conscience is clear and Bob has not performed then you need to go for the jugular. Trust me, if you didn't pay him then he would go for yours.

To have some kind of leverage it's very important that (as I've learnt to my cost) you are not persuaded to part with all your money before completion, as if you have then you can complain until you are blue in the face, it simply won't make any difference. If he fancies making good the fault then he will, and if he doesn't then he won't. It's always good to keep your builder supplied with a veritable flow of cups of tea, not to mention platefuls of biscuits. And don't give him the grotty ones from the selection that nobody else wants to eat. Or those boring dry ones that have gone past their sell-by date. He will know. In another life all builders chose tea and biscuits for Marks & Spencer. That supply of beverage and sustenance may well make him easier to deal with.

Complaining to a builder is not like complaining to a weedy lawyer or an anonymous company. He's probably right there in front of you, looming over you, all six feet and fifteen stone of sweaty, irrational humanity. But the principals are the same. Don't lose your temper, even if he has picked you up by the collar in one slab of a hand. Be rational and reasonable in your complaints without being rude. Know exactly what your objectives are. Do you want him off site with a view to getting another contractor in to finish off the job or do you want him to re-do what he's done or just finish it more speedily? If he is part of a bigger company then you need to be speaking to his boss. And for what it's worth, put it all in writing even though he may rip your complaint letter into confetti before your very eyes (that is assuming he doesn't gouge them out). That letter may be useful if your complaint technique fails and the matter ends up in court. But don't forget my maxim. If you have to sue then you have failed as a complainant.

As far as your letter is concerned, then with regard to builders, it's always best to stick to the plain facts. They don't appreciate sarcasm. It's not a trait much valued on the terraces of whichever football club they support. They all support someone. You can either tell from their tattoos or the flags or stickers on their vehicles. Whichever club it is it can be prudent to pay lip-service to their support, at least as long as Bob and his boys are in the house.

So what are your bullet points, the check-list you draw up as you wander through the debris of your half-finished loft-extension. Actually, in the case of most builders I can think of a better use for bullets than making lists of them.

1. Have you got something in writing to prove the agreed price of the job and the time it will take?
2. Have you seen all the receipts for materials?
3. Has Bob and his team turned up every day they said they would and have they been punctual?
4. Have they tidied up at the end of the day?
5. Have they nicked anything or made any unauthorised phone-calls?
6. Have they carried out the work according to the plans and any local authority consents that were needed?
7. Have they kept within their budget?
8. Have they rectified any faults as they went along?
9. Have they upset the neighbours with blaring radios or unnecessary noise?
10. Have they taken away all the rubbish at the end?
11. Is the quality of the work what you expected and have they delivered what you paid for?
12. Do you feel you've had value for money?
13. Have they agreed to come back to do any snagging and have you kept back some money to cover that?
14. Have they provided any written guarantees that they said they would?

And finally, in your heart of hearts are you happy with their work and would you recommend them? That in itself is the final and most telling point in your decision as to whether or not to complain.

Oh, and if you do complain, is your life insurance up to date?

27

THE QUEEN AND I

I have a headache. It's not because I've been staring at a computer screen for hours on end writing this book. It's because of The Queen. Now she doesn't know it and it's not as if I'm going to write her a complaint letter either. But I have written to The Crown Estate and I suppose they are working for her so I reckon it all boils down to the same thing. It's all about noise. I hate noise. In fact I'm writing this in the village of Blockley in the Cotswolds looking out over an old mill stream and up into a field where lambs are gambolling quite happily. At least they are happy until someone comes along to remove their wool as the first step to them ending up on a plate as a Sunday joint. I didn't like lamb before we bought this house, but now I positively can't eat anything that reminds me of these cute little creatures nestling up to their mummies on their wobbly little legs. There you go, another blow for vegetarianism.

Noise is relative. My friend Colin complained about the noise of the birds when he spent a weekend in the country with us. The birds ignored his complaint. My wife complains at the noise emanating from tennis players as they grunt their way through Wimbledon. They ignore her complaint too, and anyway they earn much more money than she and I so they can afford to. But I have been complaining about a massive building site just off London's Regent Street which backs directly on to my office. It's so close that I can see the tools they are using, huge pile-drivers which have been smashing through cement for what seems like months. In fact, upon reflection it has been months.

Matters came to a head a few months ago when at noon my office began to shake. I was in the middle of a telephone conversation when I suddenly realised that I was shouting to be heard and in any event, even if I was heard, I couldn't hear a word of what the person on the other end of the line was saying. I looked out of the window and saw the pile-driver in action, doubtless being operated by what my wife would call real men. I had already written a couple of mild complaint letters to City Of Westminster Council's Environmental Health Department, but largely as a paper trail to obtain a Council Tax reduction for the interference with my quiet enjoyment of my business amenities. This noise, however, was something else.

I phoned Westminster and, would you believe it, found myself connected to a call centre. I left a message and awaited a call. It didn't come and I wrote to them on the 9th June.

Dear Sirs,

I refer to my earlier correspondence regarding the work on the building site adjacent to our office at 4 New Burlington Street.

For the past week, the noise level has been quite intolerable. Work has started on site as early as 7.45, making it quite impossible to work in my office with the window open (and this in temperatures of over 80 degrees) and, indeed, very difficult to work even with the window closed. Work continued, unabated, all day and this is severely disrupting my business.

I am quite sure that the noise levels are unacceptable and I should be grateful if you could check the matter once again and revert to me as soon as possible,

Yours faithfully,

Matters did not improve, although I was contacted by a charming young lady (here we go again) called Anuja. She was an Environmental Health Officer at Westminster City Council and she was a member of their 24 Hours Noise Team, a truly crack regiment to which to belong. On the 22nd June, after I had consumed several packets of paracetemol, she e-mailed me. We had obviously hit it off because she called me Mel.

Dear Mel

Thanks for your letter dated 9th June 2004. I apologise for the delay in responding.

Construction sites are permitted to work between the hours of 8am to 6pm Monday to Friday and 8am to 1pm on Saturdays. No noisy works should take place on Sundays and Bank Holidays. We are also able to limit the hours that noisy works are carried out during the day, if this will help your business.

If work is being carried outside of these times or if the noise levels are unacceptable then please contact the office and an officer will contact you.

I hope this information is helpful to you.

Yours sincerely

By the time I'd received this I had endured the most terrible morning of noise. It was a hot day and I had to keep the windows closed but even through the glass the level of the drilling and demolition meant I could not talk on the phone, dictate or, indeed, even think. In the heat of the moment I went down to the street with the full intention of confronting the contractors on the site. Foolhardy? Perhaps, but you must understand my desperation. A few builders were sitting around smoking fags whilst the noise continued unabated. On the wall I saw a sign telling me that the development was being managed by a company called Skanska UK Buildings Ltd. They had kindly provided a phone number, doubtless in anticipation of the complaints they were certain to receive, and the name of the site manager was Trevor. I rang and was put through to Trev. He sympathised. His office was nearby and he was being affected by the noise as well. I pointed out to him that he was being paid to be affected. He was still sympathetic and told me he was employed by The Crown Estates. Doubtless he thought that would stop me in my tracks whilst I stood to attention and sang the National Anthem. It didn't. Even if I'd sung the National Anthem nobody would have heard me, as the song would have been drowned out as effectively as the English fans submerge any rival countries' anthems in football internationals. He did tell me that he could only really carry out very noisy works between noon and 2 pm. I told him in no uncertain terms that somehow or other I was determined to find a way to be able to work in peace and quiet. Although he didn't actually say so I almost imagined him muttering "Good Luck" under his breath. I returned to my office to wait for 2 o'clock. At least I might be able to hear The Archers if I turned the radio up a bit.

The following morning I responded to Anuja.

Thank you for your e-mail of the 22nd June.

The noise from the building site in New Burlington Place became so intolerable that, eventually, I was forced to go down into the street and get their phone number so that I could call the site manager, of Skanska UK Buildings Limited.

He told me that he was employed by The Crown Estates. He told me that he had been told by yourselves that they could not do noisy demolition work between the hours of 10 am and 12 pm, and 2 and 4 pm. I pointed out to him that "noisy" was relative. Even without what he termed the "noisy demolition work", I was unable to open the windows in my office as I could neither hear telephone conversations nor indeed dictate.

I asked him why he could not do these works at weekends and he told me that, up to last weekend, he had only been allowed to work on Saturday mornings by you and not at all on Sunday. Last Saturday, it appears, he was allowed to work all day but he was still not allowed to work on Sunday. The area is simply not a residential area and almost completely commercially occupied and I fail to see why you should have given such a directive, as the weekend would be the obvious time for the noisy works to take place.

As you are aware, this work has been going on for months and we have been severely disadvantaged because of it. For me now to find out that noisy work has, in fact, been Council-driven and with your approval, seems to me utterly outrageous.

I must also point out that the telephone number you gave me, merely took me through to a Call Centre where I was transferred to a switchboard, thence to the Environmental Health Department when you were not available. I do now have your telephone message and will call you back today.

Something must be done about this immediately as we do not in any way benefit, as neighbours, from the huge profit that will doubtless fall to The Crown Estate in building this development. I would welcome a visit from you to our offices so that you can gauge the level of noise this week.

Yours sincerely,

To my delight she told me that she and her partner, I assume this was her work partner and not her life partner, Ken Agnew would come to visit at 11.30 am that day.

I also wrote to Trev, as having started our relationship and gained his sympathy I had no wish to bring it to an end, at least not without causing him maximum inconvenience.

Re: Crown Estate Building works – New Burlington Place

Further to our telephone conversation of Tuesday 22nd June, the noise from your building site became so intolerable that I was forced to go down into the street to use my mobile to call you to complain because I simply could not hear in my office, even with the windows closed.

The fact of the matter is that your building site has caused us considerable inconvenience for many months and has caused me to write several letters of complaint to Westminster City Council. However, the noise reached new levels last week and this week, which has meant that, despite the heat, I have been unable to work with my windows open in the office and, even with them closed, when the noise levels are at their peak, I can neither hear myself talk on the telephone, nor, indeed, dictate a letter.

You advised me that you had been told by Westminster City Council that you could only do the "noisy" works between the hours of 12 pm and 2.00p.m but the noise begins before 8 o'clock every morning when I arrive at the office to do some complex work and continues well into the early evening.

You advised me that you were operating under the instructions of The Crown Estate Office though you told me that your office itself has been affected by the noise. As I pointed out to you, we do not in any way share in the profits of The Crown

Estate and I am amazed that you have allowed these noise levels to commence and continue without some consultation with the neighbouring owners and occupiers.

I am sending a copy of this letter to The Crown Estate as I simply cannot continue to accept the negative impact this is having on our own business.

I do expect a reply <u>by return</u> and do not expect you to wait until you feel you have carried out the noisy work and I am likely to cease my complaint.

Yours sincerely,

I also wrote to The Crown Estate. I had no real chance of being in the Queen's Honours Lists so I decided I had nothing to lose. As you will see I had read their environmental policy with interest as it seemed to bear little or no resemblance to what they were actually doing in the real world.

Re: New Burlington Place

I enclose herewith copies of letters I have sent both to the Westminster City Council Environmental Health office, the project manager for the W5 development which is being conducted on your behalf by Skanska UK Buildings Limited.

We really do have to come to some kind of accommodation with regard to this work as the effect on my own business is becoming critical.

I note with interest your environmental policy and, in particular, that you will:

"Adopt measures to achieve continual improvement of environmental performance and pollution prevention.

Manage and control environmental impacts systematically by setting objectives and targets, monitoring progress, reviewing and auditing performance.

Ensure that our staff and service providers have the appropriate levels of expertise, are <u>aware of our key impacts on the environment</u>, understand their responsibilities and are committed to applying our policies and meeting our specific objectives."

The comments I make to the project manager obviously apply to yourselves and I am not prepared to wait until you see fit to reply once the "excessively noisy" works have been completed.

Yours sincerely,

Anuja and Ken came to visit. They introduced themselves. They declined my offer of a cup of tea. I told them about this book. Ken seemed to be quite concerned.

"You didn't get my surname, did you?" he asked anxiously. I hadn't but later found it in Anuja's e-mail.

There didn't seem to be a lot they could do. Astonishingly, despite the fact they are on 24 hour and presumably 365 days a year, noise watch, there are no limits on noise levels in Westminster, just time periods and days when noise is not permitted. They did, however, agree to go to visit the site and see what could be done and it had to be said that things did improve a little after that. The only problem was the false dawn I was promised. I was told that the "very noisy" works would be finished by a Thursday of one week and by the Tuesday of the following week they were still proceeding merrily along. My new friends at Westminster were similarly peeved and withdrew permission for Trev and his mates to work all day on a Saturday as retribution. Much as I wanted to cause Trev grief, I couldn't understand the logic of that as it just meant more noise the following week.

However, I did get some kind of result from The Crown Estate so maybe my O.B.E is still a possibility. They wrote to me on 30th June:

New Burlington Place

Your letter of 23 June has been passed to me, to respond to as I am responsible for the above development.

I am sorry our work has been causing you inconvenience. Whilst construction operations are inherently noisy, we do endeavour to arrange operations to cause as few problems as possible. Noisy work is organised 2 hours on/ 2 hours off; that is to say 8.00-10.00 am; 12.00-2.00 pm; and 4.00-6.00 pm. Unfortunately we are not allowed to undertake noisy work at the weekend (other than Saturday morning) or in the evenings by Westminster City Council, due to potential disturbance to residents. This is a city wide rule.

The work which has been causing the problems over the last few weeks is the demolition of the building. Initially, this was undertaken by John F Hunt, our demolition contractor, but the site was taken over by the main contractor Skanska on 10 May. They have been undertaking the demolition of the basement walls. This work will be completed by the end of this week. We have moved into a different phase of work and are undertaking piling. This work is not as noisy, and for technical reasons has to be undertaken continuously. We will not therefore be undertaking this work two hours on / two hours off. This will continue until 16 August.

Overall the contract is due for completion in December 2005. We do have serviced office accommodation at Linen Hall which we could make available to you on an "as and when" basis if, for example, you have a meeting. If this would be of assistance, or if there is anything specific we could do to mitigate the problem, please let me know.

The development is an important part of the Regent Street Vision, a £500 million investment strategy to allow Regent Street to build on its role as a unique international destination to deliver a world-class environment, combining quality, heritage and style with success for businesses and people alike.

After this difficult period, we hope you will enjoy the greatly-improved environment in New Burlington Place.

Yours sincerely

Development Surveyor – Regent Street

As you can see they offered me a free office. Some people who have known me well have suggested that one day I would be occupying space at Her Majesty's Pleasure and here we are; they have proved to be right.

If noisy building works are a cause of concern then so are noisy neighbours. We had a young family move in a couple of doors away who decided to hold a Christening party with a marquee in the back garden and a live band. It was, as I recall, a Jewish holiday and we had the family round and were just sitting down to lunch when the music started. Plates rattled on the table, wine glasses threatened to shatter and only my elder lad Nicky nodded approvingly at the choice of music and actually went out onto the patio to listen. But then he is a music lawyer and maybe he was talent spotting. The noise continued unabated for hours and finally I said I was going in to sort them out. My wife blocked my path.

"No way," she said, "we'll have them as neighbours for years. I'll deal with it in my way."

Right, I thought. That means they'll still be playing at midnight and will have invited the Massed Bands of the Coldstream Guards along to join in.

But, not for the first time in our marriage, I had underestimated her. In she went and almost instantly the noise levels reduced. She returned smiling.

"They had a big sign in their entrance hall which said 'God is Love' and I told them it was a Jewish holiday today and bingo."

The next time they had a party they put a note through our door advising us. The buggers didn't invite me though. I wonder why?

Paul, my younger son, recently bought a flat with his girlfriend, as I may have mentioned. Hopefully, another step on the way to his mother getting to use the dress she's chosen for the wedding. They did say the other day that if, not when, mind you, they got married they weren't going to have the National Anthem played, so we took that as another indicator that things were on the move. They were inordinately proud of the flat until they found they had the neighbours from hell in the flat above. They were three young French girls who seemed to think that every night was party night and even asked for access to the scaffolding outside Paul and Jenny's window when somehow or other they managed to drop their cheese (yes, cheese) out of their window. Finally, Paul and Jenny could take it no longer. I checked their lease through for them and drafted a letter to the Managing Agents.

Hayward Property Services
31 Plympton St
London
NW8 8AB
20th November 2003

Dear Sir

We acquired the lease of Flat 11, XXX, earlier this year. Our flat is on the third floor and immediately above is Flat number 15. This occupied by three students who sub-let from the current lessees.

Since we have been in occupation we have had cause to complain to the occupants on many occasions in relation to the noise levels at unsociable hours. Often music and shouting continues until the small hours of the morning.

Matters came to a head on Saturday 15th November when they played loud music and sang until 1am. We went to complain and, although they agreed to reduce the noise level, we were woken again at 4.30 am by singing, shouting and loud music.

Clearly this is not only unacceptable but is also a breach of the lease of Flat 15 and at the moment there is also a breach of our covenant for quiet enjoyment of our flat. We must insist therefore, that action is taken on behalf of the landlord to enforce the covenants in the lease of Flat 15 which relate to non-disturbance of other occupiers of the building.

Would you please reply within the next seven days, failing which we would have to take the necessary action ourselves and would obviously produce this letter in court and look to the relevant third parties for payment of our costs.

Yours sincerely,

The noise stopped, the girls' tenancy was not renewed and silence reigned in Kilburn, or Mapesbury, as they prefer to call it.

Noise is not something we should just accept as a part of our daily lives. Of course, some things do involve noise but it must be reasonable, and the works must be conducted with some thoughts for neighbours. Love thy neighbour. But only if he shuts up when you ask him to.

So, remember:

1. You are entitled to conduct your work in reasonable peace and quiet. If the noise gets too much for you complain to the local authority.
2. If you can't get them to stop then insist on alternative accommodation being provided.
3. Don't forget to appeal against your Council Tax to get it reduced.
4. If there is a lease involved check to see what the lease says to get their landlord to take some action.
5. If your domestic neighbours are noisy then tell them nicely and only complain to the local authority if they won't be quiet.
6. If you live in a block of flats again consult your lease and ensure the landlord or the managing agents enforce the appropriate covenants.
7. If you rent accommodation again ask the landlord to take action and request a reduction of rent for any disturbance.
8. Don't just accept neighbours who play music loudly, practise the drums or have screaming drunken, or sober, rows with the windows open. Speak to them, then drop them a note, and if all else fails got to the local authority.

And remember the mantra. If you have to consult your solicitor or threaten an injunction then either your complaining techniques need to be improved or the offending neighbours are madder than a bunch of barking snakes. Oh, and if you are going to complain personally, do size up the opposition. You will need to read the disclaimer in the small print of the Introduction to this book. I cannot be held responsible for violence against your person.

THE SORCERER'S APPRENTICE:
EPILOGUE

Nothing gives me greater pleasure than to know that a friend has followed my advice and brought a complaint to a satisfactory conclusion. I had lunch with Patrick Kielty, the stand-up comic and TV presenter (oh, how I do love to name drop) just before this book was finished and he gave me permission to tell the story of a complaint that he had recently made where he followed my tutelage to the letter.

Patrick knew all about the book because I had bored him stiff with it every time we met, in the vain hope that he might think some of my material was good enough to put into his act ... or if he was really desperate, invite me on to his show. Thus, I was delighted when he turned to me somewhere between the starter and the main course to say:

"You know, Mel, I had a problem recently and your words were echoing in my mind."

A problem. My words. Bit worrying that when it comes to a superstar. What on earth had I told him to do? Had it cost him his job? His career?

It appeared that I needn't have worried. Patrick had ordered some mirrors for his new house in Ireland. You see, if you're successful you can buy properties in the most exotic locations. He'd ordered two of them (not that he's vain or anything, but I suppose it's easier to decide which is your best side if you have two reflections). He'd specifically asked if they could be delivered to Ireland. The <u>man</u> (not sexist, but relevant) to whom he spoke said he would check, made a call whilst Patrick was on the line, and said they could. Patrick then gave his credit card details, paid in full and waited with bated breath for the delivery of his mirrors.

The mirrors didn't come. Patrick phoned through. They weren't coming. It appeared that it was impossible to deliver them to Ireland. Now, the mind boggles as to why this should be such an impossible task. Build a bridge across the Channel? Bit tricky? Open a laptop dancing club in the midst of the Sahara Desert? Small challenge. Bloody hell, the Irish have managed to deliver almost their entire population to us so why couldn't this company have managed two mirrors?

This was when Patrick thought of me. He kept calm and my mantra raced through his mind. Be polite, be firm, be sure of your facts and ask to speak to somebody senior to whomever it is you are speaking. He followed the advice every step of the way. He was told that the girl who had taken his order had been a temp and had made a mistake. They were sorry, but the girl to whom he was now speaking had spoken to a director and they couldn't send mirrors to Ireland. Where else might he want them delivered? Patrick was sure of a couple of things. The bloke with whom he'd placed the order was competent. He'd taken the trouble to check that delivery was possible. He was a bloke and not a girl and a) he hadn't sounded like a temporary employee and b) he was fairly sure he hadn't had a sex-change operation in the intervening period of a few weeks.

Patrick remembered I had told him he had to persist. He did. Eventually they admitted there had been a mistake and they would make a special exception for him and deliver to Ireland. Both Patrick and the mirrors were relieved. But there was a sting in the tail. It would cost £100 and Patrick would have to pay. For a moment he was tempted. Just pay the money and have done with it. Put it down to experience. But then the words of Obi-K'nobi came back to him. It's not the money, it's a matter of principle. He stiffened his sinew and resumed the battle.

"So, let me get this right," he said. "You've made a mistake and I have to pay £100 to put it right."

The mirror company reflected (get it?) on that for a moment and agreed. Suddenly from being impossible to deliver the mirrors to their new Gaelic home it was a question of money. Shades of George Bernard Shaw there then. Up to this point Patrick had done splendidly and was about to graduate *cum laude*, but he then made a near fatal error. He tried to compromise when he was totally on the side of the angels.

"Tell you what," he said, "I'll pay a third if you pay the rest," and with alacrity the mirror company agreed. Patrick's guests can look at themselves to their hearts' content. As I pointed out to him, as he sat beside me looking a little crestfallen, the fact that they virtually snapped the £33.33 pounds out of his hand meant they knew they were on to a hiding to nothing.

Still, I did give him seven and a half out of ten for which he was grateful, but delayed his passage from apprentice to fully qualified complainer for another term.

But that shows what can be done if you follow the advice and precedents in this book. There's a whole new world our there for you. Go forth and complain, my readers. And to be effective complain *to* people, not about them. Complaining *about* the service in a restaurant to a friend isn't really complaining, it's just moaning. And please, don't hesitate to let me know how you get on. I need the material for a sequel.

I've been thinking a lot as I've been writing this as to whether I'm being reasonable in my approach to life. I think I'm looking for perfection and I realise now that I'm not going to find it. All I can hope is that every complaint I've made edges me just that little bit nearer along the primrose path to Utopia and I hope you accept the invitation to join me on my journey. Complaining is so much more fun when you have company.

POSTSCRIPT

So , here I am. It's 2005. A year since I began this book and so many loose ends neatly tidied up. I am driving a brand new Audi car which has covered over 5000 miles without having its oil topped up even once. I have a new friend at Loew's Hotel in the shape of Jonathan Tisch and I stayed at his company's excellent hotel, The Regency, in New York after the demise of The Stanhope though I forgot to take my nice new Jaeger jacket.

I get an upgrade or a price reduction when I stay at the Doubletree in Tallahessee after telling the manager, who proudly wore a badge that said "We aim for 10" that he'd achieved nought after my room had not been made up by 7.00 pm on two consecutive days. Though on a recnt stay, my wife and I did find hairs on the pillow, left by a previous occupant and the only fruit on offer for breakfast (in Florida, mind!) was tinned mandarine. Sadly though I can no longer eat at Judy's.

I have a very effective Lloyd's Gold Card that gives me money every time I request a magic hole in the wall to deliver it. My wife is treated politely every time she goes into the Alliance & Leicester. I still bathe and shower quite contentedly in my Dolphin Shower and Bath. My son has a Fossil watch and strap he really likes and has no noisy tenants above him (though he does have a lady who sings hymns at 2.00 am a couple of doors away) – and he and Jenny are engaged.

I've just returned from a holiday in South Africa where I stayed at the perfect Grand Roche in Paarl, and the newly discovered (at least for me) perfect Hunter's Lodge near Plettenberg, Cybele Forest Lodge in White River and Earth Lodge in Sabi. I couldn't muster a complaint about any of them (possibly because I told them I was writing this book, but more likely because they are establishments which rarely receive complaints) I will be writing to the Plettenberg in Plettenberg Bay, mind you, because they forgot to give us a requested wake-up call on the day we were catching a plane and also allowed their guests to "bag" poolside loungers with books. Horst Frehse at the Grand Roche would never permit that and he has loads of German guests.

And finally, and almost unbelievably, I've just been appointed a food consultant to Virgin Atlantic, to the hysterical amusement of my wife, my sons and anybody else to whom I mention it. Talk about poacher turned gamekeeper.

Complain? Not me. What on earth do I have to complain about?

REFERENCES

ACCOUNTANTS

You should always ensure that your accountant is a member of a professional body.

These organisations have rules their members should abide by, and although self regulated, they are responsible for the qualification and discipline of their members.

All chartered accountants are members of the Institute of Chartered Accountants and there are other bodies, including:

Chartered Institute of Public Finance Accountants
Chartered Institute of Management Accountants
Association of Chartered Certified Accountants

Bookkeepers may belong to the Institute of Chartered Secretaries.

Should the organisation concerned find in your favour, following a complaint, they can instruct a refund of your accountant's charges but cannot enforce any compensation. You would have to pursue this through the courts.

Useful Addresses

Institute of Chartered Accountants in England and Wales

Chartered Accountants Hall
PO Box 433
London EC2P 2BJ

Tel: 020 7920 8100
Website: www.icaew.co.uk

Scotland

CA House
21 Haymarket Yards
Edinburgh
EH12 5BH

Tel: 0131 3470100
Website: www.icas.org.uk

Association of Chartered Certified Accountants
29 Lincoln's Inn Fields
London
WC2A 3EE

Tel: 020 7396 7000
Email: info@accaglobal.com
Website: www.accaglobal.com

Chartered Institute of Management Accountants
26 Chapter Street
London
SW1P 4NP

Tel: 020 88492251
Email: cima.services@cimaglobal.com
Website: www.cimaglobal.com

Chartered Institute of Public Finance and Accountancy
3 Robert Street
London
WC2N 6RL

Tel: 020 7543 5600
Website: www.cipfa.org.uk

For Ireland

Institute of Chartered Accountants in Ireland (ICAI)
The Secretary
CA House
83 Pembroke Road
Dublin 4
Republic of Ireland

Tel: (01) 637 7200
Fax: (01) 668 0842

Email: fayj@icai.ie
Website: www.icai.ie

BANKS AND CREDIT

In 2003 Banks earned in the region of 30 billion pounds in the UK, yet they still take 5 days to clear a cheque while they invest in overnight markets to earn interest.

£20 charges for accounts overdrawn by £1 are not uncommon.

In addition, when Barclays Chief Executive openly admits that credit cards are expensive, you have to wonder to what extent we are being taken for a ride.

The Financial Services and Markets Act 2000 has led to the introduction of a more powerful regulator, notably the Financial Services Authority (FSA). A new Financial Ombudsman Service has also been created.

As with Estate Agents the code for good practice is voluntary for the banks.

The code contains the following commitments: They should:

1. Act fairly and reasonably in all their dealings with you.
2. Help you to understand how their financial products and services work.
3. Deal with issues that go wrong quickly and sympathetically.
4. Publicise the code and ensure their staff are trained to put the code in practice.

Copies of the code can be obtained on line at www.bankingcode.org.uk or from any bank.

Study the code and quote relevant points in any complaint letter you might send to your bank.

Over charging, varying interest rates without notice, money transfer clearance times and incorrect statements are all issues you should pursue with your bank. If enough customers complain when they receive bad service the banks, like any other service, will be encouraged to change. If they don't, take your business elsewhere. Options exist in the financial services market.

All banks should have their own complaints procedure.

In the first instance you should contact the Customer Service staff of your local branch, or your personal manager if you know his or her name.

If your complaint remains unresolved you should contact the Financial Ombudsman Service. In addition you should consider contacting the National Association of Bank and Insurance Customers, who can offer advice at any stage of the complaint process.

Credit

Before entering into any credit agreement check the background of the company involved, and the interest rates quoted, to ensure they clearly state the APR. For mortgages ensure the lender subscribes to the Mortgage Code of Practice. Check also to see if the mortgage brokers are regulated by the Financial Services Authority (FSA).

The Mortgage Code Compliance Board (MCCB) can offer advice for mortgage complaints.

Credit Refusal

If you are refused credit you are entitled to ask if a credit agency was used and if so which. The lender should inform you of the reasons for turning you down.

You can request a copy of any file they have on you.

Check this information for errors and inform the agency accordingly.

If you are not satisfied contact the Office of the Information Commissioner.

Complaints Procedure

If local contact at branch level or head office customer service departments fail to achieve results you should resort to the Financial Ombudsman Service.

Useful Addresses

Financial Ombudsman Service (FOS)
South Quay Plaza
183 Marsh Wall
London
E14 9SR

Helpline: 0845 080 1800
Email: complaint.info@financial-ombudsman.org.uk
Website: www.financial-ombudsman.org.uk

Financial Services Authority
www.fsa.gov.uk

Building Societies Association
www.bsa.org.uk

National Association of Bank and Insurance Customers
PO Box 15
Caldicot
Mon NP26 5YD
Helpline: 01291 430009
Email: enquiries@lemonAid.net
Website: www.lemonaid.net

For Ireland

Ombudsman for a Credit Institutions
8 Adelaide Court
Adelaide Road
Dublin 2

Tel :   01 478 3755
Fax: 01 478 0157
Email   ombudsman@creditombudsman.ie

ESTATE AGENTS – SURVEYORS

A code of practice was set up in 1988 to put an end to unscrupulous practices committed by the industry. With this in place you should contact the National Association of Estate Agents if you feel the rules covering buying and letting have been breached. The problem in the UK, unlike many other European countries, is that UK estate agents are not licensed, though they have to be licensed for any financial services they provide.

Some common problems are:

Over-valuing properties
In order to secure the house an agent may tell you the property is worth more than it is. This inaccurate valuation may convince the vendor to select this agent. The results of this are obvious but the impact not only means the house will not sell, but valuable time has been lost.

It is important to get two or three valuations and come to a realistic figure on the basis of the information provided. It is also important to be satisfied that a sale is at arms length, and not under value to favour a friend of the estate agent.

Under-valuing properties
Some agents work with property developers to secure the property for the developer at a lower than market price, despite being paid by the vendor to get the best price.

Again it is important to do your homework. Check the local market and similar properties and seek advice from more than one source.

An important consideration when choosing an agent is to see if they are signed up to the National Association of Estate Agents.

Although the standard fees tend to be 2% of the selling price many agents are prepared to negotiate. Suggest a sliding scale of charges for example:

Full asking price 1.5%

Up to 10K less than the asking price 1.25%

Between 10K and 20K below the asking price 1%.

This ensures that the estate agent does his best to get the right price and indeed establish the right price at the beginning. The more money received, the better everyone does, so why should the agent get 2% when they have achieved less than the asking price?

If you have experienced a problem with your estate agent and cannot resolve the issue directly with the branch, or with their head office, you should seek advice from your local Trading Standards Office or Citizens Advice Bureau.

A series of letters to the local newspaper is something the agent can do without, and may encourage them to resolve the issue.

313

Useful Addresses

www.oea.co.uk

The Ombudsman for Estate Agents: can only deal with complaints against its members.

www.naea.co.uk

The National Association of Estate Agents

www.tradingstandards.gov.uk

The Trading Standards Institute

www.bioa.org.uk

The British and Irish Ombudsman Association

For Ireland

If the company is a member of any of the organisations listed below, a complaint can be made directly to the association concerned.

IAVI – Irish Auctioneers & Valuers Institute
38 Merrion Square
Dublin 2

IPAV – Institute of Professional Auctioneers & Valuers
129 Lower Baggot Street
Dublin 2

SCS – Society of Chartered Surveyors
5 Wilton Terrace
Dublin 2

AIRLINES

The airline is responsible for you and your luggage arriving at your destination.

There are guidelines as to what you are entitled to and you should make a point of checking the customer charter compiled by the airline. This document will explain their complaints procedure.

If a problem arises at the Airport you should make your complaint at the time with the airlines duty officer.

Ensure your air travel arrangements are covered by ATOL, which will cover you against failures of tour operator/agency. This will ensure a refund is provided, or enable you to continue with your travel plans if problems occur during your trip.

Make sure you register your complaint with someone in authority, for example a cabin service director or the customer relations team at the airport.

You are entitled to compensation if you have lost your seat due to overbooking or for avoidable delays to your journey.

You should contact the Air Transport Users Council and can do so via their website.

For lost luggage you need to fill out a PRI form. Keep a copy and contact the Airline with your claim within seven days. You may not be able to claim the full value as airlines can pay out according to weight rather than value, so always try and put in place your own insurance. If you have bought goods on a credit card you may be able to claim the value from the credit card company or their insurers.

Useful addresses

Air Transport Users Council
Room K705,
CAA House
45-59 Kingsway
London
WC2B 6TE
Tel: 020 7240 6061

Email :   admin@auc.caa.co.uk
Website : www.auc.org.uk

British Airports Authority
130 Wilton Road
London
SW1V 1LQ
Tel: 020 7834 9449

Website: www.baa.co.uk

ATOL (Air Travel Organiser's Licensing)
You can find detailed information on your ticket/air holiday protection if bought through an ATOL-licensed agency/operator.

www.atol.org.uk

Civil Aviation Authority
www.caa.co.uk

For Ireland

Irish Aviation Authority
The Shannon Centre
Ballycasey
Shannon
Co Clare

Tel: (61) 366 226
Fax: (61) 366 097
Website: www.iaa.ie

JUNK MAIL

Every time we fill in a form of any kind that requires our personal address it is more than likely that at some point this information will be passed on to companies who buy and sell personal details. The same applies when you give your personal details over the phone. Big Brother is not only watching you, he is learning everything about you as well.
          Consider how many times you might do this in a year.
Competitions, general application forms, internet websites, store cards, credit cards etc, with all of these, we increase the risk of adding to the 250,000 tons of junk mail that is forced through our letter boxes everyday. It may come as a surprise to learn that information taken for the Census is also sold on.
      Store cards may seem like a good idea to the customer but they are an even better idea for the store. Over a period of time they can build data on your purchasing activities.
      At present there are no legal requirements restricting companies from using personal information. Invariably the more vulnerable are targeted, and it is not uncommon for this to result in old people being defrauded of large sums of money. The Data Protection Act will probably not protect you in this instance.

What can you do?

There are various measures.

Contact the Direct Marketing Association's Mail Preference Service and ask to be removed from the national mailing lists.

Contact charitable organisations and ask their customer service departments to remove your name from their lists.

Contact Redirect Mail for previous owner's mail to be re-directed.

You can request not to have your name showing on the public copy of the electoral role, which is sold on to companies. At the same time write to your MP asking that the law be changed to prevent this.

Always tick the opt-out box so your details are not passed on to third parties.

You can complain directly to the Information Commissioner if a company continues to send you junk mail when you have asked them not to.

Ensure as part of your computer protection that you use a filter to block Spam mail.

Useful Addresses

Information Commissioner
www.informationcommissioner.gov.uk

Direct Marketing Association Mail Preference Service
www.dmaconsumers.org/offmailinglist.html

Royal Mail for Redirect Mail and Door-to-Door Service
www.royalmail.com

For Ireland

Data Protection Commissioner
Office of the Data Protection Commissioner
Block 6
Irish Life Centre
Lower Abbey Street
Dublin 1
Ireland

Tel: (01) 874 8544
Fax: (01) 874 5405
Email: info@dataprotection.ie

UTILITY COMPANIES

The deregulation of the utility companies has caused considerable confusion for the consumer, particularly in relation to supply and pricing.

Complaints regarding water, electricity or gas supplies should initially be directed to the companies, who are required to have formal procedures for any consumer complaints.

Most complaints for the utility companies should be resolved at this level.   If this fails you can contact the Gas and Electricity Consumers Council (Energywatch which offers independent help and advice).

The Office of Gas and Electricity Markets (Ofgem) strictly regulates both industries. Energywatch and Ofgem will determine any disputes requiring compensation awards.

Note that all gas appliances, by law, must be fitted by someone who is Corgi registered (which stands for Council for Registered Gas Installers).

With reference to water you must contact Watervoice, the consumer division of the Office of Water Supplies, (Ofwat) who will investigate specific complaints.

Oh and by the way, if you have a gas leak don't light a match to discover the source!

Useful Addresses

British Gas
House Contact Centre
P.O. Box 50
Leeds LS1 1LE
Tel: 0845 604 0304
Website: www.house.co.uk

Office of Gas and Electricity Markets (Ofgem)

England and Wales
9 Millbank
London SW1P 3GE
Tel: 020 79017000
Website: www.ofgem.gov.uk

Scotland
Regents Court
70 West Regent Street
Glasgow G2 2QZ
Tel: 0141 331 2678

Energywatch
4th Floor Artillery House
Artillery Row
London SW1P 1RT
Email: enquiries@energywatch.org.uk
Website: www.energywatch.org.uk

Other useful websites

Council for Registered Gas Installers
www.corgi-gas.com

National Inspection Council for Electrical Installation Contracting
www.niceic.org.uk

Institute of Plumbing
www.plumbers.org.uk

Electrical Contractors Association Ltd
www.eca.co.uk

Association of Plumbing and Heating Contractors
www.aphc.co.uk

The Health and Safety Executive
www.hse.gov.uk

Ireland
Commission for Electricity Regulation
Plaza House
Belgard Road
Tallaght
Dublin 24
Tel: 01 4000 800
Fax: 01 4000 850
Email: info@cer.ie

ESB Customer complaints Arbitrator (ELCOM)
39 Merrion Square
Dublin 2
Email: complaints.com@esb.ie